A PLUME BOOK

BEAUTIFUL MADNESS

JAMES DODSON is the author of *Final Rounds*, the 1996 bestseller that was named the Golf Book of the Year by the International Network of Golf. He is also the author of *The Road to Somewhere*, *The Dewsweepers*, and *Faithful Travelers*, which was selected as one of the Top Five nonfiction book titles of the year (1998) by *Reader's Digest*. His book, *A Golfer's Life*, a collaboration with Arnold Palmer, was a *New York Times* bestseller. Dodson is a former winner of the T. H. White Award for Public Affairs Journalism and a four-time winner of the prestigious Golf Writers of America Award for his profiles and his regular column, "The Golf Life," in *Golf Magazine*. He was the recipient of the 1998 Golf Reporter of the Year award from the International Network of Golf. He lives on the coast of Maine with his two children, Maggie and Jack.

To see photographs of Jim's travels through the plant world, please visit JamesDodsonAuthor.com.

Praise for *Beautiful Madness* and the works of James Dodson

"Dodson has a wonderful style, never supercilious, totally personal, and often sneakily funny."
—The Courier-Gazette

"Dodson's prose is as smooth as Hogan's swing, and his attention to detail will impress even the most persnickety of golf fans." *—The Washington Post*

"Dodson reconstructs the great moments of the champion's career with brilliant drama and clarity . . . Sheer pleasure." *—Chicago Tribune*

"One of the biggest names in sports journalism peels back the layers and family secrets of the greatest shot-makers of all time and scores an ace."
—The Seattle Times

"Dodson uses a master's skill to tell us a lot about golf and even more about ourselves. *The Dewsweepers* is an experience to treasure."
—Maine Sunday Telegram

"Dodson brings a rare sensibility to the craft—equal parts expertise and humanity." *—Austin American-Statesman*

Beautiful Madness

JAMES DODSON

A PLUME BOOK

PLUME
Published by Penguin Group
Penguin Group (USA) Inc., 375 Hudson Street, New York, New York 10014,
U.S.A. • Penguin Group (Canada), 90 Eglinton Avenue East, Suite 700, Toronto, Ontario,
Canada M4P 2Y3, (a division of Pearson Penguin Canada Inc.) • Penguin Books Ltd.,
80 Strand, London WC2R 0RL, England • Penguin Ireland, 25 St. Stephen's Green,
Dublin 2, Ireland (a division of Penguin Books Ltd.) • Penguin Group (Australia),
250 Camberwell Road, Camberwell, Victoria 3124, Australia (a division of Pearson Australia
Group Pty. Ltd.) • Penguin Books India Pvt. Ltd., 11 Community Centre, Panchsheel Park,
New Delhi – 110 017, India • Penguin Books (NZ), cnr Airborne and Rosedale Roads,
Albany, Auckland 1310, New Zealand (a division of Pearson New Zealand Ltd.) • Penguin
Books (South Africa) (Pty.) Ltd., 24 Sturdee Avenue, Rosebank, Johannesburg 2196,
South Africa

Penguin Books Ltd., Registered Offices: 80 Strand, London WC2R 0RL, England

Published by Plume, a member of Penguin Group (USA) Inc.
Previously published in a Dutton edition.

First Plume Printing, February 2007
1   3   5   7   9   10   8   6   4   2

Ⓟ REGISTERED TRADEMARK—MARCA REGISTRADA

The Library of Congress has catalogued the Dutton edition as follows:
Dodson, James.
Beautiful madness : one man's journey through other people's gardens / by James Dodson.
p.   cm.
ISBN 0-525-94935-6 (hc.)
ISBN 978-0-452-28802-7 (pbk.)
1. Gardening.   2. Dodson, James.   I. Title.
SB455.D55 2006
635'.09741—dc22   2005034369

Printed in the United States of America
Original hardcover design by Leonard Telesca

This book is dedicated to Pat Robinson,
friend and advisor.

Contents

Contents

"There are no happier folks than plant lovers and none more generous than those who garden."

—Ernest "Chinese" Wilson

Beautiful
Madness

Introduction

Plant Nerds in the Mist

As I FOLLOWED our guide through the waist-tall grass toward the edge of the cliff where the others had suddenly vanished, he casually remarked over his shoulder, "Mind your step in places like this, Jim. This is an ideal spot for snakes, you see. Just a word to the wise. Are you squeamish about snakes?"

In the three days Cameron McMaster had been leading us from dawn to dusk into some of the most forbidding bush and rain forest of the remote Eastern Cape highlands in search of rare plants, I'd affectionately come to think of him as He Who Must Be Obeyed because there didn't seem to be anything the rugged sixty-eight-year-old naturalist didn't know about South Africa's spectacular flora and fauna. With boots on the ground and already struggling to catch up with my fanatical companions, however, one thing I frankly hadn't given a whole lot of thought to was deadly snakes.

Until now.

I glanced down and noticed my legs were missing; only my glistening bare knees were visible as they passed through the lush and dripping savanna grass as we proceeded to the spot where the others had worked over the cliff's edge into the mist of the passing cloud top.

"So what kind of snakes, exactly, do you have around here?"

It seemed, under the circumstances, a reasonable question to ask. I tried to keep my voice light and generally unconcerned. Back in my teenage scouting days, after all, I was fairly accustomed to handling snakes of various kinds, though nothing I had met at Camp Wenasa in the late sixties had prepared me for the savage unspoiled beauty and apparent dangers of the South African bush country and upland rain forest. In a word, everything we'd encountered thus far—the vast silent Great Karoo, the endless washed blue African sky, the extraordinary exotic flowers found wildly blooming on crag and cliff, the blisters already forming on my instep—seemed at least *twice* as big as anything I'd ever experienced in half a lifetime of travels through the American wilderness.

"Of the hundred and thirty or so species found in Africa," Cameron helpfully amplified, "there are really only two you need to concern yourself with in this particular area. One is the puff adder, a big lazy brute with a very dangerous bite who doesn't move for anyone. The other is the Cape cobra. Equally dangerous, of course—quite venomous, in fact—but you have the advantage that he rises up before he strikes."

"Good to know," I said with a forced cheerfulness, suddenly lonely for the sight of my booted feet, which felt as if they might be traversing a field of unseen boulders where God only knows what was crawling around and poising to strike.

"A larger concern in terrain like this is ticks," the guide continued as a series of eerie wails and barks suddenly erupted from the mountain slopes somewhere in the mist over the cliff.

"If a tick bites you there is the distinct possibility of tick bite fever, I'm afraid, a nasty business that comes with severe headache, high fever, and sometimes delirium. Rarely fatal in humans, but you will need to get immediate attention and antibiotics straightaway. I'd check myself regularly if I were you."

"Will do," I promised, hurrying to catch up. "By the way, what's that strange barking noise down the mountain?"

"Chacma baboons. They're down in the mountainside above the waterfall. We may see them later this afternoon when we hike up to the river to see some simply stunning *Haemanthus*. This is their domain, you see, the baboons, and they probably aren't terribly happy we are up here."

"What happens if *they* bite you?"

He failed to catch my little funny, because suddenly there came a very different kind of sound from over the cliff's edge—this one unmistakably human, a voice shouting excitedly, a human exclamation point of pure Edenic discovery.

Someone had discovered a rare and perfect plant species clinging bravely to the misty mountainside and was having, as a result, to use expedition leader Tony Avent's wonderfully descriptive field language, a "hortgasm" heralding a fabulous discovery.

Cameron was off like a shot over the rocky precipice. By the time I reached the spot where he disappeared, I spotted Cameron and three other members of the team huddling together forty yards down the sheer mountainside on a narrow ledge of moss-wreathed rock beneath an overhang of lush trees and vines. Three thousand feet below them, somewhere along the flanks of the bending, mist-girdled river, the baboons were keeping up their protests.

"What is it? An orchid?" I called down, remembering how Cameron claimed this Afromontane wildflower reserve was teeming with the exotic flower, but truthfully feeling a little like the fat kid left on top of the monkey bars during play period while everyone has loped off to look at something interesting the new kid threw up on the shiny cafeteria floor. Hans Hansen, a lanky and easygoing Minnesotan, one of America's leading *Hosta* hybridizers, grinned up at me beneath his faded ball cap.

"*Drimea unifora*," he called, screwing on a new camera lens. "A hyacinth. The world's smallest flowering bulb. You've got to see this."

He was right, I did. In the three days I'd been tagging along after the celebrated American plantsman Tony Avent and his group of seasoned plant explorers through some of southern Africa's most unspoiled terrain, I'd been cut, scratched, punctured, gouged, and bruised in places I didn't even know I owned.

But aside from the simple yeoman gardener's pleasure of coming to such a fabulously remote place believed to be the birthplace of perhaps as much as one fourth of the earth's flowering species of plants and flowers and having the chance to encounter several of the world's most rare and stunning flowers in their native habitat, an unmistakable botanical buck fever had even begun to take possession of my own brain as well.

Thus I hurried over the edge, too, a bit too hastily as it turned out, eager to see the latest magnificent specimen my companions had found. When an unseen rock shifted underfoot, however, I was suddenly pitching and tumbling out of control through the prickly brush, falling toward the angry baboons below.

Lucky for me a small tree of some kind was conveniently growing from the side of the cliff. It was a sturdy tree with handsome, thickly gnarled black bark that recalled Spanish cork, and a beautiful arching umbrella-like canopy full of waxy elongated leaves. I had an unexpected opportunity to examine its unusual bark pattern up close because I seized the little tree by the throat and hung on for dear life, hoping its roots were both deep and strong.

Dangling in the misty air, trying to catch my breath and collect my wits, I actually had to smile at the sweet irony that some exotic if unknown African tree had spared me a most unwelcome landing. Wild asparagus and rare paintbrush lilies sponsored ecstatic hortgasms in my learned field companions, but beautiful trees evoked a similar response in me. Improbable as this may sound, I owed my unusual predicament at that moment on the far side of the world to a beloved but ailing American beech tree back home in my snow-covered yard in Maine.

This African plant safari was simply the thrilling and wholly unexpected conclusion of a personal quest that began when I innocently set forth from home in Maine one late winter day exactly one year before to ask a gardening friend how to save a cherished but dying family tree. I soon found myself wandering down a winding garden path of discovery at a moment some believe is nothing less than a Second Golden Age of personal gardening. I had no way of knowing if that was true or not; I simply hoped to find useful plant wisdom to aid my ailing tree and per-

Plant Nerds in the Mist

haps make me a better keeper of the garden. But as the quest wound its way to many fascinating people and places, I began to realize mine was really a search for something *much* more comprehensive and timeless in nature—a broader understanding of a garden's magical ability to enchant and elevate the human spirit, not only explaining where my own growing love of landscape gardening came from, but also perhaps where the nature of my obsession just might be headed.

This hunger to know more sent me behind the scenes of the two most important garden shows on earth and placed me at the feet of a renowned plant philosopher in the heart of America's so-called Fertile Crescent of Gardening. Among other encounters and inspirations along the way, I got to know the "Botticelli of Bulbs" and encounter the kindred gardening spirits of Thomas Jefferson and John Bartram, providing a powerful historical perspective on what is simply America's latest popular love affair with all things gardening. Following in the philosophical footsteps of a simple self-guided gardening monk I only knew as Brother John, I chased over to England to the splendor of Britain's most extraordinary walled garden on that nation's celebrated national gardening day, took a living legend of garden writing out to lunch, pursued a fabled roadside yew, billeted on the grounds of a queen's private island estate with a man affectionately called the Mad Man of Kew Gardens and his brilliant gardener wife, encountering one of the great homemade botanic gardens of the world.

In the course of these chimerical investigations into how plants grow and why we love them so much, I'd happily lost myself for hours on end in the creation dramas of at least half a dozen of America's finest private and public gardens and arboretums, happened upon poets and crackpots, met a man spreading his wife's ashes over the roots of a famous ancient ginkgo tree, bartered with a guy in a darkened parking lot hauling rare daylilies, swiped cuttings from a Founding Father's boxwood, thieved a redbud from a dying friend's forgotten garden, been adopted as a mascot by a clutch of indomitable Yankee gardening dames, constructed three ambitious new gardens of my own, probed the mysteries of my own family's considerable gardening roots in North Carolina, and generally rejoiced in the wit and generosity of perhaps fifteen or twenty of the world's most accomplished gardeners.

That's a lot for one year of harmless fun in other people's gardens—just to try and save a lowly ailing beech tree, no less.

But when Tony Avent, a major figure in the world of horticulture, suggested I cap off my year of living botanically by tagging along with his group of veteran plant explorers to hunt for the exotic flowers and cutting-edge garden plants of tomorrow in the wilds of Africa's rugged Eastern Cape, the aspiring everyman gardener in me didn't hesitate to delay my scheduled return to the golf world where I've made my principal living for the past two decades, to grab my rucksack and leap, as it were, at a rare opportunity to trek off to the "birthplace of flowers" on the far side of the planet for a solid month in the honorable company of a group of crazy men who were the horticultural world's equivalent of Tiger Woods and John Daly.

"THERE'S A SPOT you can safely drop just below you," Hans Hansen called up to me helpfully, interrupting this little reverie. I suppose he was grinning because he realized the only serious peril I faced was either to my dignity or my dodgy knees.

"Just try and avoid wiping out the grandmother of all pelargoniums."

Sure enough, just below the soles of my boots, stood a magnificent monster of a wild banded pelargonium, exactly the kind of thing I'd come to Africa hoping to see along with the mammoth trees I'd read about as a boy in Edgar Rice Burroughs and H. Rider Haggard—an impressive specimen probably six feet tall and half that wide, exploding from a small shelf of turf and positively covered with beautiful iridescent violet flowers, antecedent of every geranium patio plant in America.

A few minutes later, after I'd narrowly missed flattening this rare and probably highly endangered species and gathered myself up in one piece to join Hans and Cameron by the face of the mossy cliff, I discovered the other three members of the team had already photographed and collected a bit of seed from the fruit of this latest discovery and pushed on down the steep green slopes of the mountain in anticipation of other extraordinary finds. I could hear Carl Schoenfeld, in fact, hooting from a small meadow fifty feet further below us, and saw Wade Roitsch beneath his wide Texas straw hat tilting over a rock outcropping to hone in on a specimen with his camera's lens. Tony Avent, as usual, was nowhere to be seen—lost in his own world somewhere down the dangerous slopes in search of native asparagus plants. "Put a plant nerd in a place like this," he told me the first day out, "and you won't see him for long."

"Amazing, isn't it?" Hans said quietly, aiming his camera directly at what appeared to be a host of tiny opaque white hairs growing from a mossy fissure in the shaded stone. At the tip of his finger grew the smallest flower I'd ever seen, a tiny hyacinth bloom whose stem was no larger than your average sewing needle.

"Well, I'll be," I declared, breathing a little easier now that I'd more or less caught up with the expedition. At fifty-one, having grown up in scouting and done most of the Appalachian Trail in my youth and recently even nearly scaled the summit of Mount Katahdin in Maine with my teenage son Jack, I wasn't *that* much out of shape. But trying to keep up with this bunch of fanatical plant hunters was an exhausting enterprise at best, at times even futile. Every time I caught up, they were already someplace else.

"Hey," Hans said calmly, pointing down at my leg, "you're bleeding."

This wasn't news to me. I'd been bleeding for days from various nicks and cuts. In this case, however, sure enough, there was a bright new red coin of blood among the multiple scratches and puncture wounds, just below my left kneecap—the one belonging to my *good* knee.

As Hans blankly watched, I plucked a small black tick from the bloody flesh and sent it spinning on down the mountainside to visit the baboons.

"Do you think you'll get bush fever?" Hans wondered, grinning slyly, as if we were both fifteen again and thrilled by the exotic possibility I would wake up in the middle of the African night feverishly screaming Kim Basinger's name.

"Probably," I said, aiming my own camera at the little hyacinth.

Just then, a terrifying baboon shriek erupted mere feet from where we stood—causing us *both* to jump out of our skins. With his hands cupped to his mouth like Tarzan of the apes, He Who Must Be Obeyed was calling to the guardians of the jungle a mile or so below. Among his infinite talents, the man could evidently even speak with baboons.

"Hey Cameron," I said to him, once my heart resumed beating. "What's that tree I was hanging from back there?"

"That?" Cameron glanced and squinted where I was pointing. "Why that's *Cussonia spicata*. Better known as the common cabbage tree. Quite extensive in these mountain areas." He didn't sound particularly impressed with the handsome little tree that had saved my person from serious embarrassment and possibly something much worse.

I nodded. "Well, it may be quite common, but I really love that little tree," I said with real affection in my heart, regarding the handsome specimen that arched from the face of the cliff like the world's biggest cocktail umbrella, wishing I could somehow collect it and take it home to my garden in Maine. "Hey, do you think it would grow in zone five . . . ?"

But when I glanced back my companions had already shoved off. Horticulturally speaking, no moss ever grew beneath their feet. I quickly snapped a picture of my new friend, the common cabbage tree of South Africa, silently thanking my old friend, the ailing beech back home, for sending me on a wondrous pilgrimage that wound up here. Lest I be left behind to the killer ticks and spitting cobras, I wiped the blood from my leg and hobbled swiftly on to see what rare and fabulous things my friends the plant nerds had found in the misty birthplace of flowers.

Chapter 1

Slightly Off in the Woods

ONE OF THE FIRST THINGS you learn when you move to the great state of Maine, as I did twenty-five years ago, is that people don't move here for the timeless quality of springtime.

As winter yields its icy death grip and people in the lower forty-eight begin poking their heads out of the tool hutch and enjoying the welcome sight of longer days, budding fruit trees and tender green shoots rising promisingly in their yards, we lonely souls who reside up here in the far upper right-hand corner of America are still gazing at a landscape that basically resembles a frozen TV dinner.

Some years we're still actually digging out at Easter, and then there was that memorable Mother's Day a few years back when I phoned up our regular plow guy Earl to ask if he would mind coming over to push several inches of new spring snow off our driveway so we could drive weekend guests to the beach.

When people from other parts of America who know the beautiful Pine Tree State simply as the ultimate summer getaway spot—admired for its gorgeous rocky coast, vast evergreen forests, summer camps, and postcard lobster shacks—ask me where exactly I reside in Maine and politely wonder if, ahem, I even "stay there" during the brutally long and dark winter months, I like to borrow that old Bing Crosby line from *Holiday Inn* and explain, "I live just north of Portland, friend, and *well* below zero."

Besides, as real Mainers are happy to explain, there are only three major seasons up here you have to contend with: getting ready for winter, getting through the winter, and getting the hell over winter.

It's the getting-over-winter part—what most people in the lower forty-eight call "spring" and "summer"—that makes Maine's excruciating winter ultimately tolerable, the hope that the TV dinner will finally thaw and a nice fresh spring garden salad may eventually accompany the meal. Sometime just before the rest of America celebrates Independence Day, bulbs and flowering shrubs explode gloriously into bloom, tree frogs start singing their little hearts out in search of a soul mate, the black flies swarm like kamikaze pilots, bossy summer tourists begin arriving in droves, local restaurants quietly triple their lobster prices to adjust for seasonal inflation, and snow tires go on sale at Sears.

To be fair, springtime in Maine often lasts much longer than two days, sometimes stretching over an entire holiday weekend near the end of May. Two things have always gotten me through the interminable wait for warm weather's welcome annual return, what the rest of America rather indulgently calls the start of "gardening season," both telltale echoes and distant reminders of my childhood in North Carolina.

The first is golf, an ancient Scottish game I got hopelessly hooked on as a boy and somehow managed to find a highly satisfying career writing about as a man. For more than a decade it was both my duty and pleasure to serve as the roving golf editor for American Express's flagship travel magazine, which simply meant I could get the hell out of Dodge whenever Maine's brutal winter simply became too much for a Southerner like me to bear.

The second thing is gardening, in particular tree and flower gardening, a somewhat late-in-life addiction I evidently inherited from both my gardening-mad parents and several generations of God-fearing, church-loving, plant-crazy North Carolina farmers and preachers who believed digging into the soil wasn't just tantamount to delving into the soul but also probably essential for any hope of slipping into paradise.

"Jesus doesn't mind a little honest soil beneath your fingernails," my Grandmother Taylor used to sharply remind me in my happy-go-lucky, lawn-mowing years. "But even *He* won't abide a filthy face."

This ancestral passion for the earth, this verdure in the blood, lay relatively dormant inside me for the better part of twenty years and curiously only began to assert itself with an unexpected and wanton tenacity near the end of a brutally long Maine winter about fifteen years ago when my then-pregnant wife and I purchased an old auto graveyard on a forested hill just outside a pretty college town on the midcoast.

One sunny March day not long after I moved to Maine I hiked through the fresh knee-deep spring snow up an abandoned town road and happened upon a small clearing at the highest point of a wooded hill, discovering a beautiful meadow ringed by lovely balsam and birch trees, dramatically floodlit by afternoon sun.

Save for the two Eisenhower-era cars sitting under a fresh mantle of snow, I was thoroughly charmed by the site and quickly realized that a trio of native Whitespire birches and a stunning spreading hardwood tree with smooth gray bark that I later identified as a forty-year-old American beech was the ideal spot to site a modest cottage in the wood and finally put down some family roots of my own.

The nice lady who owned the land was a trifle reluctant to part with it, for understandably sentimental reasons—her third or fourth husband, I forget which, had cherished this spot for working on his junk cars and growing some useful medicinal herbs—but after a couple minutes of deeper reflection she agreed to part with a dozen acres of it and even haul off the cars as part of the bargain. Pretty soon we were in business on multiple home fronts. I got busy with a brand-new chainsaw thinning out the trees to let a little more air and sunshine circulate through our new forested hilltop Eden, uncovering and even rebuilding the remains of the old stone walls belonging to a vanished farm homestead that had, according to old town records I dug up, been on the site nearly one hundred years before us.

In those days, to support both family and what eventually turned out to be an even more financially ruinous outdoor hobby than golf, I was routinely traveling abroad to research classic golf courses and occasional famous display gardens on behalf of my travel magazine, often putting up at elegant British country hotels, manor houses, and even the occasional baronial sporting estate. The serene and timeless landscapes of these famous places, the signatures of Capability Brown and Humphry Repton and others, never failed to speak to me on some fundamental latter-day, post–Southern redneck gardening level, reminding me of the rural race of true horticultural maniacs I hailed from and prompting what I now realize was nothing less than a full-scale midlife personal epiphany, the beginning of a true obsession.

During a stay at a place called Gravetye Manor in West Sussex, I learned the gothic pile overhead had been the residence of none other than William Robinson, the "father of English gardening." Robinson was a revolutionary plantsman who advocated naturalistic plants of hardy perennials in settings that resembled original growing conditions and whose famous book *The Wild Garden* I quickly picked up at a local bookshop and devoured even before I checked out of the author's house. In Robinson's venerable surviving garden I also encountered my first "Jekyll" vine, learning it had been strategically planted there by none other than the great Gertrude Jekyll herself, Robinson's most celebrated disciple, who once observed that you spend the first half of your life planning a garden and the last half planting it and never really get time to enjoy it for more than the odd moment here or there. She eventually partnered with Surrey architect Edwin Lutyens to create some of the most renowned private gardens in England, the "gardens of the golden afternoon" movement whose formal classical herbaceous borders helped inspire the popular British gardening craze of the late nineteenth and early twentieth centuries.

On that same trip to England in 1990, as I look back on the stirrings of an ancestral passion claiming its own wayward son, a revealing moment occurred when, halfway through a round of golf at a posh new club over in Wisley with 1969 British Open champion Tony Jacklin, I suddenly begged off the back nine by claiming I had suddenly remembered a pressing engagement that simply couldn't be postponed. In fact, my appointment was just over the hedge and about two hundred meters down the lane at the home of the Royal Horticultural Society's home display gardens, where a friendly RHS volunteer had agreed to show me around the test perennials and a brand-new rose trial garden. As it happened, I'd just been walking around rural Shropshire getting to know a farmer-turned-rose-hybridizer called David Austin, whose modern hardier "English" roses would soon take the garden world of two continents by storm and make him wealthier—and more popular, in certain better circles—than Mick Jagger.

Following these pleasant interludes, I was hopelessly hooked on my *secret* outdoor passion; and wherever I ventured in Britain from this point on, there was forever a struggle between a boy's love of golf and a grown man's emerging ardor for gardening. During bluebell season I rambled over to Kent to play a famous links course I'd always dreamed of playing, but also spent a blissful afternoooon studying the structural plantings of Harold Nicolson and Vita Sackville-West's sumptuous gardens at Sissinghurst—a word I learned that means "clearing in the woods" in ancient Anglo-Saxon, just like my budding rock-girdled garden in the woods back home in Maine.

In due course I walked Cardinal Wolsey's amazing privet maze at Hampton Court; took the entire extended Thames floating tour of English gardens; toured Stourhead, Hidcote, and Kew, too. While venturing off to meet a club secretary at a venerable golf club near the rural Welsh border, I even bumbled upon famous Powis Castle's extraordinary terraced gardens and wound up staying in a restored abbey whose beautiful grounds had originally been landscaped by a novice self-taught gardener, an obscure middle-aged monk, no less, who simply went by the handle "Brother John," an Anglican friar whose yellowing garden log the proud new owner of the property took great pleasure in showing his interested visitor one evening over salmon and peas. Most of what was recorded there by Brother John was simply a workman's catalog of raw materials and expenses, but at one point early in his labors on the abbey grounds, the accidental gardener confided to the margin of his log book: "This task has become a holy thing, a beautiful madness that consumes this learner's soul."

Brother, I knew the feeling.

THUS INSPIRED, my scheme to build a one-hole golf course in my back-yard quickly yielded to an even more ambitious and certainly costlier idea: to fashion my very own authentic English garden in the woods of Maine, a Yankee Sissinghurst.

Propelled by visions of new perennial borders and timeless vistas of flowering trees, I basically leapt whole hog (as they say in pit barbe-cue circles down in North Carolina) into gardening, digging things up and putting things down with an almost giddy determination to shape the land the Almighty had clearly intended me to transform from junk-yard to English garden, indiscriminately murdering innocent bedding plants and squandering my present and unborn children's college funds on an impressive array of ruinously expensive ornamental shrubs and trees that had no business ever being seen further north than the state of Pennsylvania.

By the time a second hungry infant mouth appeared on our rugged little hilltop, a couple years into the secret enterprise, I'd more or less established two acres of fieldgrass vaguely resembling the Queen Mum's unmown lawn up in Scotland, and was even field trialing various roman-tic place-names for my miniature Sissinghurst of the North. I took to calling it "Three Birches," a *veddy* British-sounding appellation in honor of those original Whitespire birches and the beautiful beech tree where I'd sited our woodland cottage, while my Scottish mother-in-law, a crack gardener who fancied herself a stand-up comedian as well, pro-posed "Slightly Off in the Woods," suggesting as much about the would-be estate gardener's state of mind as the garden he hoped to build.

OF COURSE, nobody ever referred to our place by either of those landed titles. The naming business was simply *my* private bit of un-apologetic Anglophile garden worship. Most folks, to own the truth, who even bothered to wander up our winter-scarred dirt road into the forest for anything other than carnal purposes or a spot of summer wild-flower picking, in fact, seemed genuinely mystified to discover a wood-land cottage so extensively landscaped but completely hidden from view by a couple million trees. In Maine, where frugality ranks considerably higher than having all ten fingers and most of your natural teeth as a visible indication of your chances of succeeding in life, such horticul-tural extravagance is generally frowned upon as a sign of true mental instability—unmistakable proof that you do, in fact, hail from some-place else, probably Massachusetts.

"Who the *hell* is gonna see any of this but you and the deer?" the FedEx guy demanded to know one afternoon after he came up the hill to collect my latest travel story.

"The deer aren't the only ones looking at it," I came back pleasantly, regarding my own humble horticultural efforts. "*You're* looking at it, too, aren't you? Besides, the only reason to build a garden"—I gave him a bit of my dirty fingernail philosophy, in the spirit of good old Brother John—"is to please yourself. Across the ages, you see, pleasure gardens have invariably been places of personal retreat and spiritual renewal—an essential expression of the creator who made them."

"You must be one *lonely* dude," said the FedEx guy, quickly retreat-ing to his truck.

Gardening in Maine and raising children, it began to dawn on me about this point in time, gives a man two fairly indispensable qualities: unnatural patience and dogged perseverance in the face of acute public ridicule, a desire to press on when nobody but the hosta-loving deer or the golden retrievers who keep digging up your spring bulbs and eating them like breadsticks really seems interested to know what the hell you're actually up to or why.

Proof that gardening gets in the blood and the apple perhaps doesn't fall far from the tree after all was aptly revealed when my young son Jack, of all people, finally came up with the perfect name for the beloved old beech tree that had triggered my own version of *beautiful madness*.

This happened one cold gray afternoon around Thanksgiving as yet another New England winter descended with the biting sharpness of a woodsman's axe. I'd just finished erecting my Rube Goldberg plant protectors over a group of tender young yew bushes and was attempting to string Christmas lights through the bare limbs of our beloved monarch beech, whereupon my fingers lost feeling and I gave up and simply flung the the damn ropes of lights into the upper branches. Father and son then retreated to the kitchen porch to warm up with hot chocolate and ceremonially hit the juice.

Truthfully, I'm always a little surprised when cheap outdoor Christmas lights actually work the way they are intended to work, and this time turned out to be far more of a revelation than normal. The plug went into the socket, the juice surged, the old beech magically lit up, and Jack grinned from ear to ear beneath his chocolate moustache.

"Look, Dad," he said quietly with the complete wisdom that comes from the mouths of a babe reared in a faux English wood, ". . . an elephant angel."

I looked at our magnificent lighted beech and realized the little cuss was right. My insouciant holiday decorating technique had somehow produced a glittering mythological pachyderm in a rapidly darkening world, the likes of which no one had perhaps ever seen—unmistakably an elephant with wings, flying away into a cold blue winter night.

You can perhaps appreciate my surprise and profound anxiety when, several years further down the garden path of life, as both Jack and my horticultural ambitions lengthened and outgrew their britches, I realized this very same tree we were so emotionally attached to was slowly but inexorably dying—Maine's celebrated hard weather once again being the leading suspect in the crime.

On the heels of the two driest summers in the state's history, the beautiful old tree had suddenly turned yellow and dropped all its leaves in a matter of days, giving up nearly two whole months ahead of normal.

Call me a sentimental boob or a sappy tree hugger who anthropomorphizes stationary living objects, but I hated to see the Elephant Angel go without putting up a decent fight, so I phoned up a couple tree experts.

The first expert who showed up at Slightly Off in the Woods walked around the ailing beech nodding his head with solemn understanding. He made careful notes with his company's official logo pen and then presented me an estimate of $4,712 to save our ailing American beech. He said I could keep the pen free of charge.

"That beech is in critical condition, friend," he explained, grimacing for effect, then ran me through an intensive program of radical tree therapy that sounded more complicated than saving an arctic ecosystem. I thanked him for his time, lied that I would be in touch real soon, and filed his estimate in my wife Wendy's mulch pile. Kept the pen, though.

The next guy, also a commerical tree "expert," had an even simpler solution to the problem. "That tree's a goner," Kev declared, clucking his tongue. "If it was me, why, I'd just cut the sucker down and plant something better there." I politely escorted him off the property.

Only the expert from the state forestry service seemed to feel my gathering arboreal pain. "Why anybody gardens up here in Maine," he sympathized as we stood looking at the visibly struggling tree together, "is one of the great mysteries of this life. They say hard weather makes good timber up here in Maine, but what they don't tell you is it also shortens the life span of most trees by ten or fifteen years. I figure this old fella must be, what, already fifty."

"I'm already fifty, too," I pointed out rather pointlessly. The forestry guy glanced around my nicely landscaped yard.

"Geesum crow," he said. "You do all this *work*?"

He was admiring a decade's worth of relentless English-style landscaping or at least looking at it all a bit puzzlingly. He couldn't have known that I secretly live for the day the phone call comes from the roving chair of our local midcoast garden club asking—no, *begging*—me to consider placing Slightly Off in the Woods on the annual Village Summer Garden Tour simply because some highbrow summer visitor took a wrong turn and discovered that the Sissinghurst of the North is just two miles off the interstate.

"My wife's a gardener," he said, ruefully shaking his head as if that explained something about his life.

"So's mine. Flowers or vegetables?" I asked sunnily.

My wife Wendy and I are not only a second marriage, but a mixed marriage as well. She does vegetables while I handle all manner of flowers, grass, and trees, a separate but equal division of labor save for high weeding season, at which point we cross briefly into each other's domains to lend an extra hand as needed.

"Mine does *both*," he said with surprising bitterness, and went on to reveal how by New Year's Day every year his house was "ass-deep in gardening catalogs and seed trays, with gro-lights going twenty-four a day, lighting us up like, *geesum crow*, Portland Jetport." He added that by April, when he annually moved his things to the basement to watch the Red Sox and get away from their dining room jungle and kitchen greenhouse, his wife even quit cooking meals because this took valuable time away from all her spring garden preparations and elaborate indoor fertilizing schedules.

"I hate gardening," he said with the mineral simplicity of a longtime sufferer.

"Gardening *is* the most addictive thing I've ever seen," I countered, feeling some obligation to convey both male solidarity with his marital plight and yet express loyalty to a fellow aspiring garden nut.

"Problem is," he went on, "she gets *worse* every year. Next spring she intends to try mushrooms in the basement. This keeps up, I'll be sleeping in the garage till Memorial Day."

"Sorry to hear it," I said, thinking I got worse every year too, or at least more horticulturally ambitious, hoping to nudge the conversation back to the subject of my dying tree.

"So is there anything you can do for my troubled beech?"

"I don't know," the forestry guy admitted, thoughtfully rubbing his unshaven chin. "Where you from, anyway?"

"North Carolina," I said, wondering what this could possibly have to do with saving the beloved Elephant Angel.

He smiled sympathetically, giving me a fleeting instant of hope.

"Maybe you should move back there," he suggested. "I hear the winters are mild and the growing season is nearly twice as long as ours. That's where my wife is bugging to move. Geesum crow. If I tell her, she'll probably want to move down there *with* you."

WHICH EXPLAINS WHY one sunny but arctic February day near the calendar end of the most punishingly cold and worryingly snowless winter in years, I fired up my truck and drove out to the peninsula to North Creek Farm hoping my garden muse on call, Suzy Verrier, might be able to cheer me up and give me some useful advice on a number of topics, including and especially what to do about my dying Elephant Angel tree.

Suzy is a nationally acclaimed garden author and former adviser to the famous White Flower Farm catalog folks, a world expert on rugosa roses, and an old friend despite the fact that I wrote in *Town and Country* well over a decade ago that she owns "a noble Gallic nose."

The charming ramshackle saltwater farm and boutique plant nursery and garden shop she shares with her German boyfriend Kai Jacob and an indeterminate number of friendly cairn terriers, barn cats, and various caged singing canaries is the kind of place that artfully peddles everything from fancy English garden tools to exotic Italian pole beans and makes wealthy visiting summer people yearn to chuck the rat race down in Stamford and run away to live on the romantic rocky coast of Maine.

I routinely go see Suzy for inspiration and insight on a range of topics at the start of every season whether I need Italian pole beans or not. She listens patiently and ultimately gives unerringly sound advice on any number of ostensibly unrelated subjects, but particularly my *other* favorite outdoor activity of gardening.

I asked her about my ailing American beech, the dying Elephant Angel.

After I'd fully described the tree's worrying symptoms, she nodded understandingly.

"The real problem, of course, is George W. Bush," she said, diverting the discussion down a familiar lane. "He and his bunch in Washington are systematically destroying the environment, you know. Every gardener in America ought to be worried and up in arms about their shenanigans—including and especially you. Aren't you a gardener *and* a Republican?"

For the next ten or fifteen minutes, my brilliant fiery personal garden adviser sketched out a complex governmental conspiracy theory that made both Martha Stewart's investment problems and the Kennedy assassination both look about as complicated as lunch with Katie Couric. If I absorbed it all correctly, military planes from a New England military base were covertly engaged in a diabolical plan to seed the clouds over northern New England with mysterious chemicals that would permit them to control the weather—a coup de grâce of clouds, as it were—presumably to prevent a third successive severe summer of drought or maybe to simply render us all involuntary Tom DeLay campaign contributors. Basically, as usual, she lost me roughly somewhere in the middle of her grand conspiracy theory.

In any case, if you believe Guru Suzy—and I usually do, because (a) she keeps her ear to the ground on an astonishing array of topics and is, botanically speaking and otherwise, flatly one of the best informed people I know, and (b) she might part my hair with a fancy imported English garden trowel if I didn't—stranger things have happened in America lately, which might not only explain the mysterious death of my beech tree *and* my sudden precipitous loss of anticipation regarding my golf game but also explain why, due to the frightening absence of winter snowfall, the winter frost had penetrated an unprecedented five *feet* into the ground, meaning we would have real hell to pay if and when the gardening season ever arrived.

Calming down and refilling our tea mugs, Suzy asked if I'd given any thought to how I might spend the upcoming year in the garden.

I admitted to my counselor that lately I'd been fantasizing about enrolling in a special two-year horticultural program down at Longwood Gardens in Delaware I'd just read about in *Horticulture* magazine. Once I emerged from hort school, I would be be qualified to hang a shingle and design other people's gardens—possibly even take up a side career designing golf courses for a living.

The good news, however, I swiftly injected before Suze could get passionately wound up again on how "we need more trees and fewer Bushes," was that I'd signed up and been more or less accepted into a local master gardener's program that was supposed to be starting up sometime in the future. The bad news was, the program had been placed on hold for another two years due to local budgetary cuts that may or may not be the result of You Know Who's domestic economic cutbacks and profligate Pentagon spending. But I wasn't dumb enough to open *that* can of worms again.

"In that case, maybe you could just take off and educate yourself," Suzy remarked a touch impatiently, as if the solution to my little dilemma should be as patently obvious as the nose on her face. Being naturally slow on the uptake, not to mention a golfing Republican with unfortunate clothing tastes, I asked her for a bit of clarification.

"I *mean*, you could go attend seminars and hang out with the experts, check out real gardeners in their own gardens! That's the only way to learn about gardening, after all—go see what they're up to and learn from the source. Successful gardening comes from trial and error, and, frankly, *all* the gardeners I know are show-offs at heart, not to mention the friendliest people on earth. The folks I know would be delighted to tell you everything they know. You'd simply be amazed at all you could pick up in a year just hanging around other people's gardens. Just take off down the garden path and see where it leads you! Almost all the world's great gardeners, by the way, are self-taught."

Suzy Verrier is nothing if not convincing. Frankly, I'd hate to have to sit across the table from her and negotiate new fuel emissions standards on behalf of General Motors. But as she beguilingly sketched it out, even *I* began to see the beauty of such a radical self-tutorial—a plan that would have warmed the very heart of my spiritual mentor, Brother John, the accidental gardening monk. After all, snooping around other people's gardens was something I'd been basically doing regularly on the sly for decades.

"I have to make a speech at a golf club down in Philadelphia the first week of March," I explained, the seed of the idea starting to germinate.

"The Philadelphia Flower Show will be going on about then," Suzy put in, smiling coyly. "They call it the Super Bowl of botany, you know. Every serious gardener should probably at least go once."

"Nothing much is going on *here*, that's for sure," I agreed.

"I could make a call or two for you, if you like—get some names together on a list. You'll have fun, and so will they. Every great gardener enjoys an eager learner getting in the way."

"Great," I said, as we actually clicked mugs. "But what about my troubled Elephant Angel tree?"

"When spring comes," she prescribed, "you might try cutting off all the dead limbs and removing some of the heavier soil around the base of the tree. Beeches have shallow roots and need air and moisture. Let the old girl *breathe* a bit. After that, I'd leave it alone—give it time to heal on its own. Nature has a way of fixing everything, you know—sort of what you're hoping a year in the garden will do for you. Less is definitely more in gardening."

"It's that simple?"

"Time will tell."

We paused by the door of her cozy little shop, the snow was finally beginning to pile up with a vengeance, far too late to help insulate the tender plants and border shrubs up in my Sissinghurst of the North. For the moment, though, I simply chose not to think about the winter kill I would eventually face. That was still *months* away, and I was headed off to Philadelphia in search of friendly gardeners and their cheerful natural wisdom.

"So what can I bring you from the Super Bowl of botany?" I asked, by way of saying thanks to my longtime garden muse.

She thought for only an instant, smiled, and sighed.

"Either news of Bush's resignation or an early spring," she said, voicing the foolish perennial hope of many gardeners living in the upper right-hand corner of America.

Chapter 2

❧

The Botticelli of Bulbs

THE 175TH EDITION of the Philadelphia Flower Show, at least for this eager rookie showgoer, began forty-eight hours before the official start of the show in the cozy, fragrant basement of Walt and Linda Fisher's modest suburban brick house on Roberts Road just off the Main Line in Bryn Mawr.

That's where I found, rising like an anthem from paradise, the sweet strains of Vivaldi's *Spring* Concerto oozing seductively from a portable boom box radio as Walt Fisher, a tall, lean, white-haired, retired AT&T executive who bore an uncanny resemblance to Abe Lincoln, ducked his Penn Relays ballcapped head and led me down a dim set of narrow wooden steps into a subterranean world suddenly transformed into blazing colors and dizzying scents of flowers in full lusty bloom. I was there because a mutual friend affiliated with the show thought Walt was the very embodiment of Philadelphia's philosophical mission—to dazzle ordinary folks and get them hooked on gardening. She'd playfully called him the "Botticelli of Bulbs" and said he was a perfect one-man introduction to the show itself.

"The tulips prefer classical music by day, the hyacinths like jazz at night," my genial host explained, immediately taking hold of the tapered

barber shears slung round his neck on long athletic shoelaces and bending to snip off a tiny blemish from a spectacular grape hyacinth plant.

"What do the daffodils get?" I ventured, a little taken aback and
wondering if perhaps my winter-numbed senses were simply playing
tricks on me.

"The daffodils don't have serious musical tastes," Walt explained,
continuing to poke through the blooms in search of minuscule blem-
ishes the way a champion showdog groomer would hunt for stray hairs
moments before Westminster. "So I don't really worry about them too
much. They take whatever they can get and seem to enjoy it. Musically
speaking, daffodils are very undemanding."

Fanning out across this Bryn Mawr basement beneath buzzing ranks
of low-slung gro-lights suspended from the floor joists overhead stood
several worktables freighted with dozens of pots of spring bulbs
blooming their silly heads off in a staggering affront to the calendar
and the still-bracing late-winter temperatures outside the walls of the
Fisher house. I saw—better yet, *smelled*—hundreds of magnificent
tulips, hyacinths, and daffodils either at peak-of-bloom stage or very
close to it.

The second question out of my slightly gaping mouth was one of
pure logistics. With the mother of all flower shows just hours away from
its grand-opening, black-tie gala, how and when did he hope to get all of
this splendid peaking horticulture all the way downtown to Philly's
bristling new convention center and assembled without damaging paradise and spoiling all the tender blooms?

Walt smiled cagily. "*Very* carefully. That's for sure. But, remember,
Linda and I are old hands at this. I think this is my thirtieth show. We'll
start taking these things down to the site first thing in the morning." He
continued his barberly ministrations. "Those of us who are scheduled to
compete in the various competitive classes, you see, can officially get
into the convention center and begin assembling our displays at eight
tomorrow morning—earlier, if you know what you're doing. Truthfully,
it's well-ordered madness. You'll see people and plants moving everywhere. We basically only have one full day to get our exhibit completely

assembled and groomed, from eight to about five o'clock. And this year we're competing in a new category that will be tougher than ever."

"We're up against a tough group," chipped in Walt's wife, Linda, who'd suddenly appeared on the basement steps behind us. "We're talking some of the toughest folks in the hall, including the Ameys."

Linda sounded like a worried manager summing up a dangerous contender in the locker room before the big title fight.

"Who are the Ameys?" I asked.

Snipping and squinting, Walt said, "They're kind of the first family of the Philadelphia Flower Show. The father, Stan, is a major figure in the Men's Garden Club of Philadelphia and longtime veteran of competition, while several of the Amey children are involved in their own displays at the show. A talented bunch, the Ameys. They literally grew up at the show. We happen to be up against the Amey Siblings, two of the daughters, in the new terrace class." He snipped gently at an arching tulip stem and added, "The others in the class aren't slouches, either, let me tell you."

"What's 'terrace class' mean?" I hated sounding so dense, but the world of big-time competitive gardening was a major step deeper into beautiful madness.

"It means we actually build a terrace at the show," Linda helpfully explained, smiling tolerantly as if she understood it's a gift to be simple.

"Our terrace is an exact replica of a Savannah terrace our little group saw when we made a field trip together down to that city following the show last spring. That's how far ahead you have to plan these sorts of things, by the way. Sometimes even longer than that. Sometimes it requires years of planning."

"You have a *group*?"

The Botticelli of Bulbs smiled. "Oh, *quite* a group. There are at least seven of us—a top nurseryman and his wife, an architect and his interior decorator wife from Philadelphia, Linda and myself, plus the doctor whose late wife brought us all together. She was a multiple Grand Sweepstakes winner—that's one of the biggies. He, the husband, is the crack taxonomist of our little gang. Once you get your exhibit fully assembled and your garden intent written and posted, see, it's important to properly identify every plant in the exhibit. The point of the show, after all, is to educate as well as entertain people with flowers. They're coming to see great gardens but also to learn about plants. We call ourselves, by the way, *The Inforcers*. Get it?"

It took me a moment, I confess. He meant, of course, that their terrace garden was the result of all of these subterranean *forced* spring bulbs.

"We like to have fun," Linda put in, still lingering on the lower step. "Some of us go along just to drink the wine and eat the cheese."

"We do drink some *excellent* wine," Walt agreed affably, still fussing with the shears. "But for most of us who are veterans of the show, while the competition is major league and about as serious as you can get, the social stuff that goes on around it is pure pleasure—a lot of fun and joking around behind the scenes, like an annual reunion of friends, people you maybe see once or twice a year when we all converge on the convention center to battle it out with flowers. It's a blast, to tell you the truth, something we construct our entire year around and all live for. It certainly gets us through the winter."

"And your job in the group, I gather, is to provide all the spring bulbs."

"Something like that." He grinned lopsidedly, *very* Abe Lincoln–like. "I'm the bulb man."

"Would you two care for a tuna on marbled rye?" Linda asked pleasantly. "That's really why I came down here. It's almost lunchtime."

"T minus eighteen hours and counting until we move the bulbs," Walt intoned, smiling slyly, calm as a watchmaker on holiday deadline. Moments before this I learned that Walt Fisher serves every year as an offical timekeeper at the famous Penn Relays track meet, which failed to surprise me in the least. To judge by the coordinated magnificence of his flowers, this was evidently a man who had the cycle of life calculated down to the minute, perhaps even the split second.

"That would be nice," I said to Linda, but turned back to the bulb-master of the Delaware Valley and asked the question I was suddenly dying to have explained to a rapidly thawing brain.

"But how do you make *all* of these bloom exactly at once, like stage performers on cue?"

"Good question. It's either magic or total madness, I'm not sure which after all these years," Linda Fisher declared with a girlish laugh and turned to proceed back upstairs to the kitchen.

"I'll call you boys when lunch is ready."

OVER THE NEXT HOUR or so, the Botticelli of Bulbs patiently explained to me how he did it—how he annually fooled Mother Nature at her own game and made hundreds of spectacular and, near as I could ascertain with the untrained eye, visibly flawless "Calgary" and "Holland Chic" tulips, "Pueblo" narcissi, "Pink Pearl" hyacinths, and "Salome" daffodils erupt into bloom on the eve of their big Philadelphia debut.

By Veterans Day every year, Fisher has no fewer than three *thousand* spring bulbs ordered from a variety of sources ("whoever is cheapest is basically the one I usually go with") safely planted in upward of one hundred and fifty special clay azalea pots. These are then stored in a homemade refrigeration unit, not unlike the kind used by mom-and-pop grocery operations everywhere, that hums along for successive months at the south end of Walt's basement, keeping the bulbs in the suspended animation of a false 48-degree autumn until they begin to show significant root growth, at which point the unit thermostat is cranked artfully down another eight or nine degrees to simulate the onset of winter in the Delaware Valley. Once top growth begins to appear, the temperature is lowered to 34 degrees Fahrenheit and the plants grow extremely slowly for another five or six weeks.

"Bulb forcing is as much an art as a science," Walt explained as I ducked my head inside his refrigeration unit, where a few pots were still cooling their heels on special shelving. "You need the suspended cold to fool the bulbs into thinking winter has arrived, because, like all living things, they have an internal clock and this is their resting or gestation period, the time they recollect their energy required for producing flowers. For that reason, this is a crucial time. You have to stay close and constantly monitor the temperatures and growth rates. If you go away, for example, and there is a power outage and the unit heats up—well, you could throw everything off and ruin the whole lot. That's why I have an emergency backup unit. But you can't always rely on that. You have to *be* there."

"So you and Linda rarely make Christmas in Bermuda."

Walt laughed. "Sometimes just driving downtown to Philadelphia feels out of the question. This is the nerve-wracking part of the process."

At some point following five or six weeks of "winter" refrigeration, the first clay pots come out of the unit and are placed on the basement floor, permitting them to warm uniformly to room temperature. "The idea is to produce a gradual warmup that resembles Mid-Atlantic spring."

Depending on the species and particular cultivars, he expanded, pots are shuttled to a special greenhouse table, where they begin their sweet bath in fluorescent glo-light warmth and the strains of jazz and classical music day and night. They are given no fewer than twelve hours of heat and light per day, all run off a temperature and time-monitoring system that would favorably compare to anything found in the controlled-atmosphere laboratory of a midsize university.

"By now it's mid-February and this is the home stretch of bulb forc-ing," my host continued, picking up the dramatic narrative of creation. "You always want to err on the side of having things coming out a little too early, because it's a whole lot easier to slow flowers down than to speed up their blooming."

From a competitive standpoint, the last thing he could afford to do, he emphasized, was to take flowers to the show that have achieved bloom stage before he and his mates have finished assembling their ex-hibit. "One of the major logistical challenges for any competitor is to make things bloom just as the judges are showing up to do their com-petitive assessments. This is the holy grail—and nightmare—of every class competitor. You see, the show runs for a week, but there are two separate judging periods that add up for a final accumulated score and determine a best-of-class award. An initial first judging takes place Sat-urday morning—at which point ribbons are placed and other prizes awarded—followed by a second judging on Wednesday. Under the rules, you're allowed to replace plants after the first round of judging. The trick is to keep the exhibit fresh and at its peak for nine full days. No easy task. Most flowers have only a day or two when they are at their peak."

He waved to another worktable where ranks of pots full of healthy-looking tulips and daffodils were just beginning to open, while many others were still in the budding stage. "Those, for instance, will come downtown later in the week."

"What about those?" I pointed to several pots of magnificent "White Parrot" tulips that already looked as if they could have lined the front walk leading to the Pearly Gates. They were spring perfection, almost good enough to eat.

"I'm afraid they've missed it. They won't be coming downtown with us."

"What will happen to them?"

The master shrugged. "Some I'll give away to friends. Others will just get tossed."

Tossed? Had I heard the man correctly? As I stood there staring at these magnificent Dutch flowers, I suddenly realized that I hadn't just ventured into the blooming heart of America's gardening Olympics, I'd also wandered into a ruthless world where a perfect flower could simply get pitched out for the sin of being perfect a few hours too soon.

OVER TUNA on marbled rye, I asked Walt and Linda how they'd become such fanatical bulb-forcing folks. This particular passion, this little corner of the specialized gardening world, struck me as an even more exotic and fascinatingly narrow subspecies of the genus commonly known as *garden nut*.

"This is really Walt's thing." Linda gave another of her youthful laughs, as if the vast botanical operation buzzing along one floor below us still both gently baffled and amused her. "I just got into it because he did. My job is to hold the flashlight and bring the wine."

"Beg pardon?"

"It's something I started in middle age," Walt spoke up, chewing his sandwich thoughtfully and thinking back to a simpler time when his bulb wizardry wasn't everything. "But the seed got planted when I was a kid in northeast Philadelphia."

As cheerful spring sun splashed into their kitchen from a pretty suburban yard where the budding trees suggested there would soon be a stunning panorama of flowering bulbs a month behind the blooming specimens below, I learned the Botticelli of Bulbs had been twelve years old and nuts about baseball and basketball when gardening unexpectedly intruded on his life.

"The war was on, and like just about everybody else on that side of town, we still had a victory garden where we raised vegetables and a few flowers. But then my older brother Charles went to work at Worsinger's Greenhouses after school. They were a big commercial outfit, with twelve greenhouses, who specialized in forcing things like poinsettias for Christmas and lilies for Easter.

"A short time after my brother went to Worsingers, I did too—picking up odd jobs and potting up bulbs, mostly. To begin with, it was just a job for us both, a way to bring home some extra money to the family."

One perk of his new after-school job was free tickets to the city's annual flower show, distributed by the area's commercial nurserymen, the sponsors of the flower show in those faraway postwar days. "The flower show, as far back as anyone can remember, was always the biggest social occasion in Philadelphia, when the blue bloods and the common folks all came together and rubbed elbows with a mutually shared enthusiasm. But for us kids it was initially just a great place to go to get out of the cold and see things actually growing, like going indoors to a great big park. In those days it was held over at Horticultural Hall. You saw everybody you knew, all your pals, and you also got to see some great exotic plants you'd never heard of—a jungle of things you couldn't name but eventually wanted to know about."

Walt took a bite of his sandwich and reflected for a moment, glancing out at his thawing yard. "I mean, how could something *so* beautiful be blooming at such a bleak time of year? That was the hook that got some of us, and we didn't even realize it."

He looked at me. "In my opinion, that's how a deep passion for gardening starts in almost anyone. It frequently begins quite innocently in youth and lies dormant for some time, often for years." As he said this, I remembered reading somewhere that Abe Lincoln was deeply pleased to have a native American rhododendron named for him toward the end of the Civil War, a tough flowering native American shrub that stands up to anything man or nature can dish out.

"For one reason or another, you somehow get introduced to growing things, and the beauty and pleasure of horticulture just gets quietly into your blood," Walt elaborated, obviously having pondered the subject. "Sometimes it takes many years to reemerge and establish itself—not unlike some plants themselves. But once it does, you're usually hooked for life." He chewed for a moment more and added, "Almost every gardener has some version of this story."

It wasn't until Walt Fisher had completed his industrial management studies at MIT, done a stint in the U.S. Army, and gotten married to Linda that his own horticultural yearnings began to reassert themselves. "By 1964, we had three of our four children and were living in our first house over in Radnor. It had a little yard with a sloping hill and that's where the kids and I put in our first garden—a bunch of things at first, being completely new gardeners—potatoes, blueberries, vegetables of every sort, a few bulbs and flowering shrubs, too."

A decade later, on something of a lark, Fisher and his youngest daughter, Amy, exhibited their first homegrown vegetables in the Pennsylvania Horticulture Society's annual harvest show, a much-loved autumn show that no longer exists. Over the next half dozen years, they were regular competitors in the show, carting home a barrel of first-place ribbons. About this same time, Walt's old interest in forcing spring bulbs began to reemerge. In 1979, he formally submitted his first pots of forced bulbs, daffodils, and tulips, and took home a handful of prize ribbons. Horticulturally speaking, he never looked back.

In the early days of his obsession, lacking a proper greenhouse of his own, Fisher developed a system of cold storage involving a pair of old refrigerators in the basement and several outdoor cold frames, where he would bury potted-up bulbs in perlite every November, digging them out again in late January or early February.

"I remember some years seeing Walt out there in the yard," Linda reminisced, chuckling gently and shaking her head, "using a flashlight and a pick to hack frozen pots out of the ground. Sometimes it was *me* holding the flashlight, trying to find those buried pots because we couldn't remember where Walt had put them." Once they were properly retrieved, the pots were brought indoors and arranged on a makeshift worktable, in those days the family's Ping-Pong table, which had holes drilled through it to permit warmth from space heaters on the floor below.

"This wasn't the most reliable system," Walt allowed. "There were years we lost everything. But that's horticulture for you—the only way to learn is by failing and getting better at it, learning the tricks."

By the early nineties, Walt had designed and built his state-of-the-art underground commercial refrigeration unit, kicking his horticultural capacities and ambitions to a whole new level of expertise.

By this point, not surprisingly, he'd also begun to fill up shelves and bureau drawers with blue ribbons and trophies from his bulb-forcing wizardry, and lecturing and speaking to garden organizations and horticultural groups across the Delaware Valley. As if that wasn't enough to keep him busy preparing for the annual spring extravaganza, he also began serving as the roving photographer for the big slide show and awards luncheon that closes the mother of all American flower shows.

"How many ribbons do you suppose you've won?"

"I've never counted," Walt allowed mildly. "I suppose it might be somewhere around five hundred or so, give or take."

"*Five hundred?*"

"They're everywhere in this house," Linda said. "Open a drawer, there's a pile of ribbons Walt won."

I asked how he kept so keenly interested in competing year after year, given this level of competitive success. He wasn't just the Botticelli of Bulbs. He was also the Arnold Palmer of spring gardening.

"As I said, it's the most intensely competitive family reunion you've ever seen, friendly plant nuts you haven't seen for at least a year coming back to try and beat you with something they've cooked up in their imaginations. Every year, it seems, you have to not only get better but more creative. That's why we've assembled our own little team of stars to build our Savannah terrace. The Inforcers have been working on this project for well over a year."

He sketched out how, commencing at eight o'clock tomorrow morning, they would be working from an architect's blueprint that had been drawn to the square inch, a detailed schematic that called for assembling a perfect Savannah terrace garden in less than a single working day and involved, among other things, the transport and assembly of nearly half a ton of ornamental brick, a large ivy-covered trellis, a large antique gate, several mature crab trees, a dozen or so large flower shrubs, Walt's bulb wizardry, and a real working stone fountain.

"It ought to look wonderful," Linda put in, clearing away the lunch plates.

"Can't wait," I said, my own sense of floral drama already beginning to build.

"You've never *been*?" She seemed flatly astonished by this admission.

"No, ma'am."

"Oh," she said, smiling like a wistful schoolgirl, "you probably won't believe it when you see it for the first time. I truly think there's *nothing* on earth like the Philadelphia show. I wish I could go back to my first time."

THE PHILADELPHIA FLOWER SHOW began shortly after a group of that city's prominent like-minded citizens founded the Pennsylvania Horticultural Society in 1827 with a stated objective "to inspire a taste for one of the most rational and pleasing amusements of man, and to facilitate the means of cultivating that taste."

Because gardeners even as far back as days of the Lewis and Clark expedition (which was completed just two decades earlier) were natural show-offs, it quickly became fashionable for fledgling society members to exhibit their achievements at early meetings, a custom that gained currency with every passing year and soon evolved into the first public one-day display of "fruits, flowers and plants" in 1829. This event was the first of its kind in the nation's history and included several specimen plants rarely if ever seen before on American shores, including the bird-of-paradise flower, exotic euphorbia plants of one kind or another, and a bold red-leafed plant named by Joel Roberts Poinsett, the U.S. ambassador to Mexico. Within a few years, the poinsettia was the rage in American horticultural circles and, as a Philadelphia newspaper evangelized, "Those who witnessed this exhibition enjoyed the opportunity of comparing together a greater variety of plants than has at any time before been assembled among us in a single view." A newspaper as distant as Baltimore—a two-day ride on horseback—concurred: "The magic of flowers and fruiting plants recently displayed in our sister city to the north was most wondrous and enviable in regard to its effect on the public spirit."

Due to overwhelming popularity, the fledgling PHS decided to make the exhibition an annual affair and held it at various venues around the city until the society built its own venue, Horticultural Hall, next to the Academy of Music on Broad Street, two years after the end of the Civil War. Beginning in 1872, the PHS mounted two major exhibitions a year, a spring and an autumn show, and began promoting competitive classes with cash premiums for the best-judged entries in individual classes on the rough theory that competition would stimulate local interest in horticulture and raise money for the society. By the spring show of 1885, these cash prizes ranged from one dollar to thirty dollars for a major exhibit best-of-show award, and nurserymen and private gardeners from as far away as New York and Washington began to haul their horticultural handiworks to Philadelphia.

When America at large began to spread out to rural fields beyond burgeoning city limits around 1910, prompting the nation's first housing boom and the first widespread measurable growth in popular gardening habits among all classes (a plant fever inspired by the suburban Victorian gardening craze that was then sweeping over Britain), the PHS wisely sensed the zeitgeist and added a host of additional competitive exhibitions and shows to reflect its membership's rapidly expanding tastes, including rose, peony, and dahlia shows, thus playing a major role in influencing the formation of local garden clubs around Philadelphia.

In 1916, the National Flower Show, as it was popularly called, staged the largest horticultural exhibition in America to date and did the spadework for an even more ambitious and expanded four-day event. Officially christened the Philadelphia Flower Show in 1925, that year it drew an estimated 83,000 patrons to the city's Commercial Museum.

By the time the show was legally incorporated two years later, near the bottom of the Great Depression, the area's powerful commercial gardening interests—nurserymen and unionized commercial florists, mostly—had wrested control of the show from the originating society and expanded the national event to encompass six days, relegating the PHS to simply managing the show's popular amateur and gardening competitions. The powerful flower unions, as one critic dismissed them, saw the show as little more than a stage for peddling the latest horticultural developments and the latest plants to a citizenry deep in the throes of America's first gardening craze.

Despite suspensions of the event owing to manpower and fuel shortages during World War II, the show chugged along in this manner delighting all classes of Philadelphians and Mid-Atlantic gardeners until 1965, at which point the city fathers of Philadelphia announced plans to demolish the Commerical Museum, the cavernous home of trade shows and conventions since 1897, and build a new civic center on the site.

Inside the palace walls of the show's governing hierarchy, meanwhile, an insurrection that had been quietly building for years finally came to the breaking point when the existing board of the show—still dominated by the ruling commercial interests—voted to suspend the annual spring show for three years pending construction of a new and permanent home, giving the PHS's plucky executive director, Ernesta Ballard, exactly the opening she'd hoped for. Stepping into the breach to convince the society's own board that it couldn't afford *not* to stage the beloved rite of spring it had faithfully mounted for more than a century,

Ballard had the society break off and conduct its own flower shows at several makeshift locations around the city while cagily negotiating a binding new space and time lease with the management of Philadelphia's Civic Center, effectively staging a bloodless coup that wrested control of the show from the nurserymen and powerful florist unions and returning it to its founding principal.

"DON'T LET ANYBODY TELL YOU horticulture is a gentle business in Philadelphia," Jack Blandy wryly observed as we rolled through the misty spring darkness from his commercial nursery south of the city toward the *latest* permanent home of the Philadelphia Flower Show, the new Pennsylvania Convention Center in downtown Philadelphia.

This was just after six in the morning, twenty-six hours and counting until judging commenced, and I had hooked up with Blandy and his son Joe of Stoney Bank Nurseries to get yet another unique perspective on the mother of all gardening shows. Jane Pepper, the PHS's current president, had arranged both my delightful afternoon with Walt Fisher and this morning commute to the show with the Blandys, explaining that they nicely represented each end of the spectrum of Philly show participants—the amateur competitors who had hope and pride on the line at one end of the spectrum, and the large commercial outfits like Stoney Bank Nursuries that had big bucks and years of horticultural experience and planning invested at the other.

The older Blandy, a former English major who chucked teaching to become a trained horticulturist in early midlife, had not only largely built his business on the exposure the show had given his firm over the previous decade and a half, but also had won numerous awards in the all-important major exhibit category, including a trio of coveted best-of-show awards. Blandy was now also on the show's executive committee, having "grown up along with Philadelphia's most famous rite of spring," as he summarized, during the very two decades the show registered its most explosive growth.

"I remember meeting Ernesta Ballard once and thinking she was one determined little lady—to go up against those union guys," Jack mused as we passed the gritty Philly shipyards in the gloaming. "That was sometime around 1980, the year she retired from the executive director's position and handed the job over to Jane Pepper. That was also *our* first year at the show, and it was still being held at the old Civic Center in those days. The Civic Center had a spectacular escalator that carried arriving show visitors dramatically down to the Civic Center floor, so that the effect was like descending into a botanical paradise. Very effective—*beloved* by many Philadelphians, an annual tradition for thousands."

Blandy smiled at the memory as we angled up a downtown off-ramp into a flow of vans and panel trucks that were clearly headed to the same destination. "The problem with the old Civic Center was, the parking lots were below the main floor, so every time all those acres of plants and horticultural exhibits got watered, the cars below got washed for free."

Joe, twenty-seven, a newly married and recent Temple University's Ambler College of Horticulture graduate, Stoney Bank's heir apparent, eyed the line of vans and trucks torturously waiting just to get near the service bays of the sprawling convention complex and observed dryly, "And now you're lucky if you can find a parking place within a few blocks of the show. Every year, parking just gets worse."

In the chilly morning darkness south of the city, two hours before, I'd watched as the Blandy crews filled the last of two twenty-eight-foot rented panel trucks with an extraordinary array of gorgeous live shrubs, flowering plants, and trees, the final ingredients for the "classic Delaware woodland estate" they aimed to complete before day's end.

The theme of the septaquintaquinquecentennial edition of the Philadelphia Flower Show was "Destination Paradise" and the title of Stoney Bank's major 2,500-square-foot exhibit was "Pathways to Paradise," describing what Joe called "a classic Delaware estate garden with a novel twist—*three* distinctly different garden experiences flowing together in one space, linked by a series of woodland garden paths."

I couldn't picture what they had in mind any more than I could imagine what the floor of the sprawling Pennsylvania Convention Center must look like, what with setup crews and major exhibitors and creators of several special noncompetitive display gardens having access to the place all week. (It's only the amateur competitors like Walt Fisher and their ilk who have only a single day to assemble their gardens.)

It all sounded highly orchestrated and not a little overwhelming to my admittedly modest horticultural sensibilities, evidenced by the fact that the Blandys and their crews were "planting" over three hundred different species of shrubs and flowering plants in their New Age–replicated Delaware Valley estate garden, including a dozen fully mature trees plus a major water feature. I couldn't wait to see how their "Pathways to Paradise" panned out.

Meanwhile, as we waited to just get *into* the place, I tried to get my mind around the volume of plants involved to make this magic happen.

"We basically forced six greenhouses full of plants for the show," Jack allowed, "though probably only two or three houses wound up being loaded on trucks and brought downtown to the show."

"Isn't that sort of extravagant, not to mention expensive?"

"It will cost a major exhibitor about eighty thousand dollars to compete in the show this year," Jack explained. "But the PHS offsets some of that expense by subsidizing about half the cost. We absorb the rest—in fact, this is basically our entire advertising budget for the year, spent in one fell swoop." A pleasant Irish-looking man with a youthful air about him, Blandy suddenly grinned. "For that price, though, we get free signs and all the mulch we can use."

"They say," Joe, behind the wheel, chipped in, "there is more theatrical lighting used at the Philadelphia Flower Show than anywhere in America."

"I believe it," agreed his father, grimacing a little at the long line of panel trucks inching up the service ramps to the rear of the massive convention center. "I just hope we can get things wrapped up and the lighting done before dinnertime. I'd love *not* to be here working at midnight, for a change."

Even before laying eyes on the show, I was awed—even a little intimidated—by the scope and organizational dimensions of this mother of all flower shows. With fifty major exhibitors and roughly three thousand entries in hundreds of competitive categories ranging from the smallest houseplant in a four-inch pot to the largest horticultural display garden with fifty-foot trees, it required more than thirty-five hundred show volunteers plus an army of technical advisers, set designers, lighting experts, caterers, carpenters and electricians, maintenance crews, union laborers, garden advisers, and individual commercial crews to piece it all together.

The heart of this spring's extravaganza, the show's thematic masterpiece and major "Central Feature," was already being widely heralded as another Philly first in American horticulture: a sweeping seven-thousand-square-foot Polynesian temple ruins displaying over a hundred thousand blooming orchids, believed to be the largest display of blooming orchids ever seen. Jack Blandy had done Central Features in his days at the Philadelphia show, and I naturally wondered if the time and expense involved with mounting something that big was worth it. The Central Feature, after all, didn't compete—it merely served as the centerpiece of the show itself, the splashy garden most visitors saw when they first came through the doors.

"I suppose in one way it is a large financial gamble," Jack mused as we waited outside the hall to get in. "The expense and time and worry that goes into this show takes years of planning and basically exhausts everyone. On the other hand, there's no question that I owe my company's success to the exposure we've enjoyed through the flower show. And being asked to do a Central Feature is the ultimate compliment. The PHS is probably the most respected gardening organization in America, full of people who know everything about gardening—primarily because they've been *doing* this sort of thing longer than anyone else."

He paused and thought a moment. "If we're lucky, five or six major landscaping jobs will come directly out of this show. I'm talking about projects that will carry my guys through much of the rest of the year into next winter. That's no small payback." He gave me a quick Irish grin and a wink, and suddenly we were parked and everyone was jumping out to unload plants and join the long queue of paid workers, volunteers, and family members bearing what seemed to be an infinite array of plant material through the gaping rear doors of the 33-acre exhibit hall.

Eager to be useful and part of the fun, I'd hoisted a small potted azalea much like the ones that used to grow in my own family's yard down in the foothills of North Carolina and joined the ranks of Philly's worker bees. I vaguely wondered if my voluntary participation could be viewed as an infraction of the show's governing rules—the impartial journalist, as it were, who joined the foot soldiers of a gardening revolution.

Amid this throng of horticultural humanity, I suddenly found myself following the handsomely burlapped business end of what turned out to be a stunning, live, sixty-foot traveler's palm tree that had just completed a nineteen-hour odyssey lashed to the flatbed freight truck that rolled all the way up I-95 from a commercial nursery in Florida. It was destined for the show's Central Feature.

When I turned around to comment on this amazing feat of mobility to Blandy and son, both were suddenly nowhere in sight. They'd either slipped ahead into the bright lights and intense explosion of foliage I could see spilling from an interior set of doors leading to the main hall floor just ahead of me, or else were lagging back to go over final assembly instructions with their crew members.

I decided to proceed into the main hall behind the Traveler palm with my potted Carolina azalea clutched importantly to my chest. Besides, Jack had graciously invited me to join his crew for an early supper, an annual tradition of sorts following the final prep work on their exhibit. The last thing I wanted to do at this point was get in the way of anyone working to make the completion deadline.

I walked the remaining dozen yards behind the elegant Traveler palm straight through the service bay doors into a scene of garden mayhem that caused me to stop and open my mouth in dumbstruck awe, to gasp like a rube from a dirt road in Maine for the second time in twenty-four hours.

If Walt Fisher's blooming basement had been like slipping down a rabbit hole to a subterranean Eden, the sprawling floor of the vast Pennsylvania Convention Center was like waking up in some garden-mad Ottoman pasha's drug-induced dream of heaven. It was every bit as startling, violent, and beautiful as Linda Fisher had said it would be to a first-timer's raw sensibilities.

Everywhere I looked was a massive garden of some sort, riotously in bloom, arched and preening, dramatically lit from above and below. There were whole stage sets that rivaled anything you'll see on Broad-way. They were matched only by a DeMille-like cast of hundreds— maybe *thousands*—of people and machinery swarming industriously in every direction, tooting horns and calling out instructions, waving at lighting crews, or simply hunched and working diligently over flower-beds. The smell of mulch and diesel fuel from forklifts and boom trucks was powerful.

There I stood, blocking the door, clutching my Carolina azalea, im-peding the flow of the Super Bowl of botany, as Suzy had called it, when a burly union guy on a forklift trying to negotiate a magnificent thirty-foot Cuban ficus into the hallway, gave me a waking blast of his horn and yelled out like Rocky Balboa, "Wanna move it, Mac? This tree ain't walkin' by itself."

I happily obliged, stepping safely aside to where a Mexican worker was on his knees constructing the most intricately beautiful stone wall I'd ever seen. The wall surrounded a massive zoysia yard that featured dozens of flowerbeds chock full of blooming spring bulbs. The worker was oblivious to my presence, covered from head to boot with a flour-fine stone dust, his small artisan hammer expertly chipping pieces off the stones before he inserted them into a wall that simply wouldn't be here in another week. "Everything you see at the Philadelphia Flower Show," Jack Blandy had said with a mischievous Irish twinkle, "is pure illusion. Those stunning gardens don't really exist. But that's the point of what we do—aim to make it somehow all look real and perfect."

Building stone walls is one of my favorite garden pastimes. I'd re-built my property's original stone boundary walls plus half a dozen smaller stone wall enclosures around various beds and terraces and sometimes fancied that I wasn't half bad as a largely self-taught wall builder. But this young man, working with the speed of a jeweler next door to a Vegas wedding chapel, made me look like a ham-fisted fool. He was fitting pieces of flat Pennsylvania bluestone so expertly together, the gaps between the stones were almost impossible to discern. The wall he was constructing embraced a stunning yard full of blooming perennials and spring bulbs set off by an arched gate leading to an equally enchanting backyard where a full-scale tree house presided over a real woodland brook tumbling musically over stones. Jack Blandy told me this was merely a horticultural sleight of hand; my eyes told me something else entirely.

"Excuse me, how long did it take you to build this wall?" I couldn't resist interrupting the young wall-builder's Zen-like flow.

The worker glanced up and smiled, showing a gap in his teeth much wider than anything in his wall. He looked to be about twenty years old.

"I begin yesterday," he provided genially. "I finish today."

His head bobbed, the smile widened fractionally. *Tap-tap-tap*.

Frankly, I was mesmerized by what he was doing so calmly, so expertly, so completely oblivious to the noisy scene of controlled mayhem that engulfed him.

"Unbelievable wall," I said.

He glanced up and smiled shyly but said nothing, just kept on chipping tiny pieces of stone and fitting pieces into his beautiful wall.

A horn briskly tooted again and I immediately leapt aside. A Gator cart whizzed past bearing boxloads of spectacular exotic cut flowers bearing labels that read in bright red letters FRAGILE and FLOWERS FROM HOLLAND toward a display where comic life-size doll figures cavorted among simulated clouds beyond a set of Pearly Gates where thousands of stunning white Calla lilies and trumpet vines were exploding into bloom.

What a way to enter Paradise, I thought, wondering if the real deal could possibly improve on this divine illusion.

Chapter 3

Gardenlust

W<small>ITH MY CAROLINA AZALEA</small> in hand, mere hours to go before the public opening of the 175th Philadelphia Flower Show, I vanished into the green mayhem of the final setup hours of the gardening Olympics. Like a toddler permitted off his leash at the Magic Kingdom, I ventured from one horticultural wonder to the next.

It's during peripatetic moments like these that I slip into a state of wistful longing. My wife Wendy likes to call them "involuntary *gardenlust.*" Once, at the much smaller Portland Flower Show, she found me in thoughtful conversation with a man selling Bobcat minitractors, getting the operational lowdown on an amazing rig that came with a seventy-inch mowing deck, dual bank of fog lights, major hydraulic earth-shaping capacity, and the kind of major-league snowplow apparatus that would wow the boys on a winter morning down at Frosty's Donut Shop. That object of my gardenlust came with a fully heated and air-conditioned driver's compartment large enough to accommodate both the driver and at least one grounds assistant, which in my case is a somewhat lazy golden retriever named Riley. At just under fifty-six thousand dollars, the versatile mini-Bobcat struck me as a steal, though admittedly I came to my senses after Wendy physically removed me from its hypnotic presence.

◦ ◦ ◦

My GARDENLUST INTENSIFIED in the mist over by the Polynesian temple, the dramatic centerpiece of the show's Central Feature. That's where I was standing with my azalea, admiring what was said to be the largest display of blooming orchids ever seen anywhere, when I met Walter Off, the evangelistic owner of Waldor Orchids of Linwood, New Jersey. Off was a longtime veteran of the Philly show and the designer of this year's extraordinary Central Feature—a twelve-thousand-foot Polynesian temple surrounded by a lush tropical jungle that included the magnificent ficus trees and towering traveler's palms like the one I'd followed into the exhibition hall. Crews were already positioning these spectacular trees and mulching them neatly into the jungle landscape, but the orchids were clearly the showstoppers. The lucky soul selected by the PHS to create a particular Central Feature exhibit, I understood from Jack Blandy, was normally drawn from a pool of former major show exhibitors who had a lengthy history and extensive experience of mounting large horticultural displays at Philadelphia. The creation of a Central Feature exhibit, he emphasized, could require years of detailed research and design work and logistical planning with the show's lead designer, not to mention a cost of upward of six figures, an expense that came directly out of the show's projected revenues. This year's show, officially sponsored by PNC Bank and several other corporations, was expected to generate about seven million dollars in revenue, making it by far the primary funding source for the PHS and a host of its award-winning projects like Philadelphia Green project that had transformed thousands of the city's formerly derelict byways and abandoned lots into people-friendly green spaces and handsome parks.

"Beautiful, aren't they?" Off observed. He was a large man in a sweat-stained polo shirt who clearly relished his job. Just moments before, he'd been directing a lighting crew on a boom crane, pleasantly shouting up at them as they positioned beams of theatrical lighting. For some reason he made me think of Robert Altman, the legendary film director, whom I'd once interviewed in Atlanta.

"Never seen anything like it," I agreed.

"You must be an orchid nut."

I shook my head. "They scare me to death, frankly. I have enough guilt over killing lavender and roses."

He smiled. "Where you from?"

"A dirt road in Maine."

"Follow me," he said, with a knowing smile.

We took a pleasant stroll together through his amazing jungle creation and he thoughtfully identified several of the stunning varieties of orchids in view, citing them by their unpronounceable Latin names, reminding me what a hopeless dolt I am when it comes to garden Latin— *phalaenopsis, oncidium, cattleya, paphiliopedium,* and *dendrobium.* "Those are philodendron, of course, and that's bird-of-paradise. I'm sure even someone from a dirt road in Maine recognizes *that.*" He ushered me pleasantly on through a vaulting aisle of misted tropical flowers. "And those up there are hibiscus and blue vandas."

"Spectacular." I was quickly running out of adjectives for the Philadelphia Flower Show, a place where a flawless tulip's lethal failing was blooming perfectly a few hours too soon.

"You should really try growing orchids. They're the hottest thing going in horticulture. Anyone can grow them. All you really need is a nice kitchen window to get started—maybe a greenhouse later on.

"The big misunderstanding about orchids is that they are fussy. Nothing could be further from the truth. That's why they grow so abundantly in the wild, in the most forbidding places. In fact, all they require is a kitchen with good indirect light, steady moisture, and reasonable room temperature to thrive." He amplified that the genus *Orchidaceae* contained nearly eighteen thousand different varieties, including terrestrials (earth growing) and even "epiphytic" (meaning they grow entirely in the air)—"Something for everyone!"—and insisted, with an unmistakable evangelical air, that there was bound to be an orchid somewhere just perfect for a dirt road in Maine.

I'd just finished reading a book about America's current love affair with orchids and knew the genus *Orchis* derived from the Greek word for testicles (which I apparently lacked in the metaphorical sense of the word when it came to attempting to grow them), alluding to the spherical-shaped pairs of tubers found on many species, popularly called "Hare's bollockes" and "Dogstones" by medieval herbalists and even assigned serious aphrodisiacal properties. Pliny the Elder supposedly believed, for example, that merely holding an orchid tuber would ignite a man's sexual desire in the most private but visible manner; for this reason, they were sometimes banned at public functions where ladies of the royal court were present, fearing the social consequences.

Another member of the family, *Vanilla planifolia*, was my favorite flavoring. The lovely woodland lady's slipper that carpeted the damp forest around my home in Maine were also a variety of North American orchid. The lady's slipper was so sacred to the Penobscot Indians who first inhabited my woodland retreat they were forbidden to even be touched and were harvested only for use in marriage rituals. Little wonder modern Americans were so utterly fascinated by orchids. They were the Viagra of Colonial America.

When I flaunted a bit of this pointless orchid trivia to Walter Off, wondering if any of it was true, given his encyclopedic grasp of the exotic species, he simply grinned. "It sounds like you *want* to be an orchid nut," he said, and promptly indicated several fairly commonplace cattleya and dendrobium he thought I could purchase over in the marketplace section of the show when it opened for business on Sunday.

"Better yet," he added convivially, "why don't you buzz on down to our nursery following the show and permit me to show you the family's operation. I promise to send you back to Maine with a serious case of *orchiditis*. That's what I call the condition that afflicts people like you who discover orchids and get hooked on them."

As we emerged from our stroll through his breathtaking tropical exhibit, passing beneath arching ficus trees that were weirdly chirring— electronic crickets?—and meant to simulate, I think, a balmy evening on Easter Island or in old Havana, Walter Off confided almost sheepishly: "Sometimes we actually feel like drug pushers when it comes to selling orchids. The demand has never been higher, because once people buy one they immediately want another one. You can understand why folks get obsessed with rare varieties. Pretty soon their kitchen window is full of orchids, followed by every windowsill in the house. Then the basement fills up and pretty soon they're building their own greenhouse. Orchids are *that* addictive."

Off explained how his father George had been a commercial wholesale flower vendor since the 1920s, specializing mainly in cut flowers and corsages. "In the 1970s, however, about the time I first started exhibiting at the Philadelphia Flower Show, in fact, we began experimenting with a few container-grown orchids and found a local growing interest in them that seemed to get stronger every year. Then, about ten years ago, our container orchid business just took off—I mean seriously *exploded*." He chuckled again, glancing up to check the stage lights. "Suddenly, that's all we did—grew orchids. Now it's come to this."

I wondered, from an operational standpoint, what it took to get a hundred thousand orchids to bloom precisely on cue during the same week in March. And here I thought Walt Fisher had performed garden magic in his beautiful Bryn Mawr basement.

"An interesting challenge, to be sure, especially considering that it can require anywhere from five to eight years for an orchid to reach maturity and bloom the way you want it to. Many of these orchids we grew ourselves down at the greenhouses in Linwood, but others we arranged to have flown in from a variety of other leading suppliers in Hawaii and California."

The orchid man turned and pointed to a row of closed exhibition doors, a velvet-roped area that was clearly the hall's main public entranceway.

"When those doors open at eight o'clock Sunday morning, this orchid exhibit will be the first thing showgoers see. Our aim is to knock the public's socks off with a display nobody has ever seen before."

I thanked him for the little escorted tour, said I thought he'd achieved his objective, and casually wondered how many folks the show's authorities anticipated coming through those doors by the end of the week.

"Quarter of a million at least. Could be closer to three hundred thousand before it's all said and done." He laughed robustly. "Everyone of them a potential orchid nut."

I WAS STILL CHEWING on this mind-boggling estimate—an estimate which, if true, meant the Super Bowl of botany or the Gardening Olympics or whatever silly sports moniker you wished to give the mother of all flower shows, in fact dwarfed the NFL Super Bowl for pure fan attendance—when I serendipitously bumbled into Walt Fisher already at work and well into the construction of his Savannah terrace across the vast teeming hall.

He was on his hands and knees, laying the last of the beautiful ornamental bricks and leveling them with the precision of a mason in the Inforcers' designated space in the terrace class. Arrayed around him—obviously waiting to be positioned and mulched into the faux landscape—sat several familiar-looking pots of blooming spring flowers, tulips, and hyacinths approaching their peaks, a stunning ornate black iron fence and gate, a large stone fountain, and several beautiful larger potted foundation shrubs, including a pair of lovely miniature crab apple trees with buds voluptuously bursting like the corset of a Victorian lady whose hubby had been handling too many orchids.

Seeing me, Walt hopped up and offered me his friendly lopsided timekeeper's smile and a large dusty hand, pointing out that the rest of his Inforcer teammates should be along the aisles at any moment with the final pieces of the exhibit's horticultural material—a trellis covered with English ivy, a blooming amaryllis, various potted cyclamens, more paperwhite narcissi yet to come, too. According to a notice of intent already posted in front of his terrace class 161 exhibit, the title of the Inforcer's production was "Savannah: Paradise Gained."

Having lived in Savannah for a brief time in the late 1970s, I was curious to see just how authentic their terrace was, though it already reminded me of terraces I'd often seen in the intimate hidden gardens of that famous Southern city where sin and orchids both thrive behind closed garden walls.

"This is the fun part of the Philadelphia show," Fisher explained beneath his soiled Penn Relays cap, "the race against the clock, the mad dash to the finish line." He glanced over at the adjacent space where a short woman with a face like an Irish wood sprite was kneeling and weirdly appeared to be painting small pebbles at the base of a fountain—sizing up the competition's progress, I supposed. She glanced back and smiled cheerfully at us both, obviously having heard Walt's comment.

"This *is* nuts, isn't it?" she said, laughing huskily. "My son Nick runs an addiction recovery program and says gardening is a lot like alcoholism and your level of addiction can even be measured by the same three questions he asks his potential clients. Wanna take the test?"

She was looking at me. Walt Fisher had already resumed his bricklaying. So I said, "Sure. . . . By the way," I interjected, before she could offer her test, "are you actually *painting* those rocks?"

She gave another low laugh.

"Absolutely, honey. This is an old show trick. You paint the pebbles with a clear fingernail polish so they glisten as if they are wet. As I tell my husband Jim, whoever has the best tricks usually wins. Unfortunately, I learned this little water trick the hard way. One year I used Mop'n'Glo wax on my rocks to make them shine—about too clever by half. Mop'n'Glo is also a detergent, see, so the minute real water touched them, holy cow, I had bubbles forming all over the place." She laughed again, shaking her head, still kneeling, still methodically paintbrushing pebbles. "Brother, what a nightmare *that* was. So now I'm using clear fingernail polish. How's it look from out there?"

"Your exhibit looks like . . . Nantucket," I ventured, taking note of an unmistakable New England nautical theme, wicker furniture and lots of gorgeous daffodils riotously blooming. No official exhibit intent was yet posted, however.

"That's it," she declared with clear satisfaction. "It's actually supposed to be a terrace *on* Nantucket, dear. By the way, I'm Jeanne Francis. My husband Jim is lurking somewhere around here, probably hiding out so I don't make him build something at the last minute. I design, Jim builds. I paint rocks, he eats. We're a small team where everybody does lots of jobs. By the way, are you planning to take the test or just stand there holding that lovely azalea till someone tells you to move?"

"Shoot," I said, shifting my Carolina azalea to the other hip.

"Okay."

She got up and presented me her left hand—the unpainted one, as it turned out. We shook hands. She was about as tall as Frodo the hobbit, only shorter and much cuter. I loved her instantly.

"Question one: Have you ever used family money to support your gardening habit? We're talking grocery budgets and related finances here."

It was slightly more than a habit, I admitted—but, yes, I had used family money to support my gardening habit now and again. I could recall, for instance, an unscheduled visit to my local nursery the previous autumn, near the end of the month, and being blown away by the half-price sale in progress. Without proper authorization from home, I left the nursery a short while later with a dozen small pots of false dragon-head and *Baptisia elegans* for my new English meadow inspired by Christopher Lloyd's creation at Great Dixter in England, purchased with money earmarked for the oil and grocery bill.

"So, let's see," she said. "So you've deprived your children of heat and food."

"I suppose so, though I wouldn't say it quite like—"

"Two." Jeanne cut me off, clearly not a woman to be trifled with with rocks in her hand. "Have you ever focused a family event around your garden addiction?"

Not that I could think of, I replied—unless you cared to count a backyard wedding party where the groom/yardman saved a bundle on a rental hall and earned rave reviews from the guests over his new mixed-perennial border and cross-hatch mowing pattern.

"Sorry, sweetie. *That* counts," Jeanne Francis ruled from the floor of the Pennsylvania Convention Center. She didn't sound particularly sympathetic to my adopted Yankee thrift, I must say.

"Which brings us to three. Have you ever *lied* to your significant other about money spent on plants?"

I had to pause and think about this one for a moment or two. Every time I went out to visit Suzy Verrier at North Creek Farm, it seemed like I came home with something sensational for the yard. Normally I didn't bother explaining to Wendy how much the beautiful specimens cost, hoping she might just think Suzy had provided them to me free of charge. This was, I supposed, an indirect fudging of the truth, a small lie of botanical omission. On the other hand, Wendy seldom, if ever, revealed exactly what she spent on scrapbook materials when she went off on weekends to mysteriously hook up with groups of other women, purportedly to paste family photographs into oversize books and gossip about their spendthrift husbands. Perhaps a good working marriage needed its provocative little secrets to keep the romance alive.

"Oh my lord." Jeanne Francis shook her head slowly, dolefully, tragically.

"What?"

"You're hopeless. Completely addicted, hon."

With that, she offered me her right hand—the painted one—and burst out laughing from the bottom of her wicked Irish throat. "You're one of us now, dear. Careful, or you'll soon find yourself wasting your whole life planning an exhibit for the Philadelphia Flower Show and on your knees painting pebbles with Barbie fingernail polish!"

As she dropped to her knees and resumed work, she explained how she and husband Jim got "hooked into the show—probably for life."

Ten years ago, Jeanne said, she hurt her back and was forced to retire from the catering and food business. She decided to take a master gardener's course and soon found herself answering gardening questions online for a prestigious national gardening service. That gig led to a job decorating antique cars for a friend on Nantucket every spring during the celebrated island's "Daffodil Days" festival.

"Next thing I know, a friend from PHS phones me to say she thinks Jim and I ought to apply for a competitive category in the flower show. I did it sort of on a lark, and we wound up two years ago being put in the entryway class, going up against some heavy hitters. We did an unusual entryway that featured Jersey pines and fairies, and managed a third-place ribbon. That's all it took to hook us, I'm afraid."

The next year they returned to the show in the entryway class with

"Hospitality Latin Style," an ambitious condominium front Jeanne created by exchanging e-mails and photographs with other master gardeners down in Puerto Rico. "We earned ninety-six out of a possible one hundred points, and wound up third again by a single point." She explained that every competitor begins the week's judging process with a score of one hundred points and loses points based on a judge's subjective assessment of the exhibit over two different days of evaluation (Saturday and Wednesday, of show week), taking into account a variety of factors such as chosen theme, overall presentation, quality of bloom, and—maybe most important of all—success at achieving the exhibit's stated intent.

"In other words, the smallest and most unexpected thing can sometimes cause you to lose a critical point simply because a judge didn't like something you did. Sometimes they don't like your theme, or maybe a particular plant is not placed where they think it ought to be placed. You never really know—even from his or her written comments. This thing is completely subjective, sweetie; therefore, *totally* unpredictable."

"Sounds potentially disheartening."

"On the contrary, being stuck on third only gets my Irish blood really worked up." Jeanne was now screwing the cap back on her clear nail polish and casting a quiet eye toward the two attractive young women who appeared to be also finishing up work in the adjoining space. They appeared to be placing the final touches on a tropical theme of some sort, with large showy palms and an inviting teak cocktail bar.

"That's the Amey sisters," she explained in a respectful stage whisper. "The rumor going round is that their nursery supplier failed to deliver the plants he was supposed to deliver and they had to run out to Home Depot and purchase all their plants. Whether that's true or not, let me tell you, *they'll* be tough to beat. They've got decades into the Philadelphia Flower Show, counting mama and papa. That's what really counts. Experience and history."

"Well," I said, figuring it was time to collect a word or two from the vaunted Amey siblings, "best of Irish luck with the judges." When I looked over to their terrace, however, they'd mysteriously vanished. Walt Fisher was momentarily gone, as well.

"Thanks," Jeanne said cheerfully and gave another gently frazzled laugh before pivoting to dive into a couple pots of daffodils that needed a bit of fluffing.

"I just hope the bloody judges we get aren't Italian."

IT WAS WELL after the lunch break before I actually located Jack and Joe Blandy and returned their missing azalea. By this point, I'd already spent more than an hour hanging out in the show's extraordinary Horticourt area, the busiest part of the Philadelphia Flower Show—and, some claim, its very soul. Here is where thousands of individual amateur gardeners come flooding into the hall bearing an infinite array of potted plants to be graded and officially submitted to hundreds of individual competitive categories by an army of PHS volunteers identified by their friendly yellow neckerchiefs.

After registering and formally identifying a particular plant, a quality control agent, called a "passer," helps the plant's owner prep and groom the specimen before it is sent along by human hands to the proper display area, typically staged on a series of stepped risers or pergola frames. Orchids, I noticed, commanded a huge square of stepped risers right in the heart of the Horticourt, suggesting their growing presence at Philadelphia and perhaps the windowsills of the entire Mid-Atlantic region. With my azalea still in hand, I'd edged admiringly past everything from the most exquisite tiny euphorbia plant with tiny starlike leaves to the largest Christmas cactus I'd ever seen, the mammoth plant's spangled blooms resembling something you'd expect to find draped over the shoulders of a Kentucky Derby winner.

I also saw a *pelargonium sidoides* to die for, scores of spectacular clivias, and more unusual varieties of begonia and fern than I even knew existed—each one something an amateur hopeful had spent months, if not years, quietly training and grooming for this appointed trip to downtown Philadelphia.

An older man who spotted me palely loitering by his *Baldwin Kaleidoscope* cattleya hurried over to explain, "I prayed all week over this one. It just opened two mornings ago, so I hustled it straight into the show. Fabulous, huh? That's a good omen. I'm going to take a blue this year. I can just feel it."

I could almost feel it too, his visible level of prayerful optimism was so keen.

Two women primping a miniature Cook Island pine saw me admiring their lovely little tree from the near distance. One of them called over, "Are you entering that azalea?"

"No ma'am. Just trying to find its rightful owner."

"What's the name," demanded the other woman, who was wearing the yellow scarf of a Horticourt official. "We know everybody."

This didn't seem humanly possible, but I told them anyway.

"The Blandys," provided the first woman, "are down at the end in the major exhibiting area. We're just the small-time crazies. They're the big-time crazies."

I complimented them on their little pine. I commented that it resembled the offspring of dozens of big Cook Island pines that had basically ruined my golf game on Kauai, the garden island of Hawaii, because I'm unapologetically mad about trees and suffered acute gardenlust admiring them and forgot to keep my ball in play.

"Are you here from Hawaii?" The Yellow Neckerchief seemed surprised.

"No. Just down from Maine."

"*Maine?*" This revelation seemed to please the first woman, who was in her fifties and wore a sensible blond pageboy haircut. "We adore Maine. We call it Philly-on-the-Rocks!"

"Everybody we know has a house in Maine," explained the yellow scarf. "Do you know Bitsy Bowater?"

I admitted I didn't. Then again, Maine is a pretty big state, I pointed out, even bigger than Texas—not to mention being the most forested state in the union. Sometimes you couldn't see all the people for the trees.

"Surely you know *Bitsy Bowater*! Everybody knows Bitsy. Her place is just around the cove from Martha's place at Southwest Harbour. A rock garden to *murder* for, I'm telling you."

"Martha who?" It seemed worth a stab in the dark. I just might know who she meant. As they like to say up in Maine, the population is too large to really be a family, but too small to really be a state.

"Stewart, of course. She absolutely *worships* Maine. Do you know Martha?"

Funnily enough, I did—or briefly had, some years ago. Back when I worked at *Yankee* magazine, shortly before I met David Austin, I'd slipped down to Martha's Turkey Hill estate at Westport, Connecticut, and spent a full day following her around for a profile that turned out to be one of the few intimate interviews she gave that year. Her husband had just moved out their house (bad news), but she'd just inked a major deal with Kmart (good news) that was rumored to be worth millions. So even if she couldn't make marriage work, she was about to become the most famous businesswoman in America.

"I once went with her out to a private luncheon in Hinsdale, Illinois," I explained to the two FOMs. "It was for the debut of her big wedding book. She told me something very interesting. This was way back in the mid-eighties, mind you."

"What did she say?" demanded Yellow Scarf.

"She told me flowers were going to be the sex of the nineties."

"But *money* was the sex of the nineties," pointed out the first woman who knew Bitsy Bowater.

"That's probably why she's awaiting trial for stock manipulation," speculated Yellow Scarf—evidently no FOM after all. "I guess she decided money was more reliable than sex any old day."

"It's nothing more than a stinking setup," insisted Bitsy Bowater's pal, giving her friend the tree primper a really testy glance. "With all the male crooks on Wall Street these days, they just want to make an example of a really successful woman. It's shameful."

"Maybe flowers are the sex of the New Millennium," I cheerfully offered, hoping I hadn't provoked unnecessary tensions between the two women. The truth is, despite all the awful things you read about America's domestic diva, I liked Martha Stewart and thought she'd probably done a world of good getting ordinary people interested in the lives of their homes and gardens.

"That may explain why my husband is always out poking around in the garden whenever he isn't investing online."

"Can you really *blame* him, dear?"

On this note, I took gentle leave and soon found Jack Blandy standing and chatting with two pleasant-looking people who turned out to be Jane Pepper, president of the Pennsylvania Horticultural Society, to whom I'd spoken only via telephone, and Ed Lindemann, the show's retiring chief designer.

"We were about to send a police search team out for you," Jack said playfully, introducing me to the show's main powers.

I apologized for the disappearing act but explained I'd never met such friendly informative people nor seen so many extraordinary horticultural exhibits—including, and maybe especially, the individual plants in the busy Horticourt.

"I'm *so* glad to hear you say that," said Jane Pepper, a brisk, diminutive Scot. "The big exhibits are wonderful, the reason many people come back year after year. But the individual competitors of the Horticourt are special. This show keeps growing because of the volunteers and those people. They're the *truly* serious gardeners here."

I asked Jane how many individual amateur plants would, in fact, by the time all the registering, primping, and classifying was completed, be formally entered into competition before the closing bell at six o'clock. Contestants are also permitted a final opportunity to enter plants on Saturday morning between six and nine-thirty, just prior to the start of judging.

"Could be three or four thousand plants. We never know. It grows every year," she explained with understandable pride. "That's why the volunteers are so important. They really know their stuff—extremely dedicated folks and passionate gardeners themselves. The vast majority of the exhibitors here, in fact, are amateurs, which is what gives this show its energy and enthusiasm levels."

She wasn't just spinning a line of friendly PR. I knew from browsing the show's public press clippings and chatting beforehand with several old hands of the show, including a couple longtime judges, that both the PHS and the flower show boomed when Pepper, a graduate of the pres-

tigious Longwood Gardens graduate program I sometimes idly fanta-
sized about attending, a former director of gardening for Haverford
College, got selected to be the legendary Ernesta Ballard's replacement
back in 1980. One of Ballard's final acts was to promote staffer Ed Lindemann to show designer. Like Ballard before them, both were passionate advocates of the amateur garden.

When I mentioned this inside knowledge to the two of them, Pepper
smiled but scarcely blinked. When I asked the show's longtime designer
if there was a visible turning point in the fortunes of the show, a moment when he could discern a change in the public interest in the
flower show, he came to life as if I'd asked him if flowers might not be
the sex of the New Millennium.

"There's no question about it," said Lindemann. "That would be
when we moved over here to the Convention Center from the Civic
Center back in 1996. Before that, we might get 220,000 patrons during
the nine days of the show. That first year here, however, we drew
314,000 people—significantly more than our previous record."

"It nearly overwhelmed us," Pepper put in thoughtfully, noting that
this boost in the flower show's popularity managed to underwrite bigger
and better shows and a host of PHS projects, such as the award-winning
Philadelphia Green program. This year alone, she added, roughly one
million dollars would be raised for Philadelphia Green from the show's
sponsorships and gate admissions. Every year since that time save one
the show attendance figures had measurably swelled, and Jane Pepper
thought she knew why.

"Gardening has always been America's most popular pastime, especially among older folks. For most of its life, this show was the social
event of the year for Philadelphians, and arguably still is, attracting a lot
of garden clubbers and passionate gardeners. But during the past
decade or so in particular, we've seen a major growth in younger patrons, people coming to the show not just to be dazzled by all the big
display gardens but also to learn practical information about plants and
gardens, ideas they can take directly home to their own gardens. The
Gardener's Studio, our free lecture series, is one of the most popular

features at the show. A who's who of the gardening world comes through here to speak."

She thought for a moment and then added, in a more philosophical vein, "I think it's fair to say we may be seeing the start of a new golden age of popular gardening in America now, comparable to that of a hundred years ago, and maybe even far broader in scope, reaching new classes of people. We have a saying at PHS—that seeds planted at the Flower Show bloom across the city all summer. I think it's safe to say that same thing is going on in a lot of places in America right now."

On the strength of this upbeat assessment on the ground, I asked the show's retiring maestro what his home garden was like. It must be a knockout, I said. He smiled—a little wearily, I thought.

"Frankly, I don't have one. My wife and I just purchased a cottage on Cape Cod. This show has basically kept me so busy over the years I haven't had time to create the kind of garden I'd like to. But now I'll finally get to do a bit of real gardening."

"Oh, by the way," Jane said, handing me a small envelope, "here's your ticket to the preview. Be sure and get here early tomorrow night so you can walk around and look at all the finished exhibits. That's like the calm before the storm."

B<small>Y THE TIME</small> J<small>ACK</small> B<small>LANDY</small> and I got back over to Stoney Bank Nursery's major exhibit site, my Carolina azalea had already been freshly watered and nicely integrated into a landscape that was in its own quiet way every bit as impressive as the flower show's Central Feature orchid exhibit.

Blandy father and son had created an extraordinarily complex woodland estate garden that featured three distinct garden themes adventurously blended together and linked by a trio of lighted stone footpaths leading to the heart of the garden. The title of the exhibit was "Pathways to Paradise."

Its southern flank, perhaps aimed at complementing the tropical splendor of the adjacent Central Feature, featured beautiful banana palms, banks of bougainvillea, and variegated ginger lilies plus an array of tropical vegetation and hothouse flowers swarming over a discreet entry pathway. The middle garden was dominated by a magnificent one-ton bronze sculptured gate element composed of arching ivy vines that invited the eye up a mossy-girdled stone path to a traditional garden tableau of flowering native dogwoods and magnolias and Okame cherry trees, which in turn gave over to a native woodland of clusters of elegant Heritage river birches around a fallen log and blackwater forest pond, with lots of beguiling ferns and other native woodland flora set off by the shadowy textures of magnificent Winter King hawthorns, spiral junipers, and full rhododendrons, a secret garden beckoning the viewer into the woods with all the charm of a mysterious forest in a Brothers Grimm fairy tale.

Several of Stoney Bank's crew of eight was busy installing Blue Cadet hostas and hellebores, ferns, and other smaller understory flowering plants and shrubs to complete a richly textured border, while others were already watering the garden with hoses. The floral complexity of the Blandy exhibit appeared to exceed anything his four rivals in the major exhibit competition had mounted. That said, they were extraordinary.

One was a large traditional formal rose garden with formal estate fountains, another an amusement theme park that appeared to have been reclaimed in a mad swoop of cascading ornamentals by Mother Nature herself, with blooming shrubs and wildflowers erupting in profusion from carriage rides. A third exhibit featured a spectacular old mill house as its functional centerpiece with a slowly turning water wheel straight from the pages of Thomas Hardy (the English major in me liked that one). The final competitor was a suburban scene with the magnificent stone wall and backyard tree house that had so mesmerized me upon entering the premises many hours ago.

"One of the competitive tricks you learn here over time is that some judges really don't want to see any mulch," Jack explained, as if reading my mind on the subject, as we watched one of his crew "plant" several pots of Siberian iris only a few feet from my pet Carolina azalea in its new home. "My view is, they want to see interesting use of plants. So our philosophy is to use as many plants as possible that look appropriate, unforced, and natural, leaving as little mulch as possible visible to the naked eye."

This approach had obviously paid dividends in the past. I knew from Jane Pepper that Jack Blandy was the reigning best-of-show winner. I also knew the chances of this happening again were probably pretty slim, as Jack himself confirmed a few moments later as we chatted about his competition.

"At this level, everybody is world-class. Over at the far end you've got J. Franklin Styer, Nurseries, legendary plantsmen from out on the Baltimore Pike, while right next to us you've also got Burke Brothers, some of the best landscape designers in America. The Flagg Garden Center's tree-house garden is very impressive. And then there's my friend Daniel Kepich over there—he's using my water wheel, by the way. The guy is really a genius. Go look at that pond—you'd swear it's real, cattails and all.

"Winning best of show back-to-back is basically unheard-of," he continued, handicapping a competition that was in many ways worlds away from the one Walt Fisher and the Inforcers were engaged in, considering the big prize money and professional stakes involved. "But that's exactly why we added lots of additional plants this year. We really have nothing to lose by pulling out all the stops. It's an expensive risk, I suppose, to fill our exhibit with so many plants, but it would certainly be a risk not to." He shrugged, watching his crews plant hellebores, the famous Lenten rose mentioned by Shakespeare. "We'll have to see if the judges reward us for the effort."

"Any predictions?" I said, and suddenly regretted it. It was bad form—I knew from having done so—to ask a thoroughbred trainer on the eve of the Kentucky Derby what he expected the order of finish on Derby Saturday to be. It placed him in the uncomfortable position of having to say his horse would win, which invariably brought down the disapproval of the gods, and rotten luck.

Blandy shrugged and smiled coyly, glancing around. I was fully prepared for him not to tip his hand at all, to simply say nothing. Whatever the final judgment, he'd told me that morning on our way into Philadelphia, it was likely to be razor thin.

"No worse than second," he allowed quietly, nearly in a whisper.

For the balance of the afternoon, I watched Jack and his brother Glen work on completing a complex ground lighting scheme that threw the exhibit into stunning relief. I watched Stoney Bank's crews under Joe's direction install the last of the small bedding plants and finish up the detailed process of primping and watering and properly labeling every tree, shrub, and flower.

Though it may have violated some written show rule, I even helped out a little bit by primping the *Phlox rosea*, candytuft, and various Christmas and maidenhair ferns; in doing do, I was reminded of my late mom's own backyard fern garden down in North Carolina.

By then, almost six in the evening, Jack's wife Jane and several of their friends and neighbors had shown up bearing soft drinks and snacks.

"This is a tradition we have," Jane Blandy explained, offering me a paper cup of ginger ale. "Several of our friends love to come help out with the last of the labeling and primping. You can never have enough eyes for this sort of thing. After so much hard work, it's nice to be able to toast your efforts. I mean, Jack's been planning and worrying over this exhibit for at least a year, maybe two. This is *it*, the thing he lives for."

BEFORE I HEADED OFF with the Blandys and their crew for their annual setup dinner at a local restaurant in nearby Chinatown, I wandered down to say good-bye to Walt and Linda Fisher, wish them all the best tomorrow, and hopefully meet the rest of the Inforcers. I wanted to see Jeanne Francis again and once again offer best of Irish luck in the morning. There was something about her down-to-earth passion that attracted me and reminded me of my own evolving obsession.

The Inforcers, part of the team at least, was still at it—primping, watering—though the rest of the terrace class competitors had knocked off and vanished. The hall, in fact, was noticeably emptying out. Jeanne and Jim Francis's Nantucket terrace was a thing of beauty and the Amey siblings's lovely "Cocktails on Lanai" looked like a stage setting for an Elvis film. Beyond the Inforcers' garden, another competitor's Southwestern-themed terrace was so marvelously detailed and authentic looking with its painted-desert backdrop, cacti, and other gorgeous succulents, I half expected to find a faux rattlesnake curled up and sleeping on their faux Western terrace.

"So what do you think?" Linda Fisher demanded in her usual pleasant and straightforward manner as I walked up. But before I could eyeball their handiwork and give an answer, Linda introduced me to Jim and Keith Straw, the married architect and interior decorator members of the team.

Keith had just finished misting the beautiful foliage of "Paradise Regained" and Jim was studiously going over the official final plant list and the exhibit's posted intent with Walt; under the rules this was required to be submitted before competitors completed their setup.

I wondered if authorities sounded a whistle or blew a horn indicating it was six o'clock and therefore time for all work on amateur exhibits to cease and desist. Evidently the major exhibitors—the show's headliners—were permitted to work all night, if necessary.

"No," Linda explained. "They just come by and rather bossily inform you it's time to stop." She gave her appealing girlish laugh. "Naturally *we're* the last to finish today."

"Any minute the class chairs are going to come by and say, 'No more work! No more work! It's closing time!' But, honestly, the Amey siblings really worry me," Keith Straw gently fretted, drifting back into the terrace space to adjust a pair of elegant balloon wineglasses and a bottle of Joseph Phelps cabernet sitting invitingly on the wrought iron terrace table.

She saw me checking out the vintage and explained with a wry smile, "That's a *very* good wine. If the show wasn't so persnickety about drinking alcohol we would have polished off that bottle twenty minutes ago. Love of gardening and good wine are two things that hold this little band of gardening nuts together, you know."

Charmingly, she went on to explain that not so long ago she and Jim used to compete against the Fishers, wagering dinner out and a good bottle of wine on the outcome.

"Then the competition got so strong we realized, holy cow, maybe we'd just better join forces and beat everybody else."

Linda Fisher was still at my elbow. I could see her quietly waiting for my answer.

"Your Savannah terrace looks fantastic," I said, and meant it.

"Do you really mean that or are you just saying it to make us feel better?" she insisted. I could just picture her out in her frozen backyard on a winter night, going after the ground where the buried spring bulbs were hidden. In her own sweet and adorable way, it came to me then and there, she was just as garden-show mad as the Botticelli of Bulbs.

I said I really meant it. With its stunning matching miniature crab apples, black stone fountain, lush Ivy-covered arbor, and iridesecent pots of paperwhite narcissus, tulips, and hyacinths, why, their coastal Georgia terrace looked like the real McCoy to me.

But as I reminded her, I was just a guy who'd come out of the cold from a dirt road up in Maine. Almost everything I'd seen that day filled me with awe and gardenlust and made me feel like a hopeless beginner.

"Garden *what*?" Keith Straw seemed highly amused by something I'd said, still fiddling with the wine goblets because an interior decorator's work is never quite done.

I explained that every time I saw a beautiful garden like this one and at least half a dozen I'd watched come together that day in the cavernous Pennsylvania Convention Center, part of me secretly ached to possess it. I called it *gardenlust*—or at least my wife did.

"Maybe someday soon you'll be competing against us," Linda observed sweetly, though I thought I detected just the teensiest note of a street-corner challenge in her voice.

Walt, genial as ever, asked me what I was going to do tomorrow to kill time before the judge's verdict would be revealed at the black-tie preview cocktail party.

"Off to rent a tux and try and not worry about all my favorites," I replied.

What I didn't say was that I was nearly dead certain the Inforcers would win their class in a romp and that Jack and Joe Blandy, owing to the weight of history, probably wouldn't win theirs. For the record, Jeanne and Jim Francis were my sentimental dark horses to capture the flower sweepstakes.

What I *did* admit to the four Inforcers was that, after hanging around and watching all of this come together, I was probably as nervous about how it would all eventually turn out as they were. "I'm still trying to get my mind around where all of this *came* from," I confided, somewhat inarticulately—meaning this vast accumulation of spectacular garden imagination and such impeccable horticultural execution, all of this incomparable beautiful madness contained beneath one large Convention Hall.

"I'll tell you where you should go after you rent your tux." Jim Straw suddenly spoke up. "Go across the river and see John Bartram's little botanic garden on the Schuylkill. Amazingly, it's still there nearly three hundred years later. That's *really* where every bit of this came from. That was America's first botanic garden and nursery."

"Jim's crazy for history," provided Keith Straw. "Even gardening history."

"Well," added her scholarly looking husband, the city architect, "there's probably no more sacred ground in the American gardening world than that place and possibly Monticello."

I said I would take that to heart, especially if the weather was decent. I wished them all good luck and went off to hook up with Jack and Joe Blandy and their workers for their annual Chinese supper.

"It's just our small way of saying thanks to our guys," Jack explained as we hoofed along the sidewalk in darkening Chinatown. "Our crew really busts their tails to get this right. Most of them have been with us for years, and they have a lot of pride at stake as well. At this point, though, everything is over—years of planning, weeks of execution, all the worry and anxiety that goes with competing in this thing. All we can do is wait, have dinner and a beer, make a toast, and hope for the best."

A little while later, following a rowdy dinner and just such a toast and a word of thanks from Jack to his crew, one of the older crew members from Puerto Rico nudged me and asked me to read his fortune cookie's message. His grasp of garden English was evidently about as solid as my grasp of garden Latin.

Soon you will be sitting on top of the world, it read.

I read the message aloud and passed it over to Jack, who was flush from exhaustion and relief that his setup day had ended before midnight, for a change.

"Well, how about that," he commented with a weary smile, folding the piece of paper and slipping it into his shirt pocket.

Chapter 4

✦

In a Philosopher's Garden

With temperatures pushing extravagantly toward sixty degrees and flowering bulbs suddenly threatening to make their debut everywhere you looked, spring was seriously flirting with greater Philadelphia the next afternoon when I drove out the Main Line to Wayne to pick a rental tux for the flower show preview party.

Without benefit of a street map, I decided to take Jim Straw's advice and go find the first botanic garden in America. Following a lengthy tour of West Philly's most run-down neighborhoods, I suddenly rattled across a jarring set of railroad tracks, turned left into an apparent dead end, swore most unbecomingly, and ran smack into the garden wedged against the Schuylkill River between a housing project and a construction site, a charming hillside oasis of magnificent hardwoods and peaceful winding garden paths overlooking the Oz-like skyline of Philadelphia and its charming southern flank of interstate highways and oil refineries.

Almost no one was about, save for a small group of chattering grade-school students being herded along an upper sidewalk toward the property's restored kitchen garden. An older gentleman in a windbreaker and golf cap sat alone on a bench about halfway down the sloping network of garden paths between Bartram's simple stone home and the attractive visitor center.

The garden was preparing to close for the day, by the time I arrived, roughly an hour ahead of the scheduled closing time. But I at least was able to pick up a walking-tour guide and a recent collection of essays published by the American Philosophical Society called *America's Curious Botanist*, reappraising John Bartram's vital impact on the social values of an emerging nation. Bartram was not only "the King's Appointed Botanist for North America," but also a cofounder, with Ben Franklin, of the American Philosophical Society. The great Swede Carolus Linnaeus (the father of taxonomy, or, as I fondly prefer to think of him, the lonely masochist who invented garden Latin to torture neophyte estate gardeners like me) called him "the greatest natural botanist in the world."

I assumed this meant Bartram was a self-taught disciple of the outdoors, which indeed turned out to be the case. Born in the humble Quaker village of Darby in May of 1699, not far from the spot where I rented my basic black theater-usher tuxedo 305 years farther along the official American time line, young John possessed only a rudimentary country education but found himself drawn early on to the beauty and harmony of surrounding fields and streams. His own explorations of the natural world around the 102-acre farm he acquired after his father was kicked out of the local Quaker meeting for taking a second wife and vanishing to the wilder fringes of North Carolina quickly led the young farmer to an uncommon understanding of plants and their medicinal value.

According to one slightly overromanticized version of young John's sudden botanical enlightenment, the young man was plowing his field late one summer afternoon when he paused and picked a lovely wild daisy. He spent the rest of the afternoon and evening staring at it and thinking of a brave new world of possibilities contained therein, returning home the next morning to inform his none-too-pleased pregnant bride that he planned to devote the balance of his days to collecting and studying plants and wildflowers. According to another fanciful bit of lore that simply can't be authenticated, she picked up a bowl of Quaker Oats Squares and hurled it at her dreamy husband's head.

Natural science in the so-called Age of Enlightenment that was at that very instant sweeping over Europe assumed a finite universe consisting mainly of known plants and animals, but many believe it was due to John Bartram's tireless plant-collecting expeditions from the outskirts of Colonial Philadelphia, followed by even more extensive travels and writing by his son William, that revealed such an abundance of new species of plants in the New World that the aforementioned Swedish botanist Linnaeus was forced to create a revolutionary new system of classification simply to accommodate them all. So, in a way, John Bartram was the guy responsible for making aspiring gardeners like me feel like complete nitwits when it comes to remembering the proper Latin names of plants.

I was roughly this far into the Bartram saga and halfway down the pleasantly winding path to the Schuylkill when I came upon the older gent sitting on the bench. He was wearing a faded golf cap and gazing through the lens of a digital camera at the budding canopy of mature trees down by the river flats, with the stub of a smoldering cigar clenched almost defiantly in his teeth and a small wooden box on his lap. When he heard my footsteps and saw me closing fast upon his person, however, he lowered the camera and grunted with irritation, "If you hold up a moment and look carefully down there where those saplings are being cleared, you might see a couple most interesting birds. I think there is a Yellow-billed Cuckoo and maybe an Eastern Marsh Belted Kingfisher."

I paused respectfully and looked for a long moment where he was aiming his camera.

"My goodness. I didn't know there were any yellow-billed cuckoos around here anymore."

Naturally, I had no idea what I was talking about. This just seemed like something one dedicated and knowledgeable birder would say to another in the field to establish an instant professional rapport.

He stared at me like a bothered eagle, puffing gently on his glowing stub.

"Know your birds, do you?"

"Only robins and chickadees," I admitted, closing John Bartram on a finger. "Truthfully, I wouldn't know an Eastern Marsh Kingfisher with or without a belt. But I live for that day."

He seemed remarkably immune to my sparkling afternoon wit.

"Well, they're both pretty damn rare these days. That's for sure. This used to be one of the best bird watching places on the whole East Coast, a nesting area for several species of migratory birds on the northern flyway, before they turned the Schuylkill into an industrial sewer. Now they say they're trying like hell to bring it back but, Jesus Christ, it's a slow go. Once you screw up something like a river, it's god-damn near impossible to ever bring it back."

I commiserated with him on this. Noting his faded Pebble Beach golf cap, I pointed out that it was much the same story in golf. Once upon a time not so long ago the game was played with minimal fuss and fanfare, with only a few good wooden clubs, a wee pint of courage, and a ball made from stuffing goose feathers into a top hat. Now players had their own Lear jets and staff psychologists on call. Personally speaking, I longed for the good old days when golf was played with full beards and Norfolk jackets, even among the ladies.

"What the *hell* are you talking about?"

"Your hat," I pointed out. "It suggests that you're a fellow golfer."

He scowled at me for a moment, puffing his stogie. "Not really. I just went out there once with my wife Elizabeth to a poetry conference. She lectured, I walked the beach looking at birds. I bought this hat in some goddamned overpriced gift shop by the golf course. It cost six dollars! Somebody told me they were charging *fifty* bucks to play that golf course, if you can believe it."

"That's Pebble Beach for you," I said, deciding it wasn't worth working him up by revealing that same hat would now set him back thirty-five dollars and a day on the famous links course cost five hundred bucks, counting caddy and lunch and keepsake golf towel.

"Do me a favor, son, and hold up for a few minutes before you go blasting down to the river and scare off the birds. Let's see if those fishers I spotted earlier come back."

"No problem, sir. Mind if I sit with you?"

"Take a load off."

I sat and opened my book. He hoisted his binoculars again and stud-ied the river flats. That's when I noticed the polished wooden box resting on his lap and got the creepy feeling we weren't alone. I had three boxes just like that back home on a bookshelf. The first two contained the cremated remains of my two former garden assistants, Amos and Bailey; the third, the ashes of my late mother's recently deceased lab, a disagreeable old girl named Molly. My plan was to eventually do something with all these accumulating dog ashes, though I hadn't quite figured out what.

"I'm Ed Pugh, by the way." He offered me a hand, keeping one eye trained on the river flats. I told him my name, and he grunted and released a small noxious plume of smoke.

We fell into an agreeable silence for a little while. Ed watched the river for kingfishers and I read about John Bartram, learning how he'd struck up a lively friendship and passionate correspondence with London plantsman Peter Collinson that resulted in hundreds of native American plants being shipped to European soil for the very first time, including mountain laurel from rocky ledges just up the Schuylkill and magnolias from my own dear Carolina colony. The beautiful *Hydrangea quercifolia* Bartram sent reportedly caused such a stir among London's eighteenth-century gardening elite there was a lot of nasty name calling among guys in powdered wigs.

"In case you're wondering," Ed said matter-of-factly, "this box contains my wife Elizabeth's ashes. We used to come here when she was at Bryn Mawr. It was her wish to have them spread around that big tree over there."

"I understand, sir. Not a problem. Sorry for your loss." I suddenly didn't feel quite so witty. I also wondered if I shouldn't get up and move along, leave the man with his private thoughts and river birds.

"Thanks. Good news is, she didn't suffer all that long. I'm just trying to decide whether to put all of her ashes over there or some of them up to our place in New Hampshire."

"Where in New Hampshire?" I always find it a kick and rather surprising to run into somebody who doesn't object to shoveling their way to Eastern services.

"The tribe is all descending on the cottage for a family memorial service in three or four weeks. I'm headed up there to open the place up and fix a few things."

"So you don't live in New Hampshire full-time?"

"Hell no. I'm not that stupid."

He puffed for a moment or two, then asked where I was from. I said I was from North Carolina but had lived in Maine for the past twenty-five years—" 'Philly-on-the-Rocks,' as they like to say around here," I added.

"You spend the winter up there too, do you?"

As I'd told Bitsy Bowater's tedious friend at the Philadelphia Flower Show, I did indeed "winter" in Maine. Only people who don't "winter" in Maine use the word as a passive verb, by the way—the same people who "summer" there, come July and August. Personally speaking, I don't have either the time or the money to use *winter* and *summer* as verbs, passive or otherwise.

"Yes sir. I love winter in Maine. It makes me realize all I'm missing in life."

"You must ski a helluva lot."

"Nope. My kids do. I just sit around planning outrageously elaborate flower gardens I'll probably never have the time or money to actually build and fantasizing over the White Flower Farm catalog the way I used to so enjoy my wife's Victoria Secret catalog. Guess that's a sign of incipient senility, huh?"

Ed Pugh surprised me by giving a distinctly wintry laugh—more of a mirthless grunt, really.

"Elizabeth was nuts for her hosta garden up at our place in Goffs-town. I'm thinking that's where I ought to put half her ashes—except the deer are always eating them. She had a running battle against the deer in her hosta beds."

I told him I knew what his late wife was up against. Over on the coast of Maine, I had the same ongoing scrimmage going with a family of whitetails who "wintered" in Maine, too. Hostas, in my book, are the most reliable and wonderful perennials on earth, worthy of mounting the strongest defense. They demand little or no personal attention, reward even the beginner gardener by looking great for months on end, divide and multiply with a gentle swipe of a garden shovel, and make any landscape look vastly better.

My latest strategy for keeping the deer out of mine, I explained to Ed, involved planting extra hostas at the rear of my property, hoping they would be content with that—a kind of pagan sacrifice of innocent plants to the monarchs of the forest, if you will. The funny thing was, this strategy had seemed to work nicely for years. My main garden hosta plants were the size of Volkswagens and almost the first thing like-minded folks commented upon when they wandered back to Slightly Off in the Woods.

"You could begin by not feeding the damn deer in winter," Ed commented rather irritably, as if this approach was about the dumbest thing he'd ever heard, like appeasing kidnappers or terrorists by giving in to their outrageous demands. "All you're doing is guaranteeing they'll *never* go way."

"Probably true. If I don't do it, though, they come and press their cute little faces against the windowpanes on cold winter nights. It's the baby deer who really get to you. Those parents, I tell you, have no shame whatsoever."

Ed Pugh glanced at me as if he thought I might be off my rocker, at which point I asked him where he spent the rest of the year when he wasn't up in New Hampshire defending his late wife's hosta garden.

"We have a place down in South Carolina, near Charleston. My wife used to teach history and philosophy at a small college down there. I was in the timber business for thirty years. Now I'm out. Some outfit from Belgium bought the company and laid off half the staff. They're importing pine trees now from Malaysia."

"Sorry to hear that."

"It's fine with me. Leaves me more time with the birds." His field glasses were back up. Then he asked, "You here for the flower show?"

"That's right," I said, a little surprised. "You too?"

"No. I just read it was in town in this morning's paper. Elizabeth and a bunch of her pals used to come up for that thing. They were into flower arranging big-time. I guess a lot of that goes on there."

"A lot of *everything* goes on there," I said, pointing out I just spent an entire day snooping around behind the scenes of the setting-up of the show and had never seen so many horticulturally crazed people in my life. It was like dying and going to heaven for a garden nut like me, I added, suddenly realizing how insensitive that sounded.

If he noticed, Ed Pugh didn't show it. He just grunted mildly again.

"You know that tree over there?"

I looked where he pointed. The tree was a towering hardwood with slightly yellowing peeling bark and a vast canopy of budding limbs. It looked like the trees you find scattered all around parks and squares in central London, though perhaps only a sophisticated globe-trotting tree aficionado like me would know this.

"Of course. That's a London plane tree."

"Hell no. It's American ginkgo."

"I was just getting ready to say that."

"Elizabeth once told me that's the oldest ginkgo tree in North America. The king of England sent it to the Bartrams. The story goes that Thomas Jefferson and Ben Franklin used to come across the river and sit beneath that tree during the summer Jefferson was writing the Declaration of Independence. Bartram was a close friend of both men, and this garden, they say, had a big influence on Jefferson's thinking. Elizabeth always said Jefferson probably sat right beneath that ginkgo working on his famous document. This is where he sent either Lewis and Clark before they set off—I forget which of them it was—so the Bartrams could show him the right way to collect plants. They also sent him plants down to Monticello."

So, I thought, Jim Straw had been correct about sacred ground. Not only had America's grand experiment in representative government perhaps taken shape in this very garden, thanks to an idle summer day of woolgathering on the flowered banks of the Schuylkill on the part of the lanky Virginian aristocrat, but a blueprint for botanizing an untamed continent had possibly commenced here as well. Looking around at the beautiful if somewhat neglected grounds of the place, I decided there ought to at least be a symposium hall for an annual convocation of American garden scholars, possibly a retirement home for active senior horticulturists, and maybe even an environmentally sensitive nature park for kids.

While I was busy pondering the unlimited commercial and educational possibilities, Ed Pugh simply got up and shuffled off for the famous ginkgo tree. As I watched from my bench, he opened the box, loosened the strings of a small velvet sack contained therein, and scattered his late wife's ashes around the roots of the old tree without much fanfare. He put the sack back in the box, stood looking at the ground for a long moment, then turned and walked back in my direction. It might have just been my imagination, but his step appeared lighter.

"Bartram's son William," he said, as he approached where I was now standing, "was a serious bird man and quite the naturalist. He accompanied his father on a lot of collecting trips down South, where they found the Franklinia tree that's still growing up near the main house there. Here's a bit of trivia: Believe it or not, wherever you find a Franklinia tree growing today in America, it came directly from that very tree. You'll want to have a good look at that. Incidentally, the son made some of the first and finest sketches of America's native birds—decades before Audubon. I think some of them are still in a museum over in the city."

I walked with Ed a short way down the pathway to where it split, going one way down to the river's edge and another back up to the kitchen garden and Bartram's lovely surviving Pennsylvania fieldstone house.

"I'm going down to the river to see if I can find that beautiful kingfisher," Ed said, pausing. "Want to tag along and see if I was right?"

I checked my watch and thanked him but pointed out that a rental tuxedo and I were running late for a date at the Pennsylvania Convention Center, where I would learn the fate of several garden nuts like myself who were competing in the Super Bowl of botany. I wished him an easy onward journey to the Granite State, hoping for an early spring and no marauding whitetails in his late wife's garden.

"Thanks," he said, relighting his cold cigar and puffing out new small noxious clouds of smoke. "You headed south on this trip?"

"Eventually," I said, suddenly thinking I had a new reason for visiting Monticello, where I'd visited many times both as man and boy.

"The forsythia is nearly over down in South Carolina," he provided, "but we've still got a few decent tulips in the yard. Liz planted 'em."

A little while later, when I glanced back down the hill from the base of the beautiful Franklinia tree (which I located using my walking tour map), Ed Pugh was nowhere in view, though I suppose he might have just stepped through the trees and gone to stalk his rare kingfisher along the river flats. Bird-watchers and plant hunters aren't so different, I suppose, and probably would make natural partners in any kind of collaboration, including marriage.

By the time I'd reached the gravel parking lot of Bartram's garden, it suddenly came to me what I should do with the ashes of my two former garden assistants and my mother's old guardian Molly as well.

I'd build two of them a special garden, and return the third to the Southern backyard garden she onced faithfully guarded by snoozing in the Lily of the Valley beds.

On the heels of a fine afternoon interlude in America's first garden, it was something of an anticlimax to reach the gleaming floor of the Pennsylvania Convention Center a short time later dressed in my basic black rental tux only to discover my flower show predictions had been sensationally wrong.

I'd predicted the charming Inforcers would win in a romp. They actually placed third behind the Southwest garden and the mythical Amey siblings' "Cocktails on Lanai." My new pals Jeanne and Jim Francis, alas, slipped a notch to fourth place in the terrace class.

Spacious and inviting, read the judge's comment on the Inforcers' magnificent Savannah garden. *But lack of contrasting texture and scale affects the balance and scale of the exhibit.*

"That person has obviously never *been* to Savannah," harrumphed Linda Fisher, who was suddenly standing there, dressed to kill, along with Keith Straw. "Every garden we saw in Savannah is so beautifully understated. 'Lack of contrasting texture'? *Honestly.*"

"Not to mention," put in Keith Straw, "that's a *very* good bottle of wine."

I asked the ladies how their husbands were taking the surprising verdict. Neither man was in sight.

Linda's winning smile returned. "Walt was surprised—but you know Walt. He's already somewhere off taking pictures for the awards luncheon next Sunday. But I know his mind is madly whirling. He's already thinking about what we can do to improve for Wednesday's round of judging. This happens some years. But it's not over yet. It's always when you think you've got something special that you need to worry the most."

I knew why Jeanne and Jim Francis weren't visible anywhere at the glamorous cocktail preview party. They'd told me they planned to be home across the river in working-class Cinnaminson, New Jersey, with their sore feet hoisted, drinking a *vin ordinare* of their own choosing, and watching the event on local access TV, saving the three-hundred-dollar admission ticket for autumn bulbs. "Let's face it, hon," the wood sprite said to me after I asked if I would see them there, "Jim would look about as comfortable in a monkey suit hobnobbing with the beautiful people of Philadelphia as I'd look in an NBA uniform playing basketball."

The vast hall wasn't wanting for guests, however, all dressed for either a Bond film or a fairy-tale society ball and roaming merrily through the finished exhibit aisles with wineglasses in hand. Ripples of applause and exclamations of delighted surprise broke out as the preview guests worked the aisles and made their own ribbon counts of unexpected winners.

With my own glass of Château Grace Kelly in hand, I set off toward the major exhibit area of the hall hoping I'd been equally wrong about Jack and Joe Blandy's chances of winning the show's biggest prize.

About halfway there, still fighting a feeling of letdown, I paused to admire a stunning palmlike plant that had won a blue in the Horticourt and soon found an older, elegant couple standing by my side.

"Do you fancy that?"

His accent was public school British. So was the cut of his tux. His graying hair was swept back just like Prince Charles's. She was a tired, pale, blonde person who looked as if she had fallen arches, and for a scary moment I thought it might actually *be* the future gardening-mad king and his new bride, Camilla.

"Pretty amazing," I said. "Never seen a palm like that before."

"It's not a palm, dear fellow. It's called a cycad. Hottest plants in the world at the moment. They're cone-bearing woody plants that principally come from the arid regions of South Africa and are amongst the oldest living things on earth, possibly *the* oldest dating back three hundred thousand years. Some experts believe they were a main dietary feature of herbaceous dinosaurs. This one is just a baby, of course. *Encephalartis altensteinii* possibly crossed with a common Great Karoo specimen. Quite lovely. Don't you think, darling?"

"Beautiful."

I exhaled with relief. Her accent was pure Alabama public school.

Luckily, I'd caught his brief informative spiel on a functioning tape recorder I was shamelessly holding.

"Do go on," I said, hoping he'd tell me more about the extraordinary plant.

"Quite a brisk illegal traffic in cycads going on at present, what with all these new governmental regulations being imposed and borders shutting down right and left. Collectors think nothing of paying six digits to lay hands on a lovely mature one, which is likely to be hundreds of years old. Lately, there have even been some sensational thefts from botanic gardens. The one down in Florida last autumn comes to mind. They struck during the height of Hurricane Charlie and cleaned out half a dozen mature cycads in less than ten minutes. Pretty daring lot."

I swallowed my natural urge to say *blimey, mate* and wondered instead how old he thought this baby cycad might be and what it might fetch at the Home Depot gardening center.

He smiled and shrugged like a man appraising a questionable Picasso. She glanced away to see if she knew anybody from her Birmingham homeroom, circa 1958.

"I'd say this little one is just ten or fifteen years along, undoubtedly grown from seed. A small one like this could be picked up for a few hundred dollars. Not too terribly much. It's not until you get into the large ones that the money becomes, shall we say, *serious inquiries only*."

A beat passed. The blonde looked at me and smiled.

He calmly said, "Are you interested in possibly acquiring one?"

"Sure," I said, before I realized what I was saying. It suddenly dawned on me that possbily *he* was the brilliant mastermind behind the daring botanic garden heist down in Florida and had simply come to the Super Bowl of botany to try and unload his red-hot cycads to some un-suspecting rube with lots of disposable income and a fancy for ancient shrubbery.

"How much are you prepared to invest?" he asked pleasantly. She was looking vaguely away again. Possibly on guard for formally dressed agents from Interpol.

It was true I'd probably invested far too much of my children's col-lege funds in my yard, and I certainly invested *far* too much of my valu-able goofing-off time fantasizing over the White Flower catalog while I "wintered" in Maine, but investing in living fossils and priceless dino-saur food suddenly struck me as a really bad idea.

"It might be nice to have one for my office desk," I allowed. "A really, really small one, though."

He coolly reached into his jacket, and for a moment I could have sworn he was going to bring out a slim Walther PPK or at least a badge revealing he was from the South African Secret Police, Cycad Recovery Division.

Instead, he presented me an elegant buff-colored card that had only his name and several international telephone numbers discreetly em-bossed on it. I got the distinct feeling that everything this guy did, he did discreetly.

"Once you start collecting them," he conveyed with a charming smile, "it becomes quite the addiction. I know a collector in Phoenix who has an entire house full of them."

His name was Humphrey, and he was a dealer in rare tropicals and other hard-to-find "exotics." I asked Humphrey if buying a baby cycad from him might get me locked up in a foreign country where I might never be heard from again.

"I assure you there is nothing whatsoever to worry about," he said, laughing like the debonair guy from Spectre. "All quite legal. There are many registered dealers around these days. The demand is so high, you see. I'm simply a middle agent who helps select customers find just the right specimen."

"Will you be at Chelsea too?"

This question came from his good lady, the former homecoming queen from Birmingham.

It took me a moment to realize that she meant the Chelsea Flower Show, the world's oldest flower show, which is held each May on the grounds of the old Chelsea Hospital on the bank of the River Thames. For all my years wandering blissfully around the gardens of the empire between tee times, it seemed rather amazing I'd never been to Chelsea. Then again, I'd never been to the Phildelphia Flower Show until forty-eight hours before this moment.

"Hadn't planned to," I admitted. "But I've always wanted to go. Is it like this one?"

"Worlds apart in every conceivable way," Humphrey responded, just a little too quickly to suit my patriotic tastes.

"Chelsea is fabulous," Lady Humphrey put in with a passionate drawl, scarcely moving her lips. "You simply *have* to go."

"This event is admirably hands-on," her husband explained, with just the teensiest note of horticultural condescension. "Chelsea is considerably more of a spectacle, a true flower show. The entire gardening world shows up there, of course."

"Then maybe I will too." Since I was free to roam at will through the gardening world, going wherever the winds of fate and the spirit of Brother John sent me, this didn't seem the slightest bit out-of-bounds to say. I pocketed his card and replied that perhaps I would see them at Chelsea, a trip over the pond with my own squeeze already forming in my brain.

Humphrey gave a discreet little wave and said, "Do call when you hit town, and we can show you some most interesting specimens."

❖   ❖   ❖

JACK BLANDY WAS BEAMING like a man who'd just won the Irish sweepstakes.

"Pathways to Paradise" had not only captured Best of Show in the major landscape exhibit category, but also had been awarded the prestigious Philadelphia Flower Show Inc. Silver Trophy, the Alfred M. Campbell Memorial Trophy, and the Chicago Horticulture Show Medal for the best use of plants.

"I thought we might do pretty well," Jack allowed, looking a bit shell-shocked but clearly savoring his moment in the spotlight as several photographers snapped his picture and a group of gardening reporters and TV crews impatiently waited for their turn to pepper the history-making grand prize winner with questions.

"I just never thought we'd take the top four prizes," he elaborated, grinning. "This is basically unheard-of. I can't tell you what it means for us. This is really so cool."

Before I could get another question in edgewise, the grand prize winner was swarmed with questions and made busy answering rapid-fire questions from the garden writers about the brilliance of his daring three-part garden design and how the show had grown over the years. I stepped back to wait my turn to ask the beaming Best-of-Show winner what he planned to do for an encore.

"Pretty neat, huh?" a friendly voice observed directly behind me.

The questioner was none other than Walt Fisher. I shook his hand and congratulated him on his third-place win—admitting exactly half a beat later that I thought he and his fellow Inforcers had been cheated by the judges, who'd evidently never ventured further south than Richmond. At this point in the proceedings, any hope of peaceful neutrality on my part had long since vanished.

"Oh, this sort of thing happens," he reflected genially. "Judges are only human, and everyone is entitled to their opinions. If I've learned anything about this show and maybe gardening in general, you really have to be philosophical about it or else your heart will invariably get broken. What is gardening, after all, but human beings manipulating plants to try and achieve an effect that isn't, shall we say, nature's own?

Besides, there are a few things we can do to improve here or there for Wednesday's final judging. I always try and look on the bright side. Everyone is still very close on points for the overall class award."

Walt shrugged affably and wondered what my plans were for the balance of the week. I explained that I planned to venture out to chat with Jane Pepper's old mentor Dick Lighty in Kennett Square and spend the rest of my time attending the show's impressive array of free seminars and lectures until Wednesday, at which point I expected to see the Inforcers win the second round of terrace class judging in a romp. We shook hands, and Walt wandered off to photograph more happy winners.

When I finally got to speak to Jack again, he was still aglow.

"So what are you going to do for an encore?" I put to him, already picturing a horticultural three-peat. I suppose he thought I meant, immediately following the closing of the flower show.

Jack laughed at something and then told me what it was.

"You probably won't believe this. But Jane and I are going off to golf school."

P<small>URELY FOR THE FUN</small> of seeing the gardening world's equivalent of Dead Heads—an apt phrase if there ever was one—I got myself to the convention hall's main entrance doors an hour ahead of the official eight o'clock opening the next morning, a bright but chilly Sunday.

Amazingly, as I'd been reliably informed there would be by the show's press officer, there were already a couple hundred folks waiting anxiously in line, armed with cameras and canvas tote bags, wearing sensible shoes, just itching to be the first public souls through the doors to see the spectacle of the world's largest indoor flower show.

Using my press pass to elbow politely through the crowd, I managed to get to the front of the pack, where I found Denise and Danny Spain reading *The Philadelphia Inquirer*. Turns out they were newlyweds and had driven all the way up from Maryland's Eastern Shore that very morning just to be on hand when the doors swung open.

"This is sort of a family tradition," Denise explained. "My mom and dad always tried to be the first through the door at the show and Danny and I decided to do the same."

I looked at Danny. His large moon face was shoved into the sports pages of the *Inquirer*. He looked about as happy to be there as a guy who'd been asked to give up a lung.

"We're, like, *total* beginners in terms of gardening," Denise sweetly let the cat out of the bag. "I mean, like, neither one of us has a clue what to do, ya know? But we just bought our first house in Chestertown and, like, it needs *everything* done outside. Dad just gave Danny a new riding lawn mower for a wedding present."

Danny looked blankly up at me from the final grapefruit league box scores, like a bloke waiting to use a public toilet.

"What kind of mower?" I asked him cheerfully.

"John Deere. I don't know what model."

"He's a bit moody because he had to give up his Sunday morning softball league in order to come up here this morning," Denise revealed in a shy bride's whisper. Danny glanced at her as if he suddenly had no idea who he'd married.

"Don't worry." I tried my best to lift his spirits, having been down this road myself a couple decades before him. "You'll start cutting grass, and soon you'll be building flowerbeds. Next thing, you'll have to start selling your blood to support your gardening habit, and softball and maybe even weekend golf will just be a dim but pleasant memory from your boyhood. It's just nature's way of telling you, Dan, it's time to grow up."

Suddenly the doors bolted open and we were pressed forward into the convention hall by the mammoth swelling crowds. There were collective gasps, followed by a blinding volley of camera flashes that would have done justice to a Paris fashion runway.

The doors to the 175th Philadelphia Flower Show were officially open and folks were already losing their minds over Walt Off's mist-filled Polynesian orchid island. Just off to the right, Jack Blandy's "Pathways to Paradise" looked like something from a movie set starring young

Kate Hepburn, its accumulated honors and historic silver-plated awards gleaming in the foreground of a breathtaking Delaware estate garden.

"GARDENING IS SO ADDICTIVE because nobody has ever mastered it. Some have come close. But nature always keeps the upper hand. Nature permits us close enough to *think* we may have mastered it—that's the eternal allure, the grail if you will, of gardening. That keeps us forever and hopelessly attracted."

After three days of showgoing, attending seminars at Gardener's Studio and asking horticulture questions of experts, I was sitting comfortably amid snowdrops and dense blooming beds of crocuses on a warm and sunny Wednesday afternoon, admiring Dr. Richard Lighty's woodland trilliums and several sharply pruned crape myrtles by the edge of the woods.

As a finale of sorts, I'd pried myself from the show that morning hoping to tour Chanticleer Garden in Wayne (it was still closed for the season) but ventured on out the old Baltimore Pike to Kennett Square to see Dr. Lighty, a legendary plant hunter-collector and first director of the Longwood Graduate Program in Horticulture at the University of Delaware and the founding director of the Mount Cuba Center for the Study of Piedmont Flora. We'd originally planned to meet on Sunday afternoon but it had been raining so we postponed till Wednesday, an excellent decision since the sun was out and even warmer than it had been at John Bartram's garden.

Before sitting down to talk on his sunny porch, Lighty had conducted me on a delightful stroll around his aptly named garden, Springwood, a naturalistic jewel set in a spectacular seven-acre vale he and wife Sally have cultivated over the past forty years. Not far from the Red Clay River, the vale includes a host of exotic trees and flowering shrubs and something like thirty different species and cultivars Lighty has introduced to American horticulture. As a plant collector, Lighty's travels had taken him to Korea, Japan, Central America, and Nigeria.

"One fascinating thing about gardening," he went ahead, "is that everyone who does it, at whatever stage in the evolution of their skills and knowledge, generally thinks they know what they are doing because the plants always respond. If you really care about a plant, that plant will reflect it by the way it grows and naturalizes into the landscape, and the opposite is true as well.

"I think gardening's current popularity right now is simply a reflection of the fact that, sad to say, most Americans are increasingly insulated from the natural world around them. They don't like to go out in the rain, for example, and most people choose to work in dreadful climate-controlled buildings where they never feel a puff of wind or notice a gathering thundercloud. When I was at Mount Cuba, you could always tell the real gardeners in the tour groups that came to look at the garden. They were the ones who would go out in any kind of weather to get a look at the plants, indifferent to the rain or other conditions."

I smiled at this observation, reminded of how Wendy liked to tell friends that her husband had a "dirty little secret"—a boy's love of getting filthy in the garden.

"We've laid down so much damned concrete in this country, in fact, gardens have become not only living metaphors for what we're in danger of *losing* on the planet itself, but ironically a necessary retreat from the kind of so-called progress that is cutting down forests at alarming rates and throwing up more subdivisions and shopping centers. If gardening is indeed prospering at this moment, I think it may simply be due to a backlash over our increasing separation from nature."

With visible distaste, Lighty pointed up the hill to a line of budding hardwoods, where, through his eight-foot deer fence, the peaks of several large new homes could just be seen rising. "Just over the hill there, and not so long ago at all, that was a wonderful hardwood forest filled with native ash and maple trees. But now it's a neighborhood of Mc-Mansions where every other house looks nearly identical—five-car garages with indoor swimming pools and landscapes they purchase before they ever move in, using the same half a dozen plants their neighbors have.

"Very worrying indeed, this trend, in my opinion. If, on the

one hand, we've finally begun to mature as a nation of gardeners—
evidenced by booming gardening centers and the endless varieties of
unusual plants streaming onto the market every season now, apparently
to feed an insatiable public demand for new and exotic plants—the
other side of the argument is that even many experienced gardeners
have no real sense of how we have evolved and, thus, where we might
be heading.

"In fact, all gardening is linked by a shared heritage of learning and
experimentation, a marvelous narrative thread that runs through the
story of English and American gardening, linking one to the other and
ultimately explaining how America has now emerged as a place where
some of the most imaginative gardening in the world is taking place—
particularly out west and in the American Southwest, where they are
using native plants and naturalistic planting styles to such dramatic
effect."

"Like Ariadne's thread," I said; the image suddenly came to mind
from classical mythology. It was she, the future moon and planting goddess of the Hellenic world, who helped save headstrong but foolish
Theseus by leading the young hero from the Cretan labyrinth back to a
garden in the upper world via a thread she cleverly dispersed.

"Precisely. A love of gardening is like that—a thread that leads you
on a wonderful story linking humans to the natural world."

"So, is Philadelphia the birthplace of American horticulture?" Someone at the show had told me as much; but I was also thinking of
Jefferson and Franklin fueling their own evolving passions at Johnny
Bartram's place on the lazing Schuylkill, not to mention all the fabulous
ornamental gardens started by the Du Pont family strung along the
Delaware River valley. Longwood struck me as nothing short of a national treasure, a formal garden every American ought to see and experience, and I had hopes of eventually checking out Chanticleer and
venturing into Winterthur, my late friend Winnie Palmer's favorite formerly private estate garden, just over the greening hills from where Lighty
and I sat in his garden. When I told Professor Lighty this, he smiled.

"I've got just the person for you to see at Winterthur. Denise Magnani is an old pupil of mine who not only helped save that garden from extinction but also created maybe the most wonderful children's garden in the country. Quite a story. She's on the cutting edge of public gardening, in my view—making gardens accessible to young people, drawing them outside into the natural world, enchanting them with nature's endless properties of renewal."

Over the next half hour or so, as I tried to put out of my mind the memory of the assembly-line landscaping in shopping centers and subdivisions I'd seen on my way out the Baltimore Pike that morning, Dr. Lighty explained to me how, almost from the days Thomas Jefferson retreated from public life to work on his neglected flower gardens at Monticello up until about the end of the Second World War, American homeowners and gardeners simply copied the landscape philosophy of Andrew Jackson Downing, the son of a Hudson River nurseryman whose pre–Civil War ideas about ornamental landscape gardening drew heavily on concepts of traditional English manor house landscaping and simply adapted them to native North American flora.

As editor of the influencial *Horticulturist* magazine, a rural essayist and self-styled arbiter of public good taste who gained a vast and devoted following, Downing's seminal *Treatise on the Theory and Practice of Landscape Gardening, Adapted to North America* went through no fewer than twelve editions and shaped the gardening consciousness of an emerging republic.

"It was Downing, a celebrated figure and America's best-known landscape gardener, who promoted the idea of planting an attractive shrub at each end of a new dwelling to frame a structure—a stately conifer, perhaps, or a willow or some other interesting ornamental tree in the middle of the yard for horticultural interest—an idea, for better or worse, you still see in every new subdivision in America. If anyone is to blame for the wretched manner they landscape those McMansions on the hill," Lighty joked ruefully, "perhaps it's him."

On the other hand, my host pointed out, Downing was also a strong early advocate of developing urban parks and cemeteries, areas in which the United States was to lead the world in landscape horticulture and design, and his writing and influence, among other things, led indirectly to the creation of New York's Central Park, an ambitious project many feel Downing would surely have been commissioned to design and create if he hadn't died prematurely in a tragic steamboat accident on the Hudson River in 1852, at age thirty-six. Two years before the accident, as fate would have it, Andrew Downing had persuaded a promising young landscape architect named Calvert Vaux to relocate from England to America. A short time later, Vaux partnered with a promising young landscape designer named Frederick Law Olmsted—and the rest, as they say, is horticultural history. Together, Vaux and Omsted created a revolutionary system of public parks that was not only the envy of the world but also inspired Americans to consider landscaping the land around them.

"As our own early Colonial dependence on them for sustenance and medicine illustrates, plants are a powerful medium for personal transformation—the best tool we have for connecting with the natural world and understanding where our own species came from and just where it might be headed, if we're not too careful," Lighty mused, slipping into a more philosophical eddy of thought.

"In England, a relatively small island with a rigid social structure, the best gardening was historically done on estates. The perennial border was an ideal expression of their use of plants because, above all else, it could be controlled. But nature doesn't *wish* to be controlled. In this country, on the other hand, when the first gardens began to appear around these parts about the time of Jefferson and Franklin and that bunch, you had thousands of miles of unexplored wilderness in all directions! And, not unimportantly, you eventually had thousands of immigrant gardeners who came from England and France and Italy who not only worked for wealthy landowners here—creating some of the finest formal gardens the world had ever seen, as you know—but eventually they got *their* hands on a little piece of land and changed the landscape around them!

"As this new society grew and expanded, literally pushing back borders and discovering interesting new lands, popular interest and knowledge of plants proliferated—it *exploded!*"

I loved how worked up Lighty got over this subject, waving his hands about like an old-time preacher, splashing a little lemonade on the porch from pure plant passion. It made me wish I had the time and money to take that two-year hort program at Longwood I'd read about in *Horticulture* magazine, though Lighty was now retired and gardening his patch at Springwood.

"You're saying we learned from the English and then evolved past them?"

"*Exactly*—or so we must! Look. It just took nearly *one hundred years* for the average gardener, if there is such a creature, to begin to break away from the influence of Downing and others who got us started in that direction—to *free* ourselves from the English perennial border!"

It really wasn't until after World War II, he amplified, that mail-order catalogs based largely in the Midwest and New England began to offer ordinary gardeners broader choices of plants and seeds, things they'd never seen before or imagined growing in their gardens. "By then, of course, you had men like Chinese Wilson from 1900–1933 at Harvard's Arnold Arboretum and J. C. Raulston down at N. C. State exploring the world and bringing back hundreds of new species that flourished in this country. Wilson, a Kew man, alone introduced something like five hundred different plants to to America. Can you imagine it? Talk about exciting. I began going over to Korea in 1966, and the things we found growing over there were positively inspiring. Some of it we brought back to this country and eventually introduced to the ordinary gardener. Each plant has a wonderful story behind it—but most people never realize that."

The plant philosopher sipped his lemonade again, a little breathless, smiled at me almost triumphantly, and added with vigor, "*That's* what I mean about gardening being a splendid narrative that each of us who love gardening, on whatever level, who want to know more and more with every passing season, are a vital part of. The most wonderful thing about gardening is, you can never come close to learning it all—there is always a lifetime more! It forever draws you in, and on."

The happy infinity of this prospect seemed the perfect point at which to end my time in a plant philosopher's garden—for that matter, my sojourn to Philadelphia itself. At least until I could come back and catch Chanticleer and snoop around gardens in the region even more.

"So, tell me exactly what is it you're doing again?" Lighty demanded as he accompanied me back to my truck.

I explained about my intention to spend a year traveling through other people's gardens in search of green wisdom and greater connection to the esperanto of personal pastimes. I was suddenly pondering, as a direct result of my time here, for example, a much broader field trip down south to explore my own gardening roots and reconsider Jefferson's Monticello, a place I'd visited maybe half a dozen times in my life but never considered from the perspective of a fully addicted flower gardener. With this in mind, I gave professor Lighty a mercifully brief account of my trials trying to build a Southern-style faux English garden in the coastal woods of Maine and he laughed as if I were either (a) a complete nitwit who probably shouldn't be encouraged to breed, or (b) a middle-aged crazy after his own garden-loving heart.

"Wonderful!" Lighty declared, clapping me gently on the arm. "If some of those people in the McMansions on the hill were taking the time to do what you're doing, maybe there wouldn't be McMansions on the hill."

His was a welcome observation. Then he smiled and confided, as if to reassure me, "By the way, it's fine to admire the English and important to understand where your passion comes from, because that gives you the base from which to develop your own style and creative imagination. That's part of following the narrative thread I was talking about. Just don't become *too* enamored of the English and realize *you* are evolving with your garden!"

"That's my goal this year," I agreed. "A little personal evolution."

Before I left Springwood, he conducted me on a lovely walking tour along the forest edge to look at some magnificent Korean stewartias and *Americana heuchera* fittingly named "William Bartram" he had introduced to America back in 1991.

I spent so much time looking at plants and hearing about their origins from Professor Lighty, in fact, I was late getting back downtown to the convention hall and found the show officially closed for the day when I finally got there.

Somewhere around the darkened Garden State Parkway, heading north toward my own still-frozen garden in the woods, I reached Walt Fisher on my cell phone.

"So, how did you guys do?" I eagerly asked him, meaning in the second round of official judging.

"We placed first," the Botticelli of Bulbs said. I could hear how happy he was over this turn of fortunes.

"But we lost the best of the class by a single tenth of one point."

"You kidding. A *tenth* of a point. To w*hom*?"

"The Amey siblings."

"I don't believe it."

"That's the Philadelphia Flower Show for you."

"I never even got to meet them," I pointed out, wondering if they were real people or just some metaphor for the high level of horticultural excellence one encounters at every turn at the mother of all garden shows.

"Oh well," Walt allowed with a laugh. "Maybe you should just come back next year and meet them."

Chapter 5

Garden Club Confidential

I WAS UNPREPARED for the record devastation spring eventually brought to Maine.

To be fair, *spring* didn't bring this devastation to Maine—it merely once more revealed it. The culprit was the same one working overtime to rub out the poor Elephant Angel tree. Three consecutive years of historic summer drought followed by a trio of punishingly cold and mostly snowless winters had wreaked nothing shy of horticultural havoc on my yard. Perhaps some diabolical government plot to seed the clouds had gone awry after all, or maybe this was simply a naturally occurring cycle of particularly awful weather the mirthful gods sent down for fun and laughs every forty or fifty years, just to test the resolve of aspiring landscape gardeners. In either case, on the heels of Philadelphia's insights and inspirations, it was difficult not to take the destruction of my garden bitterly hard and *very* personally. The one-two punch of winter kill and summer drought sometimes briefly mutes my normal boundless spring enthusiasm and makes me wonder if life and gardening up here is really worth all the trouble.

For three weeks after returning home from Philadelphia, in any case, I roamed the property with a broken-handled planting shovel, muttering oaths like some crazed woodland caretaker from Thomas Hardy, hauling up one murdered shrub or petrified plant after another, fashioning frightening large piles of ornamental brush that resembled something a bunch of naked pagans would set a torch to and dance around beneath a new planting moon.

Before the grim body count on my hilltop ceased, I was out *two* once-thriving fifteen-year-old mixed beds of English and French lavender, nine mature rhododendron bushes, two large Mugo pines, a dozen (allegedly) zone-four hardy heather plants, five holly bushes, a young Cortland apple tree, three English clematis vines, two young Japanese maples I'd meticulously sheathed in burlap for protection, six hardy rose bushes, a pair of pee gee hydrangea trees split by ice, and a yew shrub a neighbor assured me would require a nuclear winter to wipe out.

Luckily, I wasn't suffering alone that spring. On the radio before church one sunny Sunday morning in middle April, I listened to radio plantsman Paul Parent take call after call from distressed gardeners flung far and wide across the blasted hills of northern New England, all complaining that their landscapes and gardens had never been so brutalized by the winter elements. Parent, a popular lecturer and no-nonsense kind of garden expert, thoughtfully advised giving damaged plants a "little longer" to see if the natural growing cycle had simply been delayed by the extreme weather we'd seen of late. This was the same expert whose commonsense advice to a caller whose apple tree refused to bloom was to take a hammer and pound the flesh of the bark firmly enough to inflict a bruise—"just to awaken it up a bit, an old trick pecan growers down in Georgia use." I just happened to have exactly the same problem with a stubborn young apple tree at the time and tried out the unorthodox strategy and found it worked beautifully. I'd been a loyal Sunday morning listener of the eponymous Paul Parent ever since.

"After a winter like this one, patience is definitely a virtue," Parent counseled that morning after my week of pagan bonfire building, or something along these lines, to anxious callers who, in the face of their own piles of devastation, mirrored my discouraged state of mind. "Sometimes up here you just have to wait out the weather *and* your garden."

Was *that* ever the gospel truth, I thought. Among the first calls I'd made upon arriving home from Philadelphia with no fewer than three ambitious new garden plans churning in my head were those to two talented friends I've relied upon to help me shape the landscape of my unforgiving northern hilltop garden.

One is a lobsterman named Jim Gaudet who comes each spring to thin the woods and remove any dead trees, the other a free-spirited excavator I affectionately call Pothead Eddie. I knew from long experience that Jim Gaudet would show up with his immaculately kept chainsaws a day or two after I phoned, but Pothead Eddie might not show up until Labor Day to push the dirt around, for obvious reasons. When he did, the man was a wonder to behold, a virtuoso with backhoe and bulldozer.

Everything depended on timing with Pothead Eddie, however, including Eddie's prior commitments to the rich summer folk building monstrous McMansions out on the photogenic rocks of nearby islands and whether the spirit of financial need moved him to actually consider working that week. Eddie was a grizzled ponytailed throwback to the early 1970s, it perhaps goes without saying, your classic fun-loving latter-day hippie redneck who simply loves weed, Lynyrd Skynyrd, and his heavily tattooed "old lady," more or less in that order of affection.

Every time I grew weary of waiting for Pothead Eddie to show up and rebuild my weather-ravaged road or shape a new section of my ever-expanding garden plot, and reached for the phone book to call another more reliable excavator, some visitor to my little Sissinghurst of the North would offer a telling comment on how nicely the terrain flowed, and I'd hear myself speaking fondly about the land-shaping genius of Pothead Eddie, a landscape artist who worked more mysteriously (and far less frequently) than God. Eventually, however, I would hear Skynyrd or the Allman Brothers blaring through the trees as I rounded the bend of my hilltop drive, and there would be Pothead Eddie—bouncing along atop his equally aging dozer, sculpting piles of freshly imported loam and giving me the thumbs-up sign by way of brotherly greeting, smoking something that smelled faintly like a burning hotel carpet. The fact that I hailed from the Deep South where Lynyrd Skynyrd comes from made me okay in Pothead Eddie's book. We had other fundamental things in common that helped forge a friendship. We both liked beer, for instance, and fancied the pleasure of a nice long meditative pee off the deck beneath the winter stars. That's something you can do with relative social immunity on a dirt road in Maine.

"Well, what should I do till then?" the impatient lady caller who feared she had damaged peach trees over in southern Vermont demanded to know from the wise and avuncular Paul Parent that cold Sunday morning in early April.

For a fleeting moment, I had high hopes Paul Parent might tell the poor worried peach-tree owner to take a hammer and give her trees a good whack just to get them up and going for the season—rather like I'd seen Pothead Eddie cold-start his backhoe on several occasions after he'd had his Budweiser tall-boy breakfast.

"If it was me," Parent told her with a sympathetic chuckle, "I'd go down South and watch the dogwoods and azaleas bloom. When you get back, you might be surprised what's still alive but has only retreated for its own protection. Sometimes we're too close to things and can't see that nature has a way of taking care of its own."

PENDING THE ARRIVAL of Pothead Eddie, I left town the next afternoon, taking Paul Parent's sage travel advice and following the directives of my inner green monk. But first I drove out to pay a call on my garden guru, Suzy Verrier, out at North Creek Farm, who confirmed that gardeners up and down the coast of New England were reporting their worst winter kills in decades, possibly ever. "We've lost things we've *never* lost before—I'm talking northern species hydrangeas, even rugosas!" she fumed entertainingly as we strolled toward the greenhouse where Kai and the cairn terriers were busy rebuilding what looked to be either a mothballed nuclear silo or possibly someone's dis-

carded wood-fired boiler they'd dragged home from the village dump
and would soon have working good as new. *Waste not, want not* isn't just
the unstated employee policy at North Creek Farm—it's a lifestyle.

"So tell me *all* about Philadelphia," Suzy demanded with her usual
infectious enthusiasm.

I filled her in on what a fertile field trip Philadelphia had been, including how my time there inspired no fewer than three new and ambitious gardens that might or might not get built if Pothead Eddie showed
up to shove dirt sometime before the first snow flurries came around
Labor Day. Even as I piled up the winter kill and set it ablaze, I'd
sketched out plans for a small Japanese side garden, a Roman pergola
garden based on a design I'd pinched from the Philly show, and either a
small "Philosopher's garden" modeled after Dick Lighty's Springwood
or a "Southern arboretum" between the protected south-facing decks of
my house. Maybe even both. My garden schemes changed almost week
to week, and were forever subject to upper management review.

"Perfect," Suzy said, leading me into her greenhouse where Kai and
the staff cairns had the big metal contraption from the dump rumbling
worryingly to life. "And I've got just the plants for you." She showed me
a pair of beautiful *Virburnum sargentii*, a Carolina silver bell that smote
my heart, a Chinese quince and a pair of bareroot Northern redbuds
she'd just gotten in from some grower in Minnesota. I claimed them all,
especially eager to see how the redbuds fared in my soon-to-be-built
Southern arboretum. Growing up in North Carolina, redbuds were the
true harbingers of spring, and thus my favorite tree, iridescently lighting
up the bare hardwood forests of the Blue Ridge foothills on the grayest
spring afternoon. Twice I'd smuggled innocent redbud varieties across
state lines into Maine—*Cercis canadensis* or common Eastern redbud the first time, followed by an elegantly purple-leafed Forest Pansy
redbud—and twice I'd murdered them in cold blood. As I stood admiring these tall, elegant bareroot specimens, Suzy also gave me the good
news that some clever hybridizer had just announced he'd developed a
northern hardy variety of crape myrtle and she might soon have one of
those on hand to sell me, as well.

My spirits were suddenly elevated nearly back to post-Philadelphia levels, and then she demanded to know what was the next stop on my one-man gardening Chautauqua. I was heading south to give a speech to the sponsors of the approaching U.S. Open championship in Pinehurst, I provided, but also because it was the start of Garden Week in the state of Virginia and a friend who'd long been a power in the Garden Club of Virginia had strongly advised me to try and catch Peter Hatch's annual address on Thomas Jefferson's flower gardens at Monticello. While in that neck of the woods, I intended to look up a couple like-minded souls and see their gardens, including a woman who once had the greenest thumb of anyone I ever knew, and maybe go scouting for a couple lost gardens of my boyhood with a box of dog dust in hand.

"Right now," I told her, "my next stop is the Colonial Dames of Cohasset."

She laughed. "I forgot about the other ladies in your life. By the way," she added, "I've been thinking some more about your beech tree."

"Great. What else should I do?" I'd already trimmed the tree back and exposed the soil around its base in order for the roots to absorb more air and moisture.

"Nothing."

"*Nothing?*"

"Well, only a little more than I told you a few weeks ago." She explained that when I got back from my extended Southern field trip I ought to prune the Elephant Angel back, the way French gardeners at Versailles sharply pollarded tulip maples—a measure aimed at promoting new growth and irritating English gardeners—and maybe just give the newly liberated roots a nice drink of SUPERthrive to kick-start its damaged metabolic system the way Kai was coaxing that old boiler to life at the other end of the greenhouse.

Suzy swears by SUPERthrive, a mysterious amber hormone plant supplement that comes from some mysterious lab in West L.A. that simply sets the heart aglow with its untempered self-promotion, asserting to have won "Golf Medals at the World's Fair" and revived "billions of plants" with its top-secret formulation from the experts at the so-called Vitamin Institute. For all anyone knows, except for a few wild and crazy guys in lab coats, the stuff could be made from old diner coffee and boiled roadkill filtered through the dirty tube socks of the USC football team.

Whatever is in it does seem to work marvelously well, however. More than once this mystery juice has nicely revived plants I was certain were total goners, and more than once I've been tempted to put a few drops in my morning coffee, just to see what happens.

"That's *all* I should do?" I pressed my garden adviser. This course of action sounded like something Paul Parent might have prescribed to a glum honeysuckle vine owner whose plant wouldn't put out.

"That's it." She repeated something I'd heard her say many times over the years—that nature is perfectly capable of healing its own; sometimes the wisest course of action simply is to step out of the way and let things "have their head" in a garden. "Just be sure to expose the roots a little for fresh air, and keep them nice and damp all summer long. Especially if we get another drought courtesy of that Washington crowd.

"Take these with you too—road reading," she said, presenting me a couple garden catalogs she was keen on. One was the spring catalog of Heronswood Nursery out in Washington State, a place I knew Suzy was over the moon about because the owner, Dan Hinckley, is a true plant fanatic, explorer, and garden writer of the first rank.

The other catalog was the spring catalog of Plant Delights Nursery down in North Carolina, a glossy thick catalog full of unusual plants with a cover that rivaled a Marvel comic book. The owner there was a guy named Tony Avent, a popular lecturer and plant hunter I'd also heard Suzy and other plant cognoscenti say glowing things about.

"If you're anywhere near this fellow Tony Avent, you'd be well advised to stop in and meet him," she said by way of so long. "His catalog is a hoot."

I made a mental note to try and do so, then swung back by the house on my way out of town to drop off the new plants for my Southern arboretum and place Tony Avent's catalog on Wendy's nightstand, a cheap mnemonic trick I learned years ago. Because my wife is a special needs schoolteacher and thus has a mind like a bottle of SUPERthrive, nothing escapes her notice, and she never fails to remember important things her husband easily forgets. She was planning to join me at week's end down in North Carolina and wouldn't, I felt confident, forget Tony Avent and his colorful comic book nursery ways even if I somehow did.

According to the English historian Jenny Uglow, modern garden clubs and plant catalogs in large part evolved from the Elizabethan kitchen garden and sixteenth-century plantsmen seeking natural remedies for an ailing world. To begin with, the cottage garden of the rural housewife had long been the medicine cabinet of the empire. "Here she worked like a scientist with glasses and alembics, distilling the purges and cough medicines and potions, preparing her conserves and pickles, and making perfumed oils for scents and soaps," Uglow relates in her delightful *Small History of British Gardening*. "Everything was useful, even plants that we now consider purely ornamental. Marigolds and violets were candied for sweets, peonies were preserved as a remedy for sorrow. Elderflowers and irises and mallow were made into lotions for softening wrinkles, rhubarb in white wine was used for dying your hair blonde, strawberry and watercress were pounded into a cream to remove the much-disdained freckles." Among other things, beauty and health tonics were distilled from thyme, sage and savory, marjoram and rosemary, and a "honey of roses" made from rose petals and bean-flower water was believed to take away unsightly "spots of the face." From Holland, in 1524, came the fruit of the modest hop plant, transforming beer.

In 1673 the Worshipful Society of Apothecaries leased a site adjacent to the River Thames and the bustling market gardens of Chelsea—future site of the Chelsea Physic Garden—to study and experiment with new plant species that arrived almost every week from abroad, especially the exciting new worlds of the Americas. The gardener's gaze, as Uglow notes, now extended to the farthest horizons of exploration. "Henry Compton, Bishop of London for forty years from 1675 to 1713, packed his Fulham garden with over a thousand rarities, using his missionaries as plant hunters. The most successful, John Bannister, sent back many plants from Virginia, especially trees, including the 'sweet bay' (*Magnolia virginiana*, Britain's first magnolia) and a black walnut, which was photographed in 1894, its girth reaching seventeen feet. Bannister himself died at thirty-two, falling to his death, or being accidentally shot—the stories vary—while collecting on the banks of the Roanoke River."

By then, Uppsala botany professor Carolus Linnaeus had devised a clever binomial classification system that radically simplified and thus revolutionized the challenge of identifying plants and properly disseminating knowledge about them. The science of taxonomy was a boon to the commercial growing world and Chelsea eventually became the English center of that world. No fewer than two thousand new species alone arrived during this interval from a self-taught Philadelphia Quaker botanist named Bartram, "including phlox and helianthus, the first ceanothus, balsam fir and the luscious evergreen *Magnolia grandiflora*." And other colorful American imports included the rudbeckia or black-eyed Susan, "the glamorous Turks-cap lily, the sweet-smelling heliotrope and elegant purple *Verbena bonariensis*." Between 1730 and 1770, Uglow estimates, the number of species grown on the banks of the Thames at Chelsea rose from one thousand to five thousand plants. "The excitement," she writes, "must have been boundless."

Even before formal professional gardening societies formed to serve a European aristocracy that increasingly viewed a well-shaped landscape as evidence of one's divine right to govern, early nurserymen and growers of all classes began assembling at villages on a regular basis to share plants and seeds and to disseminate useful plant knowledge. Even as gardens became the fashion with the social elite, "florist clubs" began to form among the clothmakers and other artisan unions. One reason gardening became so deeply ingrained in the British psyche, Jenny Uglow asserts, is because, by the end of the eighteenth century, factory workers and artisans from across the country were organizing garden clubs and gathering at local inns to show off the bounty of their gardens, conducting competitions, holding dinners, and awarding prizes to the finest specimens. As the fever spread, the first garden catalogs appeared, proffering everything from Venus flytraps to American crab apples.

In America, not surprisingly, in the decades immediately following the Revolutionary War, the first garden societies and clubs began to pop up around the busy seaports of Philadelphia and Boston and Charleston. Like their fellow horticultural pioneers over in Britain, these fledgling organizations were originally loose associations of plantsmen and nurserymen largely dedicated to spreading popular knowledge about fruit trees and vegetables. But as a new nation got organized and a certain level of prosperity trickled down to the ordinary citizen, ornamental gardening gained a foothold it never relinquished on Northern estates and Southern plantations.

In late-nineteenth-century New York, Philadelphia, and Boston, visionary urban planners suddenly viewed public garden spots—sweet-smelling flowers and spicy ornamental shrubs—as a novel and inexpensive way of easing both the stench and congestion of city life and providing a bit of nature's comfort to a weary citizenry. Boston's Public Garden (a former community veggie patch and mustering field during Colonial times) and eventually its celebrated Emerald Necklace of interconnected parks and green spaces proved to be a pioneering leap forward in urban planning design. Not surprisingly, Frederick Law Olmsted incorporated this same flowing sense of natural winding countryside into the heart of New York's famed Central Park, making it the signature city park in the nation.

By the 1900s, the height of the Victorian garden boom, Britain claimed to have well over a thousand garden clubs and societies, most of whom sponsored some kind of annual flower competition, inspired by the lead of the Royal Horticultural Society that was officially formed to promote British gardening in 1804. Coming along across the pond twenty years later, Philadelphia's ambitious flower exhibition had a similar effect of boosting the formation of local garden clubs and plant societies, a trend that swept straight up the coast to Boston.

It's at this point in gardening's golden narrative thread that we find my beloved friend Polly Logan organizing a luncheon at the Red Lion Inn in pretty Cohasset, Massachusetts, summoning her formidable

South Shore gardening pals to get together and share their most intimate gardening confidences with an interested green thumb just passing through the village.

I first met Polly Logan and wrote about her for *Yankee* magazine in the late eighties when a mutual friend beguilingly described her as "an irresistible force of nature—a true mover and shaker in politics and about the only Republican John Kenneth Galbraith will speak to." A longtime Republican national committeeperson and dogged champion of women's rights who was equally known for her booming Phyllis Diller laugh, colorful men's bow ties and King Tut earrings, Polly had not only been responsible for electing dozens if not hundreds of mainstream Republicans to office over the course of several decades in a state dominated by Kennedy Democrats, but also turned out to be the most upbeat individual I'd ever met and an even more indefatigible champion of gardens, founder of one of New England's most respected clubs.

In summary, why nobody had yet thought to elect *her* president of these United States by now, or at least put her handsome New England visage on a postage stamp, was completely beyond my comprehension.

Actually, Polly is no more a daughter of the Bay State than I am a son of its northern Pine Tree neighbor. We're both introduced cultivars who have found a home in the thin rocky soil of the great Northeast. In manners of speech and dining habits I stubbornly remain a devoted son of Dixie. She, however, seems almost like a true native species despite the fact that the former Polly Peterson hails from tiny Red Oak, Iowa, and was that town's first participant ever in the Iowa Brain Derby. After graduating with honors from the state university, she became one of the first women in America to study foreign service at George Washington University, aiming for a life of public service.

By the time I first came calling on her, twenty years ago, Polly and her famous mobile party tents had been a fixture in the social and political life of Massachusetts for decades—or, as she once put it to me with her booming laugh, "at least since the ink dried on the Constitution."

After touring me through her garden off Jerusalem Road that fine spring morning in the waning Reagan years, with the rancorous New Hampshire primary mercifully weeks behind us, we sat together on her rear loggia overlooking perhaps the loveliest postcard bay in America and I learned a host of beguiling contradictions about this amazing little lady (she's well *under* five feet) including the fact that she was an ERA-touting, prochoice practicing Catholic who had married into Boston's *other* powerful Democratic clan for whom Logan Airport had been named back in 1949.

Among the other refreshing things she told me that fine spring morning, in the face of a rapidly souring national economy and dimming "Massachusetts Miracle" that would soon take Governor Michael Dukakis down in flames, she confidentially believed it might be *better* if a Democrat actually captured the presidency that year instead of a Republican named Bush.

"I don't *want* a Democrat to win, mind you. But given the economy the way it is, it may be another decade before we can win back the Oval Office." As it turned out, her political instincts were right on target. That same ho-hum economy eventually sent a senior Bush home to an early retirement at Walker's Point and produced the eight-year funhouse known as the Clinton presidency.

"Do you ever marvel at how you wound up here?" I asked Dame Polly as we sat on her loggia amid various spring shrubs bursting into bloom.

"Oh, all the time," she answered with her famous laugh. "That's half the fun of being an American. You can go anywhere you want and find a great life." And with that, she proceeded to tell me how she'd done just that.

One autumn day not long after the end of WWII, Polly took a train to Boston for the Harvard–Dartmouth football game and met a witty young soldier named Ed Logan who shared her avid interests in sports, politics, and theater. The next night, Logan tracked the diminutive Iowan down and took her out to see a production of *Brigadoon*.

In many ways, Polly Logan's life became a Boston Brigadoon. Logan, then a major in the 26th Infantry Division of the U.S. Army, came from a long line of distinguished military men, including the major general for whom Logan airport got named despite the strenuous efforts of one Joseph Kennedy (who tried to have the place named in honor of his dead son, Joe). The Logans were the other wealthy Irish Catholic South Shore family active in Democratic Party politics, though their money came from beer (the Boston Beer Company) instead of stockpiled scotch.

The family compound where Ed Logan took his *Brigadoon* date home to meet the family was a fifty-room mansion set on thirteen acres just off Jerusalem Road in Cohasset. "I thought the house was a country club the first Sunday Ed took me there," Polly remembered. "I was led into a large dining room and there were all these *Logans* everywhere. I couldn't keep them all straight. There were young Logans and old Logans. After lunch, everyone either went for a vigorous walk in the gardens, which were extensive, or played football on the lawn. The whole time everyone was either telling jokes or arguing politics. I decided *that's* why they had such a big house—to contain the whole noisy bunch."

Following their marriage in 1949 and seven years in the city, where Ed worked for the Sheraton Corporation, the couple moved out to the "honeymoon" cottage on the Logan estate. "By that time, the Logans were great obituary readers. None of them, however, drove a car. So I got pressed into service and used to read the obituaries every morning in the *Globe* to see where I would be driving them that afternoon. I remember once driving Aunt Martha to a funeral along Morrissey Boulevard when something dreadful happened. Aunt Martha was slightly narcoleptic, you see, and she fell asleep at the drop of a hat. In this instance she fell asleep and toppled right out the car door onto Morrissey Boulevard. Fortunately, the traffic was pretty light that day. When she finally died sometime later, they were carrying her casket down the steps of the big house when someone dropped their end. 'Well,' quipped one of the older Logan generals, 'if she wasn't dead, she is *now*.' "

It was because of heartwarming tales like this I'd remained in touch over the years with Boston's most colorful grandame and garden clubber, though curiously I didn't quite know how gardening had become such an integral feature of her life. All that Iowa corn in her past? It was for this reason and others that I decided to pay a call on her on my way south to Pinehurst and Monticello.

Now eighty-something, or pretty close to it, she hastily called her garden club cronies together for a morning coffee and a friendly chat with me. Fortunately, I arrived before the others at Polly's cozy shingled cottage overlooking the bay, and we once more got to sit and catch up for a spell out in her spectacular garden. During a couple other visits to Cohasset, Polly had introduced me to several of her closer friends, and a few had even taken me around to see their gardens, with promises of more to come.

"Ironically," she amplified, "it was gardening that got me into the whole party-giving thing and led directly to my political life. This was after the war—the Civil War, I mean—and somewhere either just before or after my children Malcolm and Martha came along and the Logan generals had pretty well died off. I was asked to open the family mansion for a benefit to raise money for a local garden club I had agreed to help get going.

"There was another garden club in town in those days, you see, the Cohasset Garden Club, very old, very elite"—here she paused and gave one of her signature robust laughs—"some of us younger mothers might have even said a wee bit *stuffy*. In any case, a handful of us who probably would have had to wait till *we* were grandmothers to be invited to join that one decided to strike off on our own and start a club. A real bunch of radicals with garden trowels. None of us, by the way, knew baked beans about gardening. We were all novices at best, true beginners.

"But that's half the fun of gardening. You don't *have* to know anything. You just have to think you might like it and then jump in headfirst. So that's exactly what we did—realizing some years later this is really a wonderful way to learn about the subject because others are learning and teaching you along the way. Anyway, we formed something called the Community Garden Club of Cohasset and had our little fundraiser. It was a far bigger success than I ever imagined it would be. People were streaming all over the lawn, talking about the gardens, joining up right and left. The Logan generals would have been *completely* horrified. Good thing they were under the ground instead of above it!"

In 1976, the Logan mansion was torn down and sold off to a developer who put five ersatz Colonial houses on the property. "The stairways went to Texas," she explained with a laugh that sounded slightly wistful, "the fireplaces to Califonia." With their own two children suddenly adults and gone as well, Polly and Ed lived quietly in Hingham. Then, in 1983, like the generals before him, Ed Logan died of cancer.

"I missed him so terribly much, his vast sense of fun and wonderful humor. The companions you make in life, the people who share your closest interests, are the hardest to see go, aren't they? After Ed died the only thing I could think to do was come back to Cohasset."

So Polly Logan and her beloved Newfy Cabot did just that; they took up residence in the cute shingled cottage where we'd first talked twenty years ago and Polly threw herself into even more charity work and political mentoring, using her garden by the sea and famous mobile party tents to raise money for everything from cancer research to the Equal Rights Amendment.

In her frugal red Ford Escort with mud-freckled fenders, Polly Logan also became a tireless advocate for literacy, day care for working mothers, cleaning up toxic landfills, and ending violence in public schools—one of the most influential women in American politics, according to one national newsmagazine, the irrepressible garden clubber who came through the terrace door of American politics. "That little lady," Kansas senator and presidential aspirant Bob Dole leaned over and commented to me, pointing to Logan one night as we were having dinner together in New Hampshire, "is a *major* force of nature." He got that right.

"This garden," she said suddenly, glancing around, "really saved my life. For several years I had the sweetest man helping me look after it and then he died too and I was . . . *lost*. I used to say to friends that I didn't know who I missed most. Ed or my gardener!"

I'd hoped to hear more of this story, but another Dilleresque laugh announced the arrival of her fellow garden club members, several of whom I'd previously met and become friendly with at one of her legendary Red Lion luncheons. I was seated next to Penny Place, for example, when she confided having been a young pregnant mother with "not a jot of gardening experience or clue what I was doing" who inherited an old formal garden overgrown with hundred-year-old vines and an elderly Italian gardener "with black fingers" who was utterly terrified she would give birth at any moment in his garden.

"He watched me like a hawk and let me make an awful lot of mistakes," she explained to me that day at the Red Lion, "but that turned out to be *exactly* the thing I needed because gardening is essentially about creating life and life is full of mistakes and misstarts that eventually lead to success if you don't give up."

Penny and her Italian mentor, I knew from Polly and others, had doggedly cleared the family garden of vines but left the most ancient flower beds, including the eighty-year-old peonies. Today she not only owned one of the showplace gardens of Boston's South Shore but had also designed and built an estate garden up on the coast of Maine that reportedly rivaled Martha Stewart's place at Southwest Harbour.

The first thing Penny demanded to know from me as she motored through the Logan cottage door this warm middle spring day was how my own Maine garden was shaping up. I hated to have to explain to her that the ruthless combination of summer drought and winter cold had dealt my garden hopes such a severe blow I was frankly having to briefly escape to North Carolina and Virginia for a while just to see something in bloom.

"It's hard not to take that sort of thing personally," she philosophized, patting me gently on the arm as we went together into the living room where half a dozen other garden dames were already having tea and chatting up a storm about various local political intrigues or complaining about the Arnold Arboretum recently including the self-same Martha Stewart in a display of horticultural heroes.

Most of the ladies, I noticed, were loyally sporting bright red, white, and blue lapel buttons that read *GOPolly* because their celebrated leader, who gave no indication of slowing down, horticulturally or otherwise, was once again running for office, in this case for a local party organizing post.

"The girl Polly's up against this time is a real nightmare," confided one of the dames whose face was familiar from the Red Lion luncheon but whose name momentarily eluded me. "She's one of those neocon, red-meat, Bible-quoting conservatives in vogue right now who makes all of us Republican centrists look like a bunch of left-wing atheist liberals. Goodness, I do hope Polly can beat her brains out."

I was pleased to see Pat Chase smiling at me from across the room. After this casual morning gathering, this classy grandmother and world traveler had offered to show me a couple of her favorite local gardens. I knew from Polly that Pat and her husband John, a dedicated birder, were just back from Lapland, where Pat had been stalking the elusive Marsh Marigold. Looking at her, I suddenly fondly recalled birder Ed Pugh in John Bartram's garden, gently conveying his own gardening bride to a favored burial resting place at the feet of a famous ginkgo.

"The *fragmites* here are a scandal," Ginny Gary was saying. "That's a kind of invasive pampas grass that's not native to coastal Massachusetts yet filling wetlands at a simply shocking rate. One year they got so out of control around here some desperate individual set them on fire. They never caught whoever did it but many of us were secretly quite happy about that act of civil defiance." The skinny on Ginny, according to Polly, was that many years ago she'd purchased a Lenten rose, a beautiful hellebore, and become hooked on gardening. Today her place near World's End was evidently another of the area's most outstanding gardens. I hoped to see it someday soon.

From June to September, Ginny spent her time at sea, touring the South Shore coastline on her tugboat, the *Millicent*. Ginny overheard me whining to Penny Place about my recently deceased French and English lavender beds and a number of equally dead Scotch brooms I'd found, leaned over, and declared matter-of-factly, "Broom likes sunny spots, dear, and should be pruned immediately after blooming to prevent it from getting too leggy. The trick in growing lavender, by the way, is very simple: Plant it and ignore it completely!"

As before at the Red Lion, at first there appeared to be no formal agenda at this particular informal gathering—just lots of interesting confidential conversations on a range of topics from husbands to hostas. It reminded me of a group of guys at a corporate golf outing, sharing intimate stories and gentle complaints about work and wives and regurgitating their latest exploits at some famous overpriced resort. True, I didn't hear any blue jokes being traded among the gardening women— a staple of even the most rudimentary male golf bonding experience— but I did overhear more than one juicy snatch of gossip about erring teenagers and peculiar habits of certain neighbors, proving men and women possibly aren't so very different after all except in areas where it counts most.

If more women are in fact playing golf than ever before in human history, as research seems to support, it's perhaps inevitable that more men will eventually be returning to the garden to find their succor in nature and a fellowship of the rose and spade, as they did two or three centuries ago.

Down in Philadelphia, for example, I'd met several men who were active and quite evangelistic members of the venerable Philadelphia Men's Garden Club, a tradition that harkens back to the original plantsman societies of the nineteenth century when Bartram and London draper Peter Collinson were swapping seeds and knowledge across an ocean.

Such segregated male garden clubs, I'd been pleased to learn, are apparently popping up all over the country these days, and I'd been pleased to discover there was even one forming near my place in Maine.

As I sat there having these welcome thoughts, wondering if a whole naturalistic men's movement might spring from the ground up, so to speak, Mary Hickey began explaining to me how she'd grown an *entire* yew hedge from just ten or twelve small six-inch cuttings she'd taken from an established hedge and rooted. I'd casually mentioned to her how fond I was of funky English lanes where the yews were so big and bushy they could strip the paint off your rental car when an approaching lorry sent you swerving hard into the shoulder.

"You should simply go find the nicest old hedge you can find and just cut off pieces and take them home. You'd be surprised how easy they are to root and how quickly they'll grow. . . ."

"The hedge I love is in England," I pointed out. "Isn't it against the law to bring live plant material through customs?"

She smiled daintily. "If it was cut, dear, I don't suppose they could claim it was actually *living*."

Mary had a point. Oh what larcenous *fun* these garden club lunches were, I thought. Next time I went to England, why, I'd simply load up the side pocket of my golf bag and walk through customs like a man on a busman's holiday.

Someone dinged a fine crystal goblet. It was our host.

"Would everyone please grab a seat," trilled Polly, "because we have a very special speaker who is going to talk to us about a great adventure he's been on in the world of plants!"

Following my natural feeding instinct, I picked up a piece of somebody's delicious pecan tart and found a seat by the window, giving my back to pretty Cohasset Bay and wondering who the special speaker could be. Perhaps the special speaker would be none other than Paul Parent or some other luminary of the New England plant world.

"So, without further ado, here's my old friend Jim Dodson to tell us all about his adventure at the Philadelphia Flower Show!" Polly declared warmly, and waved me to the front of the room.

At that moment, I did a fairly convincing imitation of a man choking on pecan tart. Polly seemed to think I was merely stalling for time and added cheerfully, "It's *always* great fun to see a young person get hooked on politics or gardening! I suppose it's a little like getting hooked on golf, too. Maybe I'll take that up if my career in party politics doesn't work out."

This brought a roomful of laughter.

"Isn't she *amazing*?" the woman seated on my right leaned over and pertly whispered. "Can you believe she survived that terrible ordeal with that vile and awful fellow?"

"Whaaa ordeee?" I asked her thickly, attempting to hasten the dry pastry down the little red lane.

"Why, the horrible robbery, of course. Simply dreadful. He tied poor Polly up and left her upstairs for two or three days. It was in all the papers. Anyone else would have perished. But not Polly. Something, isn't she?"

Startled by this evidently not-so-confidential information, I put down my china plate, finished swallowing my dough, got to my hind legs, and tried my level best to sound like I knew what I was talking about in briefly summarizing my various "adventures" behind the scenes at the Super Bowl of botany. I spoke about the addictive passions of the Botticelli of Bulbs and the impressive commercial artistry of Jack Blandy and his son Joe; about funny Jeanne and Jim Francis; about Dick Lighty and his philosophical views on the splendid narrative thread of gardening.

When it was over, the garden club dames of Cohasset politely applauded and went straight back to talking about their husbands and children and neighbors and gardens.

I helped Polly collect dessert plates, and caught up to the undeniable force of nature herself in the kitchen.

"What's this about you being robbed?"

She laughed and shook her head.

"Oh, *that*. The gardener did it."

I was even more shocked than being fingered as that day's speaker.

"It happened a while back. I'm fine now. The poor man was working for me as a part-time gardener, and I'd been trying to help him get established; but I guess his issues went a little deeper than anyone knew. Anyway, he tied me to a chair up in the bedroom and took some of our family jewelry. A day or two later, he phoned the police and told them where I was. I guess he feared I might die and then he'd be in bigger trouble."

She laughed and took the dirty plate from astonished hand and gave it to the young woman cleaning up at the sink.

"Did they catch him?"

"Not yet. Someone said he took off for Florida. They'll probably never find him." She smiled and shook her head. "My guess is, he'll join the circus."

"Are you okay?" I was fully prepared to go after the brute with a mashie niblick iron or my broken-handled English gardening spade and permanently part his hair.

"Oh sure. If you think my house was busy before the incident you should see it *these* days. My children refuse to ever let me be alone in the house now. I can hardly get any reading and gardening done. There's always people around, these days, and I have the most wonderful young girl helping me out in the garden."

Before I could press GOPolly for more confidential info on her gardener's crime, she added: "Frankly, the only thing that has me worried right now is my opponent for the state party post. She's quite sharp and has got all the conservative Christian Republicans worked up. They're spending some money like there's no tomorrow. Mine's a much more grassroots and kitchen operation."

I kissed her on the cheek, thanked her for yet another engaging interlude with the gardening elite of the Bay State, and promised her that if history was any judge, she was going to win her political race in a romp. The instant I said this, however, I rememered that the last person I said this to was Walt Fisher—who lost by a *hair*.

"I hope so!" GOPolly said, giving me a surprisingly firm hug for such a diminutive Iowan. "So what's your next big stop on the gardening adventure?"

I informed her I was headed home to give a speech in the Old North State and then north again to Thomas Jefferson's beloved Monticello garden, to try and see the place with the fresh eyes of a born-again gardener and see if I could find the golden thread of gardening's endless narrative.

"Wonderful," Polly Logan declared, grinning. "Thomas Jefferson was maybe our finest thinker and our finest gardener. Lovely man. I *knew* him personally, you know."

She gave me a rousing Phyllis Diller laugh for the road.

Chapter 6

✿

Lost Gardens

SWEET ALICE BROWN was in a nursing home not far from Winston-Salem. According to her second-oldest son, Anthony, who I'd tracked down through one of my mom's longtime gardening pals, Sweet Alice had good days and bad days and some days when she just went along her own way in a private fog, humming church hymns. I was disappointed to learn from Anthony that his mother had been forced to give up her cottage near the state forest up in Ashe County. It had been sold to a man who rented it out, and none of Alice's six children could even abide driving by the place, he said, due to the way Sweet Alice's gardens had been let go. When I explained my connection to Sweet Alice and asked Anthony if he thought his mom might be up for a visit from the son of an old friend, he chuckled and observed, "I'll bet she'd be very pleased to see you. Mama loves company. Just don't be disappointed if she don't remember who you are. She don't remember *us* half the time these days." He laughed and added, "But she never forgets her flowers."

"How old is Sweet Alice now?"

"Ninety-two."

The summer Richard Nixon resigned from office was the summer after I quit mowing lawns up and down Dogwood Drive and cutting grass at the golf club in order to put on long pants and take my first indoor job. I worked as a newsroom intern at the *Greensboro Daily News*. Sweet Alice had permitted me to write a small Sunday feature about her for the paper. She was my mom's friend, someone she had met on one of her occasional plant collecting forays up to the foothills of the Blue Ridge. Strangely, I had no clear memory of how my mother and Sweet Alice first met—this was something I hoped to learn—but the memory of the beautiful plants and trees my mom brought home from Sweet Alice's place in the trunk of her Chrysler Newport was vivid. I was the cheap labor who planted most of those things in our yard—lush native mountain laurels and rhododendron bushes with leaves so shiny and healthy they almost appeared blue; wild crape myrtles, a red bud yearling that grew into my favorite tree beside the house; various kinds of roses; peonies; lily of the valley; and spiky blue perennials like meadow sage and speedwell.

Someone in my mother's church circle, as I think back, must first have told her about Sweet Alice Brown, a real "earth mother" whose place was in a hollow just off the main road on the way up to the Lutheran summer camp, near Boone. Many kids from our church (except for me, the neighborhood "lawn whisperer," who wouldn't go anywhere in summer and risk losing lucrative mowing jobs) spent a fortnight getting back to nature and a little closer to God every summer. One amusing thing I recalled about Sweet Alice was how quickly, but thoroughly, she sized up anyone who wanted to buy her plants. If she liked you and sensed you would be a good caretaker of her "babies," she sold you some extraordinary plant for about half of what a commercial nursery in one of the cities would ask and gave you useful planting advice and a bit of Bible verse for the road. If not, she might agree to part with a quart of her locally famous clover honey and possibly a small basket of sweet vine tomatoes. If anyone was truly closer to God's heart in a garden—as the small sign in my mother's backyard peony beds bearing the famous verse by Edwardian gardener Mrs. Gurnsey used to read—it was undoubtedly Sweet Alice Brown.

As I sat in the empty waiting room of the nursing home while the young attendant on the reception desk went to investigate whether Sweet Alice was feeling up to having an unannounced visitor, I mused on the not-so-sweet irony that my mom, like her own garden adviser Sweet Alice, had lost her garden, too, proof that no good deed in life goes unpunished. My mother's lost garden was due in large part to a painful executive decision I'd made and pretty much regretted ever since.

Five years before, acting upon the advice of her closest neighborhood friends and more than one doctor who feared Mom's periods of growing forgetfulness might sooner than later result in a terrible fire or injury, my older brother and I had teamed up to force our stubborn widowed mother to accept the devastating verdict that it was time to give up her home and suburban garden of more than forty years on Dogwood Drive, in Greensboro, and move up to Maine where I could better look after her daily needs. My brother's life at this point was in a major transition due to various career changes and a pending remarriage to a woman with whom my mom wasn't particularly enamored.

If leaving her friends and gardens behind was the downside of the proposition, the possible upside of the upheaval was the lovely "garden" apartment I'd secured for her just three miles from my house in an award-winning senior community where I was helping design a Scottish golf course. That's what I told myself, at least, especially since my children were still young enough to want to spend time with their charming Southern "Gammy."

Mom's diagnosed dementia was relatively mild and the strategy my brother and I family agreed upon seemed like a pretty reasonable compromise under the difficult circumstances, namely that Mom would retain full ownership of the property for the foreseeable future—as our father had wished—and be free to return periodically to check up on her neighborhood buddies and beloved garden. Her longtime gardener James Faircloth would continue to look after the property in her absence. Meanwhile, my brother and his new wife were going to move into the house and keep it up. They would possibly undertake some much-needed repairs, the cost of which he and I would naturally split, inasmuch as both of us would someday, theoretically, share ownership of the property, ideally passing it on to our own children down the line. I imagined keeping up my mom's beloved backyard garden and maybe even substantially expanding it—thus having both a northern and a southern garden in which I'd get gloriously dirty.

This was the agreed-upon plan, at any rate. But days, almost hours before I drove down from Maine to fetch mom and her aging lab Molly, my brother and his new wife took her to see a lawyer who presided over a startling alteration of her living will—"gifting" all of her remaining material assets, including the house and its garden, to my brother's new wife. This woman turned out to have been married previously several times and reportedly had a son who'd been on trial for murdering an elderly woman.

By the time I mustered the legal wherewithal to do anything about this shocking betrayal of family trust—which basically left our mom exposed financially in a way that was likely to incur the wrath of the gods or at least our father from his golf course in the heavens—the woman had sold the house to unknown persons, purchased a new Mercedes, and even booted my brother out on the street.

All families, I sometimes think, are simply overgrown gardens filled with beautiful flowers and the rankest weeds, forever requiring close attention so matters don't get impossibly out of hand. Over the four difficult years since that time, my brother had apologized for his colossal blunder in judgment and even begun to try to mend fences with his own children and me. He and I are once again on good speaking terms, attempting to rebuild what once was an unusually close relationship. I've scarcely been back to Greensboro since that awful and incomprehensible time and, more to the point, had only driven down my old childhood street once since then. That was an hour after my mother's funeral. I'd stopped by the empty house on my way out of town and spread her ashes in the vast lily of the valley beds, beneath the towering tulip maples of her beloved backyard, where Molly the dog had terrorized invading squirrels and uninvited meter readers for more than a decade. By that point a new owner was preparing to take possession of the property, and I absolutely hated to think what might become of my mom's splendid garden as a result of the calamitous event I had unwittingly helped engineer.

As I sat in the empty rest home waiting room, turning these sad and complex family matters over in my head, I heard a faint tapping sound and suddenly there was Sweet Alice, smaller than I remembered, now traveling with the aid of a large wooden cane, and dressed as if she'd just been to church—which, of course, she had. This was just after noon on a warm Blue Ridge Sunday in late April. Sweet Alice, like many of my own kin scattered through the Carolina pines east and south of us, was a good Southern Baptist.

"How you doin', dear heart?" she asked as if she instantly recognized me. But I recalled that Sweet Alice called anyone who bought her plants either "sugar pie," "baby doll," or "dear heart."

I gave the tiny frail woman a gentle hug, told her my name and wondered if she perhaps remembered when I came to see her thirty years ago and wrote a little feature story about her amazing foothills garden for the Greensboro paper. Just to help prod her memory, I mentioned my mom, too—one of her most loyal and admiring customers and an old friend.

"*Sure* I remember that, baby doll. How's your mama keepin' these days anyway? We ain't talked in so long, seem like. . . ."

I explained to Sweet Alice that my brother and I had moved my mom up to Maine a few years back. She'd had a stroke a short time later, but appeared to enjoy her life on the coast of Maine with her grandchildren, although she never stopped missing her old pals back in North Carolina and her Greensboro garden for a moment.

"Well *bless* her heart," Sweet Alice declared, shaking her head and showing me a gold tooth. "Coast of *Maine*! Whew-*eee*. Bet that's colder than the top of Beech Mountain! What you doin' way up *there*, child?"

I admitted I sometimes wondered this same thing, especially in the spring when everything down *here* was exploding into bloom.

"Spring in Maine. What that like?" the flower gardener in her was awakened and curious.

"It can be nice, too. All three days of it."

Alice cackled deliciously, glanced furtively over at the administration desk, lowered her voice, and whispered, "I was just fixin' to go have me some lunch, dear heart. You want to come eat with me? They'll let me bring you, I expect. I'll say you're from the *white* branch of the family." She smiled mischievously at her own joke.

"What if I take you out for Sunday lunch?" I proposed, remembering a K & W Cafeteria I'd seen a few miles away.

"Sounds good," she said brightly. "You and Miss Alice can go to the Hardees, baby doll."

"*Hardees?*" A hamburger joint wasn't exactly what I had in mind.

"I do love that Hardees," she explained fondly, already reaching for my arm. " 'Specially them chocolate milk shakes. Oh, lordy, those folks can make a milkshake."

Safely installed into the passenger seat of my ridiculously large, gas-guzzling SUV, Sweet Alice quickly spotted a couple of potted plants sitting in the rear compartment.

"Where you get those good-lookin' daylilies from?"

"That's a funny story," I said, cranking up the truck.

"What you mean *funny*?"

"They were an unexpected gift, Miss Alice—from a stranger in a darkened parking lot. A tale of night and daylilies."

She grunted pleasantly, obviously missing my little funny.

"Tell me what you mean, child."

So I did.

Two nights earlier over in a grand ballroom in Pinehurst, I'd given a speech to the sponsors of the forthcoming U.S. Open championship and during the question and answer period that followed, I casually mentioned my plans to take a short sabbatical from golf writing in order to learn more about my *other* outdoor passion—my "dirty little secret" of landscape gardening.

Afterward, a man in a brightly checkered blazer stepped forward to get his book signed for his wife and grinned, as if embarrassed about something, possibly his choice of sports jacket.

"Interesting what you said about your dirty little secret. I think I share it."

"How's that?"

"I used to be your basic weekend golf addict until my wife got me hooked on growing daylilies. Then she started playing golf and got hooked on that. We've more or less swapped hobbies. Nowadays, you can't get her off the golf course and I've got nearly an acre of daylilies at our place up in Charlotte. I spend my weekends constantly weeding and watering. I just came from buying more."

"No kidding," I said. "Everything okay at home?"

"Terrific. We hardly see each other now on weekends. It's put the spice back in our marriage."

There was something about the guy, to be honest, that seemed rather dodgy.

"Sign it to Phil," he instructed.

"Phil?"

"Her name's Philida."

"Short for Philadelphia?" I was prepared to tell him I'd just enjoyed a wonderful time there getting in touch with my inner green monk.

"No. That was her great-aunt's name. Family deal. Very old-fashioned family, every one of 'em plum plant crazy."

He added that, if I had a minute to spare, there was something out in his car I needed to see.

For reasons that now elude me, I followed him out to the Hotel Carolina's darkened parking lot and watched him open the trunk of a Lincoln Town Car, expecting I don't know what—maybe his wife's body rolled up in a bloody hotel carpet or possibly a cache of shoulder-held rocket launchers on their way to Iraq.

The back end was absolutely full of potted daylilies.

"You're looking at some of the rarest *Hemerocallis* plants in the world," he said quietly, almost reverently, glanced cautiously around as though expecting to see the ballroom clearing out, with guys in expensive golf duds, who shared our dirty little secret, bolting our way. In fact, most of them were now standing about on the hotel's broad and handsome white wooden porches, sucking importantly on cigars the size of garden rake handles. Cigar smoking was a fairly recent phenomenon in golf that made me wonder if I wasn't stepping away from the game not a moment too soon.

I asked my fellow secret gardener where he'd gotten such rare daylilies.

"If I told you, I'd have to kill you."

"How's that?"

He laughed, pulling out something of his own to light up. It turned out only to be a cigarette. This was my beloved North Carolina, after all, where all children under the age of twelve are permitted to smoke, but only in designated playground areas.

"Guy down near the South Carolina border. Works out of a shed in an old tobacco field stuck out in the middle of nowhere. Drive to the edge of the known universe, turn left, and you're there. I'm telling you, this guy is the *king* of the daylily breeders." He said the junction was called Marietta and might not be on all maps but he could tell me how to get there, if I really wanted to go. He made it sound like trying to find the Voodoo Lily of the Lost Incas.

"This plant is an unusual diploid called 'Shuffle the Deck,' " he explained, touching one of the stems. "It's deep red purple with a green starburst throat you wouldn't believe, a total knock-out. This one is called 'Sand in my Eyes,' a hybrid tetraploid with peach blooms edged in lavender. Helluva plant. Puts out ten or twelve blooms at maturity."

It sounded like he was describing thoroughbred race horses. He also showed me "My Soul Surrendered" and "Ruth Bell Graham," named (or so I deduced) for the Rev. Billy Graham's wife, as well as "Cold Winter Nights" and "Electric Marmalade Splash." He ticked off perhaps a half a dozen more hybrid daylilies with equally festive and homespun names. "Every one of these, by the way, is a *new* introduction. Daylily collectors would kill to get their hands on 'em. Hottest thing in the gardening world at this moment."

Before I could politely stop myself from doing so, intrigued that *daylilies* and not cycads might, in fact, be considered the hottest plants in the horticultural world at this moment in time, I heard myself asking how much he'd had to shell out for a Town Car trunk full of red-hot collector daylilies like these.

"Nearly a grand," he allowed. "Maybe a little more than that."

He smiled. "Basically about what Philly and her pals will spend to play golf here for the next couple days and drink a lot of very good wine."

"So where *is* your wife?"

"Back at the room. She has an early tee time tomorrow. I'm heading home to Charlotte to get these plants into the ground. Thanks for signing her book, by the way."

"My pleasure." My greater pleasure, however, was hearing about some guy down near the border who might be the king of American daylilies. As we stood there in a darkened parking lot together, the first tingles of gardenlust began to take hold of me.

We stood there for a moment, saying nothing and gazing pleasantly into his crowded trunk. Suddenly I began to feel bad about how I'd misjudged his character and rushed to judgment about his clothing tastes.

"Hey, look," he suddenly said, thumbing away his smoke, "why don't you take a couple of these with you? Are you driving or flying?"

"I'm driving, But that's not really necessary . . ."

Under other circumstances, I would have explained to him that he was wasting his time because daylilies had never really been my thing. I knew they were among the first ornamental plants to find their way into colonial gardens. Their lineage reportedly dated back to the ancient courts of India, where they were mentioned in early Vedic poems and featured in Islamic art, but I couldn't get beyond a stubborn southern prejudice that daylilies were simply redneck flowers any fool could grow in a ditch.

True, back home in my redneck *jardin anglaise*, I had several late-blooming Asiatic lilies tucked into the lush hosta landscape of my summer "blue" garden for interesting contrast, but—aside from these few exotic and highly aromatic Asian cousins of the species—I'd frankly never given conventional daylilies much thought, save that any fool could grow them in a ditch.

"Sure you can. Take whichever ones you want. Believe me, I know where there are *plenty* more. You're not going to believe how amazing these are when they bloom."

I asked which variety had a subtle shading that would complement pale blue flowers and foliage of a late summer hosta garden. Splashy racetrack colors weren't for me. In fact, the more I went along the garden path to horticultural obsession, the less I fancied brilliant blooming flowers of any sort, much preferring discreetly flowering plants with interesting foliage, mixed textures, and complex stem structures.

"That would probably be 'Cold Winter Nights.' Cream and pale pink bloom. Velvety and lush. Late bloomer. Very subtle. Your classic diploid hybrid."

"Sounds about right for Maine," I said, wondering what the heck a *diploid* was. Clearly, I had a great deal to learn about daylilies.

"I guess I'll take one of those."

"No," he said, grabbing a couple of plastic containers and pulling them out. "Take *two*. One for you and your wife."

"You're very kind. She'll be here in a couple days."

"Is she playing golf?"

"Not this trip," I said. "We're just visiting with a few friendly garden nuts like you."

"So what you doin', baby doll, drivin' this big ol' *thing* with just a couple little bitty privvy lilies in back?"

Sweet Alice Brown was almost as famous for her plainspoken opinions as her miraculous green thumb; she'd also been an ardent steward of the environment decades before such a thing entered the popular consciousness. My gas-guzzling SUV undoubtedly offended her.

"Those are a couple rare *Hemerocallis* plants," I explained, using one of the few proper Latin names I could both pronounce and spell.

"I see." She sniffed, peering out over the SUV's vast hood at the state road, evidently wondering where our excursion was leading.

"So where we goin', child?"

"I thought we might go to Hardees for a milk shake," I reminded her.

Her tiny white-capped head bobbed and she grinned. "Oh that's just *fine.*"

I asked her if she remembered the time I came and spent a long afternoon with her in her garden over near the Bethel Church Road, not far from a little Episcopal church where I knew the rector. There were a couple amazing frescoes done by local artisans on the wall. One of the frescoes—of Mary with child, clearly showing—had caused quite a flap in the Baptist hill country of beautiful Ashe County.

"No," she said, watching the passing houses, "I don't remember that."

"But you remember your garden of course . . ."

She brightened, looking at me. "I had the sweetest old place you ever saw, dear heart. Flowers and trees, oh *lordy*. I had 'em all named."

I remembered this well. A common Carolina dogwood with arching foliage wasn't *Cornus florida*, it was Ruby Ann's Favorite. Her false indigo wasn't *Baptisia bracteata*; it was Cousin Cleavie's Wedding Bush. And so it went through an extraordinary personal garden that was really a living piece of folk artistry and included spectacular specimens of Cape jasmine, various wild crape myrtle, banks of azalea and rhododendron and mountain laurel, an arbor tunnel fashioned creatively from wild trumpet vine, purple wisteria and Concord grapes, several varieties of hydrangea, more peony plants than I'd ever seen in one place, and every kind of flowering border perennial you care to name. Sweet Alice, a Blue Ridge Carolus Linnaeus, had her own homegrown taxonomy and plant identification system, which in retrospect may have been one reason my brain, despite three years of college Latin, was averse to retaining the formal language of horticultural science. Garden Latin lacked the poetry of common garden names, in my humble opinion. But maybe everyone who can't recall a plant's proper Latin name says that.

I reminded Sweet Alice that she'd not only shown me the correct way to prune grapes on an arbor, but also how to "bruise" the root ball of a container plant before you put it in the ground. Another of Sweet Alice's nifty garden tricks I still used constantly is how, after bare-handed weeding, you could take a garden hose, pinch its flow, and clean your fingernails.

This brought a broad smile from Sweet Alice.

"I showed you *that*?" She shook her head at the wonder of such simple wisdom.

"Yes ma'am. You also helped me get over my serious aversion to weeding."

"I *did*? How'd I do that, sugar?"

"Always weed while you're passing through the garden, you said, because you may get called home at any instant and not pass that way again."

She snorted amicably, looking over the hood again. "Well that sure is true."

Ever since she said this to me, I pointed out, I'd been something of a serial weeder, at least in public places—I couldn't pass through an airport or municipal square, weirdly enough, without pausing to yank unsightly weeds if I saw them. Pulling weeds at home, however, was nigh impossible for me, especially at times when I was busy expanding the scope of the place, possibly because I naturally assumed there would always be another day when I would pass through the garden and could get the job done. If the sad saga of my mother's abruptly vanished property revealed anything beyond how quickly a garden can be lost, it also revealed how accurate Miss Alice Brown was on the wisdom of weeding as you go—before you're *called home* to account for things. A young gardener who was restoring a famous historic garden in Newport, Rhode Island, once told me there are few things harder than recovering the integrity of an old garden once it has been let go, and Penny Place of the colonial dames of Cohasset had said pretty much the same thing.

"Weedin' is just the good Lord's way of keepin' house," Sweet Alice proclaimed and fell silent, keeping a sharp eye peeled for the Hardees.

I smiled at this lovely folk wisdom, vintage Sweet Alice, and asked her when she'd last seen her little blue house by the edge of the state forest.

"Oh, lordy. . . . I just don't know. Seem like. . . ." Her voice trailed off and she shook her head making soft regretful sounds.

"Would you like to go see it?" It was only an hour or so out of Winston-Salem, and I didn't have to be at the airport in Greensboro to meet Wendy until seven o'clock that evening. My impression was, Sweet Alice didn't have anywhere she had to be except where she was at that very moment.

"Oh," she said with a little sigh, "you don't want to see that old place of mine."

"Sure I do." I cheerfully forced the issue, because I really *did*, thinking indirectly about my mother's garden, which I'd foolishly left unprotected, and was, for reasons not fully explored or comprehended, powerfully reluctant to go and find as well.

Sweet Alice's face suddenly lit up like a child's and she pointed excitedly over the vast hood of my gas-guzzler.

"There's the Hardees, honey! That's the place we're going!"

It took us a little longer than I'd hoped to find her old place in the folded hills along the Bethel Church Road, largely because the landscape had been so dramatically altered by development pushing out to the country and because neither one of us could quite remember the way. Even so, we drank our milk shakes and talked pleasantly about her grandchildren and my teenage children almost as if we really were real blood relatives, although I still couldn't escape the feeling Sweet Alice had no inkling of who I was—just some friendly guy who showed up to take her out for a milk shake.

I was startled to see her house. What was left of it, I mean to say.

To begin with, it was no longer the cheerful sky blue cottage it once had been, girdled by a lovely Appalachian jungle. The proud banks of rhododendron and azalea had been purged leaving scarred patches of rain-washed, hardened red-streaked earth, and there wasn't a Ruby Ann's Favorite shrub or Cousin Cleavie's Wedding Bush anywhere in sight. The majestic grape and trumpet vine arbor was still standing—but only barely—a shadow of its former glory. It now sheltered somebody's redneck Monte Carlo, a heap swamped by weeds which I had no interest in pulling. Meanwhile, none of the specimen flowering trees I remembered were left—probably pillaged or dug up and sold—and save for a couple small redbud volunteers growing on their lonesome beyond the unmowed lawn by the state forest boundary line, the place scarely resembled what it once had been: one of the finest natural gardens in western North Carolina.

The house was now a wreck to match its perished gardens, another living metaphor of my poor judgment if there ever was one, slapped with a depressing emergency room green paint and with sagging porches that looked about twenty minutes from collapsing in the dirt. In the side yard a yellow dog, chained dismally to a post, lay on a bare patch of ground silently eyeing us, a redneck Cerebus guarding this fallen Paradise.

No cars were in the driveway so I eased my truck into the dirt driveway and switched off the engine. For a moment, we sat listening to the engine cool, ticking gently.

"It doesn't look a whole lot like I remember," I finally said, stating the obvious.

"It ain't much to look at now," Alice agreed. She gave a little snort and shook her head with visible disappointment. "Some old trash moved in here and just let this place go."

So much for my clever plan to try and better understand the origins of my own late-in-life gardening passions. Suddenly I wished we'd dined *indoors* at Hardees and skipped this portion of the reunion party.

"Well, at least there are a couple redbuds in bloom out by the boundary," I said, attempting to put a positive spin on the grim landscape. I added, "I wish I could take those redbuds up to my new southern arboretum in Maine."

"Tell you what you do," Alice suddenly said, staring in that direction. "You just go get that shovel yonder and dig one of them redbud trees up and take it on home with you. Whichever one you like, dear heart."

"Oh, no. I couldn't do that, Miss Alice."

"Yes you can. I'm *givin'* it to you, Sugar Pie." She stared at me. "Hurry up now, child, 'cause I got to get on back and see my television program."

I studied her calm ancient face. Even if I really wanted to take a red-bud home with me to Maine, which I did, I knew from experience that the chances of it surviving the punishing winter up there were slim to none. I'd brought several small eastern redbuds north to Maine over the years, assured by Mid-Atlantic nurserymen that they would survive with a little proper protection. Not one *Cercis* had made it, and I frankly didn't need another dead redbud on my conscience.

"But somebody else owns this land now," I pointed out, grateful that whoever lived here hadn't come out the busted screen door, pulling on a wife-beater undershirt and loading the Remington.

She reached over and patted my hand as if *I* was still missing the point of her gentle earth wisdoms thirty years later. Her voice was eerily calm, almost soothing.

"It's all right, baby. We *all* just borrowing ground from God. You listen to Alice Brown and go fetch that little ol' redbud from the ground. You can have that 'Cherokee' rose near the dog, too. It'll just get trampled to pieces. No go *on*."

What the hell was a grown man on a field trip to try and find the secret garden roots of his boyhood supposed to do? I got out of the truck and did a quick scan of the premises to make sure the owner wasn't merely sleeping off his date with a case of Colt 45 in the backseat of the Monte Carlo, picked up the shovel, hurried across the yard to the boundary line, and dug up that tiny neglected redbud tree in Olympic record time for hillbilly plant theft. I hurried back with the heavy root ball clutched to my midriff like a ninety-year-old man staggering beneath a YMCA medicine ball.

Even quicker than that, I popped the dusty little wild rosebush out of the hard-baked ground and carried it back to the truck, placing it in with the world-class *Hemerocallis*. Then I shut the rear hatch doors and got safely back into the driver's seat, half expecting gunshots to ring out.

There were none, only the chained yellow dog now standing up and watching, with what appeared to be both amusement and even supportive interest, as this Clouseau-like episode of rural plant larceny unfolded. As I passed with the purloined rosebush, within a few yards of the beast, his tail had actually begun wagging.

"Just a minute," I said and picked up my melted milk shake, got back out of the truck, and made a beeline for the dog.

He turned out to be a *she*, and she was evidently perfectly happy for me to take along the forgotten redbud and neglected rosebush as a memento of our unscheduled visit, especially after I dumped the gooey remains of my melted vanilla milk shake into her cruddy, dented, and bone-dry water bowl. I watched the dog gratefully lap it up and was rewarded by the sight of a tail that didn't stop wagging. Lingering a moment longer, I also gave this gray-muzzled monarch a quick scratch behind her dusty ears and was reminded vividly of the late *Molligator*— the name my kids gave their grandmother's backyard guardian after she accompanied her mistress north to try and start a new life in Maine. If my mom at least put on a reasonably convincing show of happiness mingled with moments of pure longing for friends and garden, old Molly made no such effort whatsoever. Growing more blind and deaf with each passing winter, she rarely ventured more than a few paces from her adopted spot near the woodstove. No doubt dreaming about the beautiful, fenced domain she once fiercely protected, Molly took to snapping furiously at anyone who ventured too close, hence her nickname. She finally expired the winter before this very trip, outlasting her mistress by more than two years. Part of me was still puzzled with what to do with the Molligator's ashes. They rightfully belonged in my mother's backyard with my mom's own ashes, but I wasn't sure either one of us would ever see that lost garden again. The unexpected encounter with Ed Pugh at John Bartram's garden, meanwhile, had simply served to underscore why gardens have always been favored for a nice, long rest. Writing of her own pets planted in the garden, an old chum of mine named Patti Hagan, a Brooklyn neighborhood activist and the former garden editor of *The Wall Street Journal*, beautifully summed up the point of returning dust to dust in a garden when she wrote: "We put them in the ground, we water them, and they come up roses."

"It was *so* nice of you to come see me," Sweet Alice said, as we hugged good-bye in the nursing home lobby. A young attendant was waiting patiently to take her arm and walk her safely down the hallway to her room. I still had the feeling she had no idea who I was.

"Where you off to now?" she asked. I explained I was on my way to the airport in Greensboro to pick up my wife Wendy who was flying down from Maine.

"Whew-*ee*! Maine!" She cackled, surprised. "You live in *Maine*?"

"Yes ma'am," I said. "I used to live in Greensboro. You and my mother were good friends once. She sure loved your peonies."

"I remember you mama," Sweet Alice said, giving my hand a final firm pat. For a moment I had reason to believe she really did, too. But then she added, "How's she keepin' these days? I don't think I've seen your mama since that church supper where she sang over in Mount Airy."

"She's doing just fine. Spends all her time these days out in her backyard garden. Couldn't be happier."

"Well, child, you tell her Alice Brown sends her love and says hello. Will you do that?"

"Yes ma'am. I will."

"Good. And be sure to give that little redbud lots of love and water."

"Thanks. I will."

The pretty young attendant smiled pleasantly at me and I watched her lead Sweet Alice all the way down the hallway's shiny linoleum floor, shoes squeaking, until they turned the corner.

WENDY GOT OFF THE AIRPLANE positively giddy from the freedom of spring break and from browsing Tony Avent's *Plant Delights* catalog during her flight.

"Have you looked at this thing?" she asked. "This guy sounds great. He's got things for sale in here that will blow your mind—stuff that's not even supposed to grow in North Carolina. His botanical garden sounds just *incredible*. It's at his nursery in some place called Juniper Level. I guess that's near Raleigh. Are we going anywhere near Raleigh? I'd sure love to see it."

Wendy is nothing if not enthusiastic—a kind of Polly Logan in training. One of the things I love most about my wife since the start of the new millennium is her willingness to weed for hours on end and revise the adventure as she goes along, providing there's any hope of good red wine and some fun to be had. Come to think of it, Wendy would have made an excellent addition to Walt Fisher's Inforcer garden team.

"Do you think we have time? I'd love to."

"We can always make time for somebody's garden."

"What's with all the plants in back?" she said, looking in back of our truck. "Have you been spending college funds again on trees that won't grow in Maine?

"It was all free, I promise. You won't believe how I got these things."

As we eased into the western suburbs of Greensboro and headed for the guest bedroom of our friends Pat and Terry McDaid, I filled her in on everything from my unexpected encounter with a daylily nut after dark to my theft of a redbud and "Cherokee" rose.

"What exactly is a 'Cherokee' rose?" I asked her, hoping she knew.

"Country music song? Cheap brand of wine? I have no idea," she said. "We can ask Tony Avent when we see him."

"There's an idea."

A beat passed, and she wondered conversationally, "So did you have a chance to go by your mom's place and meet the new owner?"

"Nope. I think we'll be skipping that."

"Too bad," she said. "I brought Molly's ashes with me. I thought we could put the old girl back where she belongs and make more shelf room for books."

"You're a funny girl," I said.

"That's probably why you invited me to get married."

In the end, prior to lights-out at Pat's, I agreed we could at least drive by my scrupulously avoided homeplace to see if the new owner might be receptive to having dog remains dumped in the backyard flower beds, assuming there still were flower beds in back. Alice Brown's lost garden made me wonder if we might not arrive and discover the entire house wiped off the face of the earth and a big ugly McMansion squatting in its place, with an assembly line yard that had been fully installed by a crack crew of landscapers in less than an hour.

"You'll be glad you did this," Wendy assured me before drifting off to sleep.

"Like looking up Alice Brown," I said. "That turned out so well."

"Yes. But look at the lovely plants you got."

As USUAL, she had a point. But in the morning things didn't quite work out the way either of us hoped. Nobody was home on Dogwood Drive but, rather amazingly, the house and property looked remarkably the same, save for one glaring factor. My favorite redbud tree was gone, replaced by a large azalea bush at the left-hand corner of the house.

"Why don't you at least go look in the backyard?" Wendy suggested, as we sat in the truck trying to decide what to do. We'd already eliminated the idea of leaving a friendly note on the door with helpful instructions for spreading our dead family dog's ashes in the backyard garden. Part of me was tempted to walk over and knock on either Merle Corry's or Ginny Frank's doors to see if they would agree to do the honors. They were my mom's oldest neighborhood pals. But this was just before six on a cool Monday morning, and I wasn't certain they would even be up yet. No lights were on at either lady's house.

A tubby jogger approached us in the gray dawn light, laboring hard. His T-shirt said: IF YOU'RE CLOSE ENOUGH TO READ THIS, YOU'RE NOT MY PRESIDENT.

He waved; we waved. He probably wondered if we were casing my old childhood home while I wondered if he might be willing to sell me the T-shirt off his fat, hairy back for Bush-basher Suzy Verrier—or maybe even swap it in exchange for a stolen redbud sapling that would surely perish if I took it home to Maine.

But he jogged on, as we sat, still trying to come up with a good idea.

"I don't know if I could bear to look in the backyard," I admitted, feeling a little of what Miss Alice Brown must have felt when she saw her old place in such sorry shape. If the lovely redbud I'd planted in the side yard during my junior year in high school was missing, who could say what else might be missing from the backyard. Or, worse, what might be there instead of the redbrick planters I'd built for my mom for her fern garden. I could suddenly envision a swank new Scandinavian teak deck with a state-of-the-art outdoor jet stream Jacuzzi and God knows what else that didn't belong there.

"Want me to do it? I could just toss Molly's ashes in the flower beds and scoot."

Wendy has a natural streak of the devil in her, I'm pleased to report, which is why she's such a blast to travel with and game for just about anything.

"No. Let's just go find the daylily king. That might cheer me up."

"You sure?" Her tone suggested she thought I might never come back. That idea had crossed my mind.

"Yeah. I've done enough creative trespassing for one week."

FAYE SHOOTER WAS KNEELING in a vast beige field, digging up several daylilies with a clipboard by her side. She stood up, pulled off her work gloves, wiped sweat off her brow, and greeted us warmly.

It was shortly before ten that same morning in the flat, sandy countryside a few miles above the South Carolina border, a few miles east of Marietta, a faded junction town full of forlorn tobacco warehouses no bigger than the hips on a corn snake, as my Grandmother Taylor might have said. Clearly tobacco was no longer king in that forgotten corner of North Carolina. Faye Shooter confirmed this fact of life, when she said, "You'd think people around here would want to work, given the poor state of jobs in these parts. But even finding garden help is nearly impossible. Thank God for good old George," she added, nodding at the middle-aged Mexican man working with a hoe and hand shovel, a few yards away. "He's about the best worker on earth, otherwise we'd be swamped. We can barely keep up as it is, demand being what it is."

Faye explained that her husband John stressed the importance of digging and selling only the best-conditioned plants because the family's reputation as premier daylily breeders and suppliers was on the line, and "a mom-and-pop organization like us can't afford too many returns." She laughed and dusted off her knees. "Come meet Pop in the office," she drawled appealingly. "He likes to say hello to folks from the outside world. I keep him safely indoors."

Based on this information, I don't know what I expected from King of the Daylilies—Pa Kettle meets Norman Bates, perhaps. The large, genial fellow we found sitting at a computer terminal inside the cute shed office greeted us as if he'd been expecting us all morning and turned out to be more like an engaging blend of Sheriff Andy and Luther Burbank, with a pinch of Bill Gates thrown in for seasoning.

A sophisticated computer system was busy printing out hundreds of individual bar code labeling for young plants still in the fields and within minutes John Shooter was showing us *pages* of e-mail orders from loyal customers all over the world, plant orders that had found this forgotten little corner of the Old North State through cyberspace. The daylily season was evidently off and running like a well-oiled dot-com empire.

"We're a pretty small outfit," John deadpanned and then smiled at Wendy. "Just Faye, George, myself, and our daughter Elizabeth. She's a schoolteacher who runs the office and comes out to help dig and ship on weekends. I taught school in Robison County for thirty years before getting hooked on this crazy business. We have about fourteen acres in cultivation out there, counting evaluation fields, and maybe five or six thousand regular customers. Some of our competitors are much larger outfits but they tend to go for the established market in daylilies—Wal-Marts, Home Depots, garden centers, that sort of thing. We deal directly with our customers, many of whom want only the latest thing in hybrid development."

"Like a guy I met in a parking lot up in Pinehurst," I said, and told him about the pair of "Cold Winter Nights" I'd lucked into in the dark parking lot for the price of signing a book.

"He sounds *exactly* like our typical customer," Shooter said, with a easy drawl that was nearly identical to his wife's. "Most of our customers we never even meet. Yet we have a very intimate relationship with them, and they buy in large quantities, sometimes *very* large quantities. On our open house weekend in a few weeks we may get a couple thousand people out here, wandering around out in the fields to select their own varieties. Some come knowing exactly what they're looking for and what they want to spend. Others are looking for the latest hybrid. We don't do any horse trading or discounting. Whether it's a three-dollar daylily or a three-hundred-dollar one, we sell it for whatever it cost to develop, test, and produce that particular flower."

I asked Shooter if it was true daylilies were really the hottest thing in horticulture.

"They are, I think, because gardeners crave anything that's new," he continued, in a way that suggested he wasn't trying to boost his own product, but merely stating an obvious conclusion. "Because they are relatively easy to breed and grow, daylilies can offer a gardener a lot of choice every year. This year, for example, we have over thirty new introductions in the catalog, stuff we've been developing out in the fields for years in some cases. The other appeal of daylilies, of course, is that, generally speaking, your average daylily will keep its bloom twice as long as, say, a peony or a rose. They're proven survivors in the garden and look good even when everything else is dying off." Shooter smiled. "That's why every outhouse in North Carolina used to have daylilies around it. So folks could just sit and admire them."

I glanced up through one of Marietta's lushly illustrated catalogs to see if Shooter was shooting me a line of bull. He was trying to be funny, but he wasn't fooling around in the least. Flipping through the pages, I saw several new varieties bearing price tags in the two-hundred-dollar-range and tried to imagine myself shelling out that kind of money for a *single* hybrid privy lily, and simply couldn't fathom it. I decided to ask John about the folks who could.

"The hottest part of the market might be the serious daylily collectors. Those people will go anywhere and pay anything to get their hands on something nobody else has yet. Money is usually no object. We're talking major league connoisseurs here—the kind of people who buy a very expensive piece of artwork just to be the only person who owns it. If some daylily collectors could, they would be the only person who owned certain varieties."

Faye said, "Fortunately we're known primarily for our top-of-the-line daylilies and a large number of new plant introductions, most of which we breed ourselves." She smiled lopsidedly, wearing a cute slash of dirt across her chin. "That's why we rarely sleep around here starting about mid-April."

John lifted a printout sheet and showed me several substantial order lists from major league daylily collectors in America and several foreign countries, including France, Italy, Germany, and Canada. There was even a large order from Slovenia.

"It's a true obsession with them," Faye pleasantly added, lingering a moment more before heading back to the fields. "People who love daylilies can't seem to get enough of them. For them half the fun is finding something different."

John smiled lazily. "The poor man's orchid."

Remembering the evangelistic Walter Off from Philadelphia, I asked the Shooters if they had any theories on why certain daylilies were suddenly so popular with plant collectors.

"Easy," declared John. "One reason is the sheer variety of plants available these days. There are probably currently around eighty thousand different varieties of daylilies these days and a lot of exciting new stuff coming on the market every year. This is really only a phenomenon of the past twenty or so years—this boom in breeding, I mean." He winked at Wendy, who appeared completely fascinated by the discovery of a daylily empire in the middle of nowhere. She wasn't alone. "That's really what we're up to out here in the middle of God's country—coming up with new hybrid varieties for a world that really wants unusual daylilies."

"How many are you responsible for?" I asked the sovereign of Marietta Gardens.

"As a family we've developed maybe six hundred hybrid varieties. That's counting myself, Elizabeth and Faye, of course . . ."

These clearly weren't my grandmother's privy lilies, and I didn't hesitate when John Shooter invited me to take a ride on his golf cart through the growing fields while Wendy went off with Faye Shooter to hunt for a couple more interesting varieties that might safely relocate to the challenging latitudes in Maine.

John provided a lovely discourse on the process involved in crossbreeding and hybridizing the genus *Hemerocallis*, that once lowly field flower that rewarded soup eaters in ancient China and pioneer Americans with a brief, elegant burst of summer color in the wilderness of a new world. In most cases a new variety took anywhere from three to five years to develop and field test and reproduce sufficiently to make it into Marietta's spring and fall catalogs. Depending on the amount of labor involved, a new offering could go from anywhere from fifty bucks to five hundred dollars per plant. Of the fifty-three new varieties offered for sale in Marietta's 2004 spring catalog, however, the most expensive was something called "Sam I Am" for $125, bred by John's daughter Elizabeth. "Sam I Am" was a bold red star-shaped diploid with a vivid streak of green running from its yellow throat through the petals and sepals. *Diploid*, I was pleased to learn from the king, is simply a biological term that indicated two chromosomes in the breeding process.

When I told John how the man from Charlotte had given me two "Cold Winter Nights" for signing one book, he commented dryly, "I'm sure the book is good. But it sounds like you got the good end of the deal." He confirmed that the pale pink beauty, a cross between "Helen Shooter" and "Molino Pink Loveliness" was a middle-priced variety, selling for fifty dollars in the current catalog. "I'm rather partial to that daylily," he added, "because I bred it."

"Could you show me a five-hundred-dollar daylily?" I brazenly asked the king.

"Sure," John said mildly and graciously bounced me over several rows out to a fairly remote corner of the evaluation field, in the most remote county in North Carolina, no less. To me it just looked like a daylily coming up in a field. "It isn't named yet," the affable breeder explained of this mysterious gem of the earth. "But if it produces flowers like I expect it to, we could be looking at *the* hottest *Hemerocallis* on the planet someday soon."

"How on earth do you come up with all the names?" He refused to divulge what racehorse name he was considering.

"We usually go away on vacation and have a good time. The name just sort of comes to us."

I liked this guy a lot. He was my kind of *Hemerocallis* breeder, a genius who didn't take himself too seriously—Luther Burbank meet Jeff Foxworthy.

Even better, we made a nifty barter of our own. After hearing me describe my "Blue" summer garden and how I preferred flowers that had subtle blooms, John had Faye dig up "Circle of Friends," "Winter Frost," and a recent award winner called "Night Dreams." He let me pay full price for these plants, but threw in "Marietta Dreamer" and "Havana Day Dreaming" free of charge. "The first one is named for me, the second for the old Jimmy Buffett song," he explained.

"Not many people dream in color, they say, but I do—about *daylilies* in color," he insisted, after we'd loaded up the truck. Shooter suggested I consider meeting him and daughter Elizabeth at the upcoming meeting of the American Hemerocallis Society in St. Louis in July if I really wanted to meet the cream of America's daylily crazies.

I thanked him for the invitation and told him I just might take him up on the offer if I could get my three new display gardens in Maine built in time.

"Maine," he said, smiling. "What's Maine like?"

"Pretty much like here," I answered. "Only thirty degrees colder at any given moment."

Wendy asked him what we might send him from Maine to thank him for all his kindness in time and daylilies.

"You don't have to send us anything," Faye said. "John *adores* trying to get people hooked on daylilies."

"I love lobster," the King of Daylilies put in, though, after giving it a moment of thought. "The ones from around here are kind of on the puny side."

TONY AVENT WAS ON THE ROAD lecturing that week, we learned when we made a phone call to Juniper Level, so we pushed on north to the famed Wilderness Road in the upper New River Valley, arriving at Dr. Michael Payne's place a couple hours ahead of darkness.

There was just enough time for Dr. Payne, a small, wiry fifty-eight-year-old internist from nearby Christiansburg, Virginia, to show us around the house and grounds of his family property, a lovely old farmstead that dated from the late 1700s and had been his grandmother's home. "I took over the house from her in 1979 and moved in the following year after my first wife's death," he explained, leading us from the oldest portion of the structure into a beamed addition, which included a kitchen overlooking an upsloping garden bordered by some truly impressive trees.

"In some ways this house was a salvation for me because I threw myself into faithfully restoring it from top to bottom. This old place was on the same road Virginia settlers took over the mountains to Kentucky. America literally headed west right down on that road."

He saw me eyeing his impressive trees out back and smiled.

"Tree man, eh?"

"Oh yeah." We were like a couple guys admiring Ferraris in a showroom.

The main reason we'd stopped by Payne's on our way up to the Jefferson garden lecture in Charlottesville was because my wife's friend on the library board back home—Payne's second cousin—had said he was the craziest gardener she'd ever met. He had a collection of trees that needed to be seen to be believed—and was a dude who got addicted rather late in that game, at that. She said Payne had the restless energy of a Jack Russell.

"He sounds exactly like who you're turning into," was the way Wendy put it, proposing we stop off in Christiansburg to see what the good doctor was up to and what kind of plant obsessive she might find herself hitched to in another eight or nine years.

"The restoration of the house was fun to do," Payne explained, leading us through a sunroom delightfully cluttered with various gardening catalogs and horticultural magazines, heading toward a terrace door. "But it wasn't until I got to work out here that the real madness kicked in."

With that, he led us out into a stunning garden made all the more majestic by the dramatic shadows of the late afternoon sun. I saw fantastic conifers and Japanese maples in almost every direction and a beautiful yard that seemed to be whispering my name.

"When I started gardening in my mid-thirties," Payne confirmed, setting off at a brisk pace for a facing slope of ornamentals, "I basically didn't know anything about gardening. I was a true beginner who took up gardening primarily as an outlet from work. A country doctor, you see, basically works twenty hours a day, seven days a week.

"A cattle trail crossed the slope where my grandmother had her huge vegetable garden, and I was first tempted to just fence it off and let the cows have it. But then I bought a couple of lilac bushes, and planted them out there, and liked how they looked."

He checked up and smiled. It wasn't the smile of a weary doctor. It was the smile of a crazy man, a human Jack Russell in love with trees.

"That was roughly twenty years and two hundred bushes and trees ago."

"Are you easing up or getting worse?" I asked,

"Oh, definitely getting worse. Just ask my wife and children. If I had it to do all over, there's no doubt in my mind I would head straight off to horticulture school and forget country doctoring. This is the closest thing I'll get to a second life."

For the next forty-five minutes before the sun disappeared into the spring hills—and speaking purely for myself—I was in tree heaven. Doc Payne showed us his amazing "Henry Hicks" magnolia cultivar, his stunning dawn redwoods, and a formerly scruffy hillside that had been transformed by several paperbark maples and a rare and wonderful Thunderhead pine. "That other pine there," he said, pointing to a most unusual conifer with lightly fringed sea-green needles, "is called a Lace-bark pine—just like the one that stands near the entrance of Longwood Gardens." Then he moved on to show us a Tabletop pine grafted onto a redwood.

With more than forty different species of Japanese maples artfully scattered around his grandmother's old veggie garden, he might have gone, he confessed, "slightly overboard, although I don't think by much." Payne's *Chamaecyparis nootkatensis*—or Alaskan cedar—was about the handsomest thing I'd ever laid eyes on until I saw his *Sciado-pitys verticillata*, or Japanese umbrella pine, with its nodding glossy green whorls of needles and arching habit.

"I really really *really* want one of those," I heard someone say rather childishly behind the host's back. It turned out to be me, Wendy said later, coveting another man's *Sciadopitys*.

"Christmas is coming," she calmly said, following at a distance.

"That small Stewardia over there is just like the big one you find by the entrance to the Arnold Arboretum and, oh, let me show you a splendid boxwood with a weeping habit I stole from Monticello," Doc said before boyishly charging off toward a lush, full shrub guarding the flank of an adjacent slope. I gave close pursuit, wondering how he accomplished such a daring heist of national shrubbery. Recalling my own theft of a tiny redbud sapling from Sweet Alice Brown's decimated yard, I tried to picture this beloved country doctor and respectable father of three, hurriedly digging up a boxwood planted by the Sage of Monticello and making a mad waddle with it for the parking lot.

"It wasn't hard. I just broke off a small piece, and brought it home, and rooted it," he explained. "Boxwoods root very easily. I did the same thing with another boxwood at Mount Vernon. Beautiful, isn't it?"

Over a delicious dinner of fresh salmon with homemade ginger-yogurt sauce, which Doc Payne whipped up once darkness had chased us out of his extraordinary Wilderness Road tree garden and back into his kitchen, we drank wine and talked at length about his evolving friendship with a renowned nurseryman from over in West Virginia. He'd made several reconnoitering trips with Payne to Holland simply to "deepen my grasp of what real gardening is all about and where the great plants come from." He also mentioned how he'd simply phoned up Dr. Michael Dirr, a famous university professor of horticulture who literally wrote the bible on woody stemmed plants, and chatted pleasantly with the man for over an hour, picking up a host of useful insights about trees and shrubs. "Try doing *that* in almost any other world but the gardening world and see where you'd get," Payne summarized. This reminded me of Chinese Wilson's and Suzy Verrier's shared belief that all gardeners as a species of the genus Homo sapiens are, without a doubt, the most generous souls on earth, show-offs at heart, but eager to help the rankest beginner along the path.

While Wendy was helping Doc Payne clean up the dishes, I wandered back into his sunroom to check out his garden catalogs. One of them, I was surprised to see but really shouldn't have been, belonged to our new friends down at Marietta Daylilies, John and Faye Shooter. Several pages of a yellow legal pad were covered with Payne's small, crabbed physician's writing, listing dozens of varieties he was preparing to order.

"Daylilies are the next stage of my evolution," Payne said, seeming to read my thoughts; he was standing in the kitchen doorway drying his hands with a dish towel. "I just planted fifty of them across the road near my new boxwood nursery. That's probably the *next* twenty years of my life," he joked.

"Small world," I said, and told him where we'd been just that morning. Having begun our day by a lost family garden, it was such a pleasure to end the day with a fine meal in the company of a man whose passion for the natural world not only saved his family's land, but transformed it into a garden of trees.

"Where are you two headed now?" Payne wanted to know, as he saw us out to the truck in the cool spring darkness of the Wilderness Road. When I told him we were traveling to Peter Hatch's annual lecture on Thomas Jefferson's garden at Monticello, our host cracked a huge smile.

"He's one of us, you know."

"Hatch?"

"No, Jefferson. A true garden nut who got started rather late in life on his passion. Gardening kept him alive. He's the patron saint of late-in-life gardeners everywhere."

"So I understand." I explained to our host that I'd been to Monticello half a dozen times in my life but had never seen it through the eyes of a late-in-life gardener.

Doc Payne patted my arm like a brother in beautiful madness.

"In that case you're in for a treat. I always see something new there. I wish I could dig up the trees and bring them home."

Chapter 7

Old Men, Young Gardeners

WITH HIS FAMOUS GINGER HAIR showing the first traces of gray, and a saddle posture that remained as ramrod-straight as ever, fifty-one-year-old Thomas Jefferson met his black servant Robert Hemings in Fredericksburg, Virginia, for a fresh horse and what he believed would be his final twelve-hour journey home through the foothills of the Blue Ridge to a well-earned retirement on his Ciceronian summit, Monticello.

This was January 1794, five years after the author of the Declaration of Independence and the young nation's first secretary of state, under George Washington, returned from his important diplomatic mission to France, a job that both delighted and thoroughly exhausted him. As far back as 1768, Jefferson had begun leveling the top of his "little mountain" across the valley from Charlottesville, engineering clever roundabout roads and eventually beginning construction of a neoclassical Georgian manor house he was destined to never fully be pleased with, evidenced by the fact that he constantly tore sections of it apart and built new ones, forever tinkering with the design as new ideas came to him.

"I hope to spend the remainder of my days," he confided to a close friend about this time, "in occupations infinitely more pleasing than those to which I have sacrificed 18 years of the prime of my life." The "little spice of ambition, which I had in my younger days," he admitted to fellow revolutionary James Madison, had "long since evaporated." All he desired now was to go home to "the bosom of my family, my farm, and my books."

Two years before he purchased his five-thousand-acre mountaintop in 1766 Jefferson had envisioned a rural retreat like no other and actually begun keeping a detailed journal of notes that revealed a powerful interest in horticulture and the natural world around him. The diary seems at times written by a mad landscape designer and amateur botanist and included extensive lists of native trees and shrubs and native wildlife and various experiments on the land he hoped to conduct once this unnamed Elysium was a reality. Over the course of an adult lifetime, Jefferson's Garden Book would contain his wildest dreams and ultimately articulate his most intimate passions.

Jefferson's time in Paris, the Old World capital of seductive pleasures in the view of the widowed Virginia statesman, yielded far more than a rumored dalliance with a married socialite and an expensive appetite for French wine and cooking. His personal friendship with Andre Thouin, famed superintendent of the Jardins des Plantes in Paris, carried over to Jefferson's time as secretary of state and resulted in Thouin regularly dispatching him seeds and exotic plants from all over Europe, some of which Jefferson planted at Monticello. Others he sent on to other private gardeners who shared his zeal for self-taught botany.

At a time when the prevailing scientific attitudes in Europe dismissed wild North American plants as inferior in beauty and quality to those cultivated in the fashionable capitals and estates of the Continent and Britain, Jefferson mounted a vigorous defense of New World horticulture. He shipped back to Thouin, among other things, the first honeysuckle plants and swamp laurel ever seen in Europe.

Meanwhile, in Washington, the homesick Virginian routinely scouted Potomac basin nurseries in search of healthy and unusual trees and shrubs to convey to his evolving mountaintop retreat, and his lively correspondence with leading plantsmen of his day, including John Bartram's son William, was both evangelistic and extensive.

The roots of this botanical zeal were planted during his teenage years at Shadwell, according to his various biographers, but it wasn't until the late 1780s—precisely at midlife—that Jefferson's dreams and plans for Monticello finally began to take shape based on influences from abroad. While in Paris, for example, he used every opportunity to visit famous French château gardens, including the renowned formal treasures at Marly and Versailles, and came to love the trees, lawns, and *alles* of the prevailing French style, yet quietly yearned for something far more natural and less regimented and geometric on the land.

He found the natural influence he craved—at least, a fair approximation of the ideal rural landscape—across the English Channel in 1786 when he and longtime friend and political rival John Adams embarked together on an extensive garden tour of twenty-two English gardens. Theirs was an odyssey of discovery that dramatically shaped Jefferson's thinking and fueled his eagerness to get back to his beloved mountaintop to dig in the soil and delve in the soul.

Despite a constitutional predisposition to loathe anything English save the sweet garden pea (it was his favorite vegetable), Jefferson fell hard for English gardens on his walking tour with Adams. He confided to his journal afterward that "the gardens in that country surpass all the earth." His tour of the Blessed Isle in the spring of 1786, as it happened, couldn't have come at a more fertile moment in the life of the English garden. Between 1760 and 1800, under the design influences of Lancelot "Capability" Brown and his popular successor Humphry Repton, a pair of enterprising nurserymen who used their royal connections to become wealthy and influential estate designers, more than twenty-one million acres of open fields and common lands were closed off for private cultivation. According to English garden writer and historian Penny Hobhouse, Jefferson was deeply taken with the pastoral quality of Brown's idealized park landscapes, meant to recall the work of late Renaissance painters, and the "variety of hill and dale," which he hailed as "the first beauty in gardening."

The Virginian also found delight—yet room for improvement—in the clever serpentine garden walks found at Woolburn Farm and The Leasowes, a controversial *ferme ornee* (ornamental farm) owned by poet William Shenstone that featured pastoral walks through flowering woodlands and fields and pathways adorned with urns and pithy quotes from classical authors—a kind of literary nature trail that London's Samuel Johnson, for one, championed as a blueprint for the garden of the future but which Humphry Repton—the first authority to use the phrase "landscape gardening"—blasted as both a contrivance and a "vulgar attempt at profitmongering."

The visiting Americans, it's commonly believed, came down mostly on the side of Sir Humphry, yet several of these novel gardening ideas nevertheless found their way into Jefferson's evolving landscape at Monticello, including the informal flower walk, the concept of planting trees in groves, and the idea of constructing terraces of fruits and flowers ajacent to field crops, a working farm that blended traditional husbandry with ornamental gardening.

Unfortunately, Jefferson's own "retirement" to farm and garden during the winter of 1794 proved woefully premature. Despite the construction of roads, his property's famous U-shaped terraces and an accelerated planting scheme of trees "of the loftiest stature" and various orchards during this period, America's rural Renaissance man was summoned back to Foggy Bottom to serve his country as its third president from 1801 to 1809.

During the last two years of his presidency, in anticipation of his final withdrawal from public life to his mountaintop mecca, he began drawing up plans for making twenty oval flower beds to be placed at the four corners of his house, as well as an informal gravel serpentine walk bordered by flower beds like those he'd studied at Woodburn Farm and other places in 1786.

The publication in 1806 of *The American Gardener's Calendar* by his friend John McMahon, plantsman and the curator of the Lewis and Clark expedition, only increased the aging president's sense of urgency to get back to his ornamental farm and begin turning the soil. (The volume was believed to be the first book to address the variety of conditions and climatic challenges facing the new American gardener.) A lively correspondence and exchange of plant material had gone on between the two men for nearly a decade, but the summer his book appeared, McMahon, anticipating Jefferson's final withdrawal from public life, dispatched exciting new tulip roots and autumn planting directions to his most distinguished customer for his new Monticello flower garden.

In January 1807, Jefferson placed a large order that included day-lilies, tuberose, Sweet Williams, marigolds, anemone, aricula, ranunculus, and Belgian strawberries. From April 11th to the 15th, according to the man's own meticulously kept records, Jefferson laid out the circular and oval flower beds near the house on the west and east lawns—and by the thirtieth, those beds had been planted with flowers, trees, and shrubs. In beds positioned at the corners of his house, he planted several paperbark mulberries and horse chestnut trees, mountain ashes, tacamahac poplars, purple beeches, and even a lone redbud tree.

By the time Jefferson, now sixty-five, took his final ride home from Washington through a driving snowstorm on Old Eagle, his beloved horse, in January 1809, his flower garden was finally waiting for him. Fittingly, the story goes, one of his final acts as president was to give away various indoor plants from the President's House, including one of the first geranium plants to reach American shores from the wilds of South Africa, to a Washington socialite and fellow gardening buff.

Deeply in debt from his habit of spending extravagantly on rare books, French wine, exotic seeds and flowers, fruit trees, and other horticultural excesses, the author of the Declaration of Independence and arguably America's most celebrated figure hoped he'd finally escaped to his garden. And, for a little while at least, that was the case.

The picture various biographers draw of the retired president reveals a physically spent but mentally vigorous figure of a man who quickly shed the garb of statesman and assumed the humble field boots and corduroy breeches of a Virginia planter, making his endlessly detailed lists of chores and of changing weather observations, mounting his beloved Old Eagle like clockwork each afternoon following lunch, rain or shine, for a solitary ride around his mountaintop; supervising wheat harvests or the planting of a new orchard; pioneering techniques in crop rotation and forever battling the drought conditions that plagued his elevated retreat; chiding his daughters and grandchildren for their inattention to the weeding of his serpentine flower garden; assisting Wormley, the head gardener, to precisely align rows of flowers and vegetables with the use of a trapline; officiating footraces with his grandchildren on the evening lawn (the winner always got fruit) while enjoying three or four glasses of imported wine and maybe a little homemade cider at dinner.

Jefferson, who had no fear of death and quietly confided to friends his concerns about "living too long," slept only five to eight hours per night, rose before dawn and bathed his feet in cold water (believing this stimulated the circulation), and devoted his earliest working hours to writing letters to friends and admirers—a hopeless attempt to make a dent in the estimated one thousand letters he received through the post every day at Monticello, prompting his fellow surviving garden patriot John Adams to slyly observe that Jefferson hadn't had the foresight to make himself unpopular in office. In one such letter to a friend, months after leaving office, the retired master of Monticello described himself simply as finally "living like an antediluvian patriarch among my children and grandchildren, and tilling my soil."

Unfortunately, the world beyond his mountain couldn't bear to let him go. During the final decade of his life, an endless procession of friends, admirers, foreign dignitaries, Jeffersonian scholars, and garden-variety crackpots showed up every day at Monticello to try and see the retired Founding Father. "Even out of sight on his mountaintop," essayed a celebrated New York newspaperman, "he dominates the landscape of this nation, presiding over us all like the welcome shadow of a kindly uncle."

"THERE'S NO QUESTION that every gardener in this room, every gardener in America, for that matter, owes Thomas Jefferson an enormous debt of gratitiude," Peter Hatch told the standing-room-only crowd near the end of his annual spring talk on Jefferson the gardener. "Gar-

dening for Jefferson was a bridge from simply being an academic observer of the world around him to being an active participant. 'No occu-
pation is so delightful to me as the cultivation of the earth,' he said. 'Tho
an old man, I am a young gardener.' Whether it was counting his Carolina beans from his kitchen garden or introducing his pioneering concepts of contour plowing and crop rotation, his love and delight over his
ever-changing flower garden or his zealous quest to introduce useful
species of plants to society, we all benefited from a man who viewed the
garden as the workhouse of nature, as he called it, as the ultimate
source of inspiration and innovation."

Outside, as Hatch made this observation, nature rattled the darkening sky over Monticello. By the time the lecture crowd was filtering out
and heading for the gift shop to snap up cute Jeffersonian refrigerator
magnets and official Sage of Monticello T-shirts, Colonial cookbooks,
and other Jeffersonian do-dads, the first large drops of rain were pelting
cars and buses parked at the Monticello visitor center.

Surveying the threatening skies, I suggested to my own traveling garden mate that we make a beeline up the winding road to the great man's
house and gardens before the storm broke and perhaps gain a leg up on
the lecture crowds.

Once there, we joined a walking tour of the famous white-domed
house, at least my fifth or sixth tour of the premises, and listened to the
young female guide drone somewhat blandly on about Uncle Tom's love
of experimental gadgets and expensive scientific geegaws, reminding
me of the wonderful late garden writer Henry Mitchell's claim to have
visited Monticello no fewer than one hundred fifty times in his life, admitting a slightly unnatural fascination with the enigmatic owner that
trumped my own.

Mitchell was fortunate enough to know the garden from its desolate
postwar days of the late 1940s to its splendid rebirth two decades later,
and gently grieved for the loss of certain old bulbs and plants that were
somehow lost in translation like the wild lady tulip, *Tulipa clusiana* (possibly a gift from John McMahon) and old-fashioned double hyacinths
that were descendants of the very ones Jefferson personally planted.

I, on the other hand, had only been periodically calling to the place since an elementary school class field trip in my formative lawn-mowing years, circa 1966, when, on a dare from Woody Ham, I slipped beneath the velvet rope in the great man's bedroom and brought great relief and amusement to several fellow fifth-grade scholars by stretching out on Jefferson's novel bed-in-the-wall. My first of many visits to Monticello ended, I regret to say, with me being given rapid ejection from the building and having to sit in a hot, empty school bus, and eat my bologna and cheese sandwich.

I'd been drawn back to Monticello many times since that rocky beginning to prowl the famous estate as Mitchell had in search of . . . well, it was difficult to say what, exactly. Corny as it sounds, perhaps even early on there was something quite attractive to me about the notion of a house built on a forested hilltop and girdled by a garden slightly off in the woods where few, if any, were expected to ever lay eyes upon. Peter Hatch was clearly on to something when he observed that "every visitor who loves his or her garden can see traces of themselves in Thomas Jefferson at Monticello."

His delightful spring lecture also brought out one of the more encouraging and humanizing aspects of Jefferson's gardening experience—namely, his dogged determination to keep trying new things in the face of repeated failures and schemes that flopped.

That Jefferson the gardener exhaustively documented the planting of 113 species of ornamental trees and no fewer than sixty-five kinds of shrubs, many from other parts of the world and several unknown to the New World until reaching the soil of his Little Mountain, as well as over one hundred species of herbaceous plants in his ever-changing flower gardens and not fewer than four hundred varieties of nearly one hundred different species of vegetables, fruits, and nuts, clearly makes the fellow America's first great gardening nut; our patron saint, as Michael Payne had called him; Fiacre de Breuil dressed in the humble garb of a Virginia man of the soil.

As Hatch notes, however, among more high-minded Jeffersonian schemes that went absolutely nowhere was an altruistic effort to substitute sugar maples for traditional plantation crops down South—aimed at easing the region's heavy reliance on slave labor—and an ambitious hydraulic scheme based on a revolutionary aqueduct system designed to pump water from the river a mile and a half below to his thirsting mountaintop that never even got off the drawing pad.

While he was returning from ministerial duties in France, Jefferson actually illegally smuggled cool-climate variety of rice seed out of Europe in hopes of cultivating it in America and thus easing common malaria among traditional low-country rice growers. Various species of willow and scores of lowland Chinaberry trees also failed to survive the harsh mountaintop climate and unaccustomed landscape of Monticello, and an ambitious English maze designed to be made entirely from Scotch broom never materialized—or vanished pretty quickly, if it did.

Yet the self-taught horticulturist in Jefferson never flinched from the trial and error of developing such useful novelties as his innovative thousand-foot-long vegetable terraces on the southeastern flank of his mountain, where he attempted to grow three different varieties of his beloved English pea plus two hundred fifty other kinds of vegetables, many of which Americans at that time had never heard of, including Italian pole beans and wild strawberries collected from the flanks of the upper Rockies by Lewis and Clark.

Apples and grapes held special thrall for the man, too. He not only took a lead in propagating and grafting new varieties of apples, forever on a lonely search for what he termed the "proper keeping apple"—it was a quantum step forward in America, says Hatch, when people began "eating apples rather than drinking them"—but also planted his vineyard on six different occasions to try and establish a working grape culture suitable for wine making. No luck there.

He also planted as many as thirty-eight varieties of peach at a time when there were few cultivars available. Introduced by Spanish explorers to Florida in the 1500s and brought north by native peoples, seedlings escaped from orchards and quickly naturalized the southeastern landscape in such "wild" profusion, according to Peter Hatch, that more than one foreign naturalist dismissed the fruit tree as "North America's first weed."

Not Uncle Tom. "We abound in the luxury of the peach," Jefferson wrote glowingly after putting down no fewer than 160 young peach trees in his south-facing orchard.

ARGUABLY AN OLD MAN but a new gardener myself, it was in this spirit of ongoing struggle against the elements of man and nature—an impressive record, if you will, of costly failures interrupted by the occasional horticultural triumph—that I optimistically escaped the house tour that was as dull as I remembered, and set forth to try and gaze anew upon Jefferson's beloved flower gardens at their seasonal height.

He designed the original oval beds and serpentine flower border to serve as an ever-opening stage play of the seasons, a barometer of passing days in the garden, beginning with hyacinths and tulips and American columbine in late April that soon yielded the stage to the irises and tuberoses of early summer, followed by hollyhocks, daisies, poppies, larkspur, gladiolus, and lilies.

This day, with rain slipping off to the east, a dozen varieties of brightly hued tulips were out in full force (Jefferson called them "belles of the day," the most frequently mentioned flower in his Garden Book due to their ease of shipping and reliable bloom) and the native columbine and Virginia bluebells were coming out in profusion under the old surviving trees that presided over the winding gravel path of the west lawn. The informal winding style of the path reflected Jefferson's own interpretation of the English gardens that inspired him in 1786. The beds themselves reportedly were never cared for by professional gardeners, but principally by Jefferson's daughters and granddaughters, an elderly slave, and the master of Monticello himself. "I find that the limited number of our flower beds will too much restrain the variety of flowers in which we might wish to indulge," he wrote to granddaughter Anne in June 1808, a year before leaving office, with an accompanying sketch plan for the roundabout flower border. "And therefore I have resumed an idea . . . of a winding walk . . . with a narrow border of flowers on each side. This would give abundant room for a great variety." The winding walk and accompanying flower borders, Hatch notes, were duly laid out that spring but systematically revised into smaller more organized groupings of seasonal flowering plants in 1812.

"In some ways," Hatch told me wryly after I went up to have a few words with him following his enlightening talk, "like all true garden fanatics, Jefferson constantly overreached in his planting ambitions. He would scarcely finish one garden and be able to keep it properly cared for before he doubled its size and was off on something else. Henry Mitchell once observed something to the effect that if everything Jefferson aimed to create at Monticello had come to pass, the place would have looked like crap."

As I followed Jefferson's winding narrative path through the blooming tulip beds around the west lawn, falling in line behind one of the first dragonflies of the season, what struck the relatively new gardener in me quite forcefully—perhaps even for the very first time, despite all my previous nosing about there as both man and boy—was how perilously close to being lost forever the great man's garden came, following his death in 1826. That part of the story rarely makes it into the history books attempting to unravel the vast and enigmatic life of the man.

"The last few months [of Jefferson's life] were uniformly sad and grim," concludes Joseph Ellis in *American Sphinx*, "punctuated by one final effort to rescue at least a portion of his burdened estate for his heirs and one last and truly defiant display of the inimitable Jefferson style." Roughly about one hundred thousand dollars in debt—several million by today's standards—the overspent gardener devised a public lottery to sell off enough of his personal possessions in hopes of retaining hold of Monticello and its immediate land for his heirs, a plan that technically violated the law and required a legal waiver by the Virginia state legislature.

When the legislature failed to grant the waiver—"in a fit of inexplicable ingratitude that also enhanced his embarrassment," according to

Ellis—it took intervention by the dying man's friends and several lead-ing political figures to convince Old Dominion pols (clearly they were neither men of history or the soil) to reverse its decision. Advised of the change, Jefferson prepared his will in March of 1826 "with the expecta-tion that Monticello would be salvaged from his creditors and some of his land would pass to his heirs." In the belief that the auctioneers would sell off his loyal servants, the architect of liberty chose to legally free five members of the Hemings family.

As summer and the end of his days approached, Jefferson had but one last wish: to survive to the fiftieth anniversary of his most enduring creation, the Declaration of Independence. True to form, he accom-plished this feat, slipping away just before noon that calm summer In-dependence Day on his cultivated summit. That same day up in Massachusetts, in a feat of timing that equaled that of his political rival and English garden tour companion, John Adams also passed away.

On a bleak January day six months later, all of Jefferson's worldly possessions plus "130 valuable negroes" were auctioned off and carried away by the highest bidders. The auction lasted five days. "His grandson Jeffy," recounts Ellis, "never forgave the sad scene, which he compared with 'a great captured village in ancient times when all were sold as slaves.' "

As I nosed slowly around the west lawn's serpentine walk where Jef-ferson once proudly escorted his distinguished visitors to show off his flowers, sometimes arm in arm with aging patriots of the revolution, a soft spring rain returned and began filtering down through the few catalpa and tulip poplars that survived their owner's death, chasing some of the visitors back to the safety of the main house.

Watching them scuttle off, I thought of Dick Lighty's wry observation that he could always tell the "real" gardeners in any tour group visiting Mount Cuba because they were the ones who stayed out in any weather, oblivious to the rain or cold, poking and exploring. One can't possibly live and garden on a dry hill, as I do and brother Jefferson did, and fail to notice water falling from the sky—nor fail to gratefully rejoice in it.

So, I continued on my winding circularity, a circle both visible and unseen, dampening at shoulders and cuffs, enjoying the earthy smells and this sudden gift of rain brought forth in another man's garden, making me suddenly remember Sweet Alice's observation that we're all just borrowing ground from God.

Within a year of Jefferson's death, curiosity seekers by the hundreds showed up at Monticello, digging up virtually every shrub and flower and carrying them off to sell or put in their own gardens. Most of his rare and beloved trees were cut down and sold off for timber, and mulberry trees were planted to try and exploit the silkworm craze that was then sweeping Southern culture. His treasured lawn was plowed up and planted with corn. Notices placed in newspapers by family members, requesting visitors to desist in trespassing, did little to stem the onslaught of plant predation. A sympathetic Washington friend who hadn't visited Monticello since its horticultural peak in 1810 came to pay homage and was appalled to discover the main house nearly in ruins, its gardens vanished, almost every outbuilding vacant and tumbling down. "All was silent," she recounted somberly. "Ruin has already commenced its ravages."

In time, to further satisfy unpaid debts, the land itself passed into other hands. The domed mansion remained a vacant hulk for many years and had to be propped up to avoid toppling to the ground. It wasn't until the Garden Club of Virginia, in 1939, enlisted the help of an eminent research scholar named Edwin Betts and an indefatigable gardener called Hazelhurst Perkins to begin the process of trying to restore the property that America regained its most valulable early American garden and an unprecedented glimpse into the private passions of Thomas Jefferson.

Because the man who was arguably America's first landscape architect drew so many plans for his various gardening schemes—some of which materialized, most of which didn't—as superintendent Peter Hatch likes to regale his audiences, the lost flower beds of the west lawn walk were eventually found in a most inventive manner.

"One evening after sunset the architect shined the lights of his car across the west lawn and there it was finally—the crest of the lawn itself and traces of the raised beds around the walk. What's almost equally amazing is, they also found flowering bulbs still growing in places, almost one hundred and twenty years after Jefferson's death."

AFTER AN HOUR of poking about in the spring flower beds, I realized I'd lost track of my gardening companion. But I soon found her where I knew I would—studying the progress of early pole beans and French kale down in Tom's handsomely restored thousand-foot veggie patch on the east-facing slopes.

"You could probably use something like that up in Maine," she said cheeerfully as I came sauntering up with my brain still stuck in the early nineteenth century, pointing to Jefferson's beautifully rebuilt brick pavilion, which presides over the terraced gardens and a view that stretches leagues across the rolling Virginia hill country. The brief shower was gone and the day-trippers were filtering back out to look at the flower beds. According to Jefferson's own records, he often began his day watching the sunrise from this spot. As Suzy Verrier once said to me, the best thing about a garden is that it's "always on its own time—and clocks don't matter." Unfortunately, our clock did, the wristwatch that told me it was time to go so we could make another garden date tomorrow morning up in Delaware.

"This place isn't just a shrine to the backyard gardener," I put to Wendy, thinking of the financial grave Jefferson's restless genius dug for his family. "It's a cautionary tale for the price of overindulging in foundation shrubs."

"Remember that when we get down to the garden shop," she said mischievously.

A short while later, we set off together along a footpath descending through the man's beloved hilltop grove, passing the modest family burying ground on the way, admiring a forest that may have inspired Jefferson's own design for the arboretum at the university he designed just across the valley in Charlottesville, a forest he'd hoped would someday rival the great private woodlands of Europe. Though only a few of

Jefferson's "pet" trees today remain, thanks to the enlightened stewardship of the Thomas Jefferson Foundation and Peter Hatch's faithful
restoration work, the woodland is once again thriving.

At one point, veering slightly off the trail, in fact, we passed a large
boxwood growing wild and rather on its own. I broke off a few eight-
inch cuttings in tribute to both Jefferson's unbridled garden passions
and my new New River Valley role model, Michael Payne, not to mention generations of Monticello visitors who simply couldn't resist taking
a piece of living history home with them. I had serious misgivings about
whether English boxwood would even grow on my stern northern hilltop, but my new "Southern" arboretum scheme made the modest theft
seem morally defensible.

Down at the garden shop, in tribute to Brother John, I indulged myself a small pot of Jeffersonian monkshood, which the young lady clerk
assured me a guest to the estate in 1810 would have found growing
profusely in the late summer garden. Maybe she said that to all the
rubes from Maine. My practical-minded wife picked up several "Martha
Washington" asparagus roots, promising a feast to come in a couple
years' time.

As I was putting my small pot of monkshood into the back of my
truck, a guy about my age who'd just pulled up in a van full of arguing
kids strolled over and asked where I'd bought such "great-looking
plants," especially the nice little redbud tree whose root-ball was now
safely swaddled in wet newspapers and a plastic garbage bag.

Swiped it from a lost garden, I was half tempted to say. Instead I
said, "A friend gave it to me from her yard. She was moving."

"Man, I love redbud trees. I'd love to have a little one just like that
little fella. Half the fun is watching them grow, you know."

I knew. As Michael Payne and just about every other real gardener I
knew liked to say, the pleasure of planting a tree is in planting it small
and watching it grow large, marking your own life in the process.

"You from around here?" I asked the guy. He grinned, one big
friendly oaf in a striped polo shirt.

"Yup. Just over the mountain toward Lexington. I'm the pro at a little golf club out in the country. It used to be a cow pasture, but I'm slowly dressing it up with trees and flowers. I like to come here for ideas. Neat place, isn't it?"

I couldn't believe it. *Throw a Titleist, hit a gardener.*

"Tell you what," I said, reaching in and sliding out the little tree. "You take it. Give it a good home and lots of water. Put it on your signature hole so folks can appreciate it."

"Jeez, are you *kidding?*" He seemed so pleased I thought he might try and kiss me. His kids even stopped arguing for a nanosecond and gaped at us—two old farts getting misty over a stolen redbud yearling.

"Nope. Enjoy. Good luck with your garden golf course."

"That was very sweet of you," Wendy allowed quietly as we drove back down the mountain to the main highway and started north.

"Yeah, I guess so," I agreed, thinking I just might try and pick up a nice red horse chestnut somewhere in Pennsylvania to replace its loss, just like the ones you see lolling over the walls of Arundel Castle in England. For some reason, my brain was already thinking fondly about England, bluebell season in woodlands of the chalk downs and New Forest, the world-famous Chelsea show where I'd never been, ye olde nature bursting lustfully forth, Kim Basinger playing Queen Titania in a tight lace bodice.

"Say, would you like to go to England?" I casually asked my wife, probably much the same way Jefferson asked Adams to go on their little life-altering garden tour. Her cute button nose was once again tucked into Tony Avent's delightful spring catalog.

"Can we go home first and unload all the plants in back and maybe do a little laundry?"

"Funny girl."

"I thought that's why you married me."

I FEEL ABOUT GOING into a private garden the way Annie Dillard felt about venturing into the jungles of Ecuador. The point in going is not to see the most spectacular anything, but simply to see what is there, and in my case to try and figure out what the creator of the garden had in mind—all the better if the creator happens to be the person leading the tour.

That's exactly what happened at Winterthur, Harry Du Pont's former private estate garden and my late friend Winnie Palmer's favorite garden woodland, when we stopped off briefly during the homeward trek to meet Dick Lighty's former star pupil, Denise Magnani, and see the children's garden she created in the heart of one of America's finest if woefully under-visited gardens.

It was instantly clear why Lighty was so fond of Denise, Winterthur's curator of gardens. She had an earthy enthusiasm and vast knowledge of the history and biology of the estate that rivaled anyone's, having shown up fresh from hort school at Delaware two decades before to work as a part-time garden tour guide and became a vital part of the major restoration of the gardens that commenced about that same time.

"It wasn't a willful neglect on anyone's part," she explained as we set off along a circulatory walk that would lead us through a "sundial garden" full of flowering quince, crab apples, viburnums, and azaleas, and ultimately up to the garden's famous March Bank area. "But after Harry Du Pont's death in 1969, work on the gardens for the most part ceased. People here then assumed that because Mr. Du Pont had designed it to be a *naturalistic* garden, meaning a garden that fit the landscape in the way English garden writer William Robinson advocated, with one natural space flowing into another, a journey into the heart of nature itself, seemingly unmade by man, that everything here would more or less maintain itself." She laughed, shaking her Jeffersonian red hair. "Of course, any real gardener knows *that's* a formula for disaster."

Winterthur avoided disaster by embarking on a systematic restoration of its twelve or thirteen major garden areas—woodlands and meadows, our host was quick to point out, Harry Du Pont had played in as a boy and found incomparable pleasure nurturing as a young man upon returning home from his Harvard horticultural studies to serve as his father's land manager in 1910.

"Harry had some horticultural training at the Bussey Institute in

Massachusetts but mostly was a self-taught gardener, heavily influenced and fascinated by the natural gardens he saw in his travels through Britain and other European countries. Robinson's Gravetye obviously had a major impact on his thinking, but so did Getrude Jekyll's gardens and her views about colors blending naturally with landscape. You see that everywhere you look here at Winterthur—harmonic drifts of color set in a landscape that shifts naturally with the changing season as you go through."

Around 1902, Du Pont began spending lavishly on naturalizing hundreds of thousands of hardy bulbs and perennials in the heavily wooded slopes northeast of his ancestral home, developing the so-called March Bank, a daring horticultural experiment that today is considered one of the world's most successful renderings of William Robinson's natural gospel.

But he didn't stop there. Over the next seventy years, Du Pont created a succession of stunning interconnected seasonal gardens that artfully expanded on Jefferson's concept of nature as stage play, producing a complex living canvas of flowering shrubs and flowers girdled by a 2,400-acre sweeping hardwood forest that would sequentially bloom from January to June.

Our delightful guided hike also took us through a section called the Azalea Woods, where hundreds of the Kurume hybrids from Japan (among the first ever planted in America) were just coming out, announced by a carpet of emerging woodland trilliums, Virginia bluebells, and fading scillas. But it was when we reached Du Pont's prized pinetum that my interest peaked. Up on the hill, providing a dense green backdrop to this valed garden of flowering shrubs, were stands of monstrously beautiful conifers that looked like the druid elders in some mythical tale of forest intrigue, a crowning glory that included Blue Atlas cedars, Northern firs, Oriental spruce, towering Eastern red cedars, false cypress trees, and the largest Aborvitae I'd ever laid eyes on. These elders of the forest dated back to Harry's papa's friendship with Charles Sprague Sargeant of the Arnold Arboretum (the famous plant hunter of the early 1900s who suggested to Algernon Du Pont, Civil

War veteran and Congressional Medal of Honor winner, a U.S. senator who'd just lost his seat in Congress and retired to devote the rest of his days to horticulture, that planting "unusual" varieties of trees known largely only in the Far East and Europe would be a great service to American horticulture, showing Americans what they were capable of growing in their own yards and gardens).

In the midst of this shadowy, quiet realm of evergreens stood a lone beautiful cherry tree shedding a blizzard of pink-white petals in the late morning breeze, carpeting the pine-needled floor in a manner that seemed almost surreal, a stage setting for pure spring mischief. When I made this comment to our host, she smiled and said, "The story goes that Harry smuggled that tree into the country under his top coat, returning from one of his big plant tours abroad."

"Absolutely enchanting," I said, picking out a cluster of where I would have had my secret fortress in the forest as a boy.

Denise laughed. "No," she said, "*that's* back down the hill."

Before we started that way, however, she pointed out to an edge of the field where daffodils were blooming. "And that's where Harry had his ten-hole golf course."

"Old Harry was a golfer?" I took heart from this news. Plant thief *and* pasture pool nut. The guy was even more of a spiritual brother in arms than I'd guessed.

"Oh, *mad* for golf. So much so, he built his own course. Why it was just ten holes, I have no idea."

"Maybe that's all the time he had left after weeding his garden."

Denise saved the best, though, for final leg of our walking tour—the "Enchanted Garden" she'd worked hard to promote and finally seen become a reality.

Spread over a small hilltop of towering hardwoods, the magnificent children's garden featured an authentic thatched-roofed stone woodcutter's hut, a fairy house made from an ancient tulip tree stump, a mythical story ring of stones, a troll bridge, a "gathering" green for storytelling, a gigantic bird's nest, a green man's secret lair, and a fairy flower walk.

"Never step inside a fairy ring," our host advised, pointing to a circular group of large toadstools charmingly embowered by flowering azaleas, knowing, I suppose, I was too much of a wild green man to avoid the temptation. I stepped in and was immediately engulfed in a cloud of mist.

"The children absolutely adore that," she said, breaking into a laugh.

"So does he," my wild green wife spoke up on my behalf.

"You're a genius," I told Magnani, stating the obvious.

"A garden is made by many hands. I was just the person who agitated for this garden a long time. There were lots of others who did the design work and actually built it."

"Jefferson said the same down at Monticello. Every garden needs a majordomo."

Ironically, when Winterthur's extraordinary Enchanted Garden opened to the public in 2001, shortly before events of 9/11, I knew from conversations with others attached to the place that some of the governing board's more staid members quietly worried about the effect of attracting children into Harry Du Pont's old garden—fearing, I suppose, that they would wander off the path and get lost or injured, prompting a blizzard of lawsuits. Others voiced concerns, Denise conceded as we started back to a Du Pont mansion that is probably far better known in the public mind for its American crafts and art collections than its gardens, that having so many noisy children in a garden would be an irritation to older visitors seeking a sylvan retreat.

"It was the fourth generation of the Du Pont family itself that gave such critical support to the garden's creation," she explained. "They understood what this enchanted woodland had meant to the first two generations of their family. Without their support, this garden never would have happened."

But it did happen, and the world, so far as I could tell, was a much better place for this ingenious creation. By the end of the first year in business, she added with a sly fairy-like smile, recalling how her son Matthew grew up playing at Winterthur and for years was forced by his mother to don a steamy Easter Bunny costume for the annual egg hunt extravaganza she'd started there—Matthew was now in his twenties and expecting a child of his own—the garden had registered a 1,700 percent increase in the number of young people who came to be enchanted by a magical garden in the woods.

"That's a lot of future gardeners," she added. "I think Harry would be terribly pleased with that."

B𝚈 THE TIME WE REACHED White Flower Farm, our final planned stop, I'd added a small Delaware Valley red horse chestnut tree worthy of Arundel Castle plus three young *Sargeantii* pears and a fragrant *Viburnum carlesii* to the jungle of plant stock riding in back of my truck.

White Flower was purely a sentimental pause for me. During my happy wandering years as *Yankee* magazine's senior writer I'd been drawn to investigate and write about Boston's famed Green Necklace and Public Garden, Polly Logan, and the unapologetically rapacious Martha Stewart. But I'd never quite reached the headquarters of the legendary garden catalog in rural Connecticut that filled my early garden dreams with lovely perennials and, for a time, employed none other than Suzy Verrier as a consultant on rugosa roses.

The cottage I eventually built, not to put *too* fine a point on this horticultural homage, a simple, stark-white New England affair surrounded by ever-expanding perennial borders, was originally and quite shamelessly copied from the White Flower catalog's photos of owner Amos Pettingill's famous Connecticut farmhouse and nursery grounds. Like an immigrant wanting to see if the Statue of Liberty measured up to its publicity stills, I'd always hankered to visit White Flower and see for myself in the worst sort of way.

Fortunately, through mutual friends, the firm's longtime director of horticulture, Englishman David Smith, not only graciously invited me to stop and have a look around the property but even enthusiastically spent a couple delightful hours of his own time walking me through the display beds and trial fields and packinghouses of the legendary catalog firm. The business turned out to have been started after the war by a somewhat ill-tempered magazine writer named William Harris and his wife Jane Grant, a pair of literary New Yorkers (he was senior editor at *Fortune*; she was a correspondent for *The New York Times* and previously had been married to Harold Ross of *The New Yorker*) looking for a means of escape to the country.

"Their original thought was to just have a place they could come out to on weekends, to write and putter around in the garden, which they found here in Litchfield back in the late thirties. Like most things," Smith added with a quick grin, "once they got outside in the garden, things got out of hand, I'm afraid, and they never really went back indoors."

What began with Harris's simple desire to build a traditional English lawn soon turned into an innocent field excursion to pick blue flowers in a local wildflower meadow for a dinner party, which in turn yielded a full-scale assault on the surrounding landscape as the writers leapt headfirst into homemade horticulture, eventually transforming their perennial border from mixed colors to pure white—what's known in England as a "moon" garden, not unlike Vita Sackville-West's famed white garden at Sissinghurst—hence the eventual christening of a new name.

By devouring books and plumbing the insights of local estate gardeners and golf course superintendents, Harris and Grant were soon growing annuals and perennials of such distinction their city friends suggested they begin selling their plants to others. Not long after the war's end, as Harris details in his delightful account of their transformation into sophisticated gardeners, "One evening, obviously after one more drink of bourbon than necessary, we said, 'Let's start a nursery!' "

Their original intent was to specialize in pure white-flowering perennials and shrubs, but they realized there might be a larger market to exploit, because only a handful of high-quality mail-order catalog nurseries then offered premium ornamental stock, almost all of them in the Midwest. The industry, per se, was rife with careless mail-order outfits that shipped any old plants and committed outright fraud. Reflecting the rigid Yankee virtues of integrity and square dealing, Harris and

Grant built greenhouses and hung their shingle. "We had another reason for starting a nursery," William Grant relates. "We found that many fine English nurseries were offering many new strains that were not cataloged in this country. Also, the English offered exceptionally good species of genera that were impossible to find in the United States. So our nursery would bring in as much new plant material that we could find hardy in the colder zones."

They also decided to pay a visit to the Chelsea Flower Show in search of both horticultural suppliers and possibly a young English nurseryman they could bring home to the colonies to help with the breeding and propagation of new species for their fledgling mail-order catalog.

Enter David Smith, twenty-nine, former Spitfire pilot, apprentice gardener son of a well-known BBC "Out in the Garden" commentator, then working at renowned Baker's Nurseries in charge of daylilies and chrysanthemums, overseeing a staff of fifteen.

"They—Harris and Jane, I mean—were looking for someone to propagate and develop their herbaceous perennials. I was newly engaged to a physical therapist at Birmingham Hospital, thinking about possibly going off to Australia or New Zealand to seek my fortune. Funny how life works," he mused, smiling at the memory. "Another half hour either way at Chelsea, and I'd have missed them entirely. But I was there when they just happened by the display, and the offer was an opportunity I hated to miss, so I drove up straightaway following the show to ask Diana what she felt about the possibility of marrying me and going off to America. I think the very idea of it must have given her a small fright. It certainly did *me*. But she was terribly brave, and we got married that next month and came to America that very same September."

As we paused to admire a row of arching peonies in bloom, David Smith added, a touch wistfully, "That was 1954. Almost fifty years ago to the day."

During the half century that followed, under Harris and Grant's clever marketing strategy and Smith's horticultural direction, of course,

White Flower Farm used advertising in high-quality publications like *The New Yorker* and *Yankee* magazine to carve out its own niche and develop a following of buyers that became, with time, utterly devoted to them. When the firm's "new and improved" plant catalog appeared in 1954, White Flower enjoyed a base mailing list of about six thousand customers. When David Smith finally retired in 1990, the firm had over a million customers on its seasonal lists; today the number is roughly 1.6 million.

Among the plant introductions Smith oversaw that today are considered standards of the American garden were various kinds of top English dahlias, Simpson's chrysanthemums, George Russell lupins, rare delphiniums and begonias from Blackmore and Langdon of Bath, white salvias, and multiple varieties of garden phlox.

"Since the late sixties, the plant introductions coming out of Japan, Holland, and Germany have been nothing less than extraordinary, most of them aimed directly at the American marketplace, feeding an insatiable appetite for something new in the garden. Now you have plants being produced by micro propagation and tissue culture and sent from every place in the world. Quite literally, science and gardening have made the world a much smaller place than when I was a lad at my grandfather's potting bench at West Dean Cottage."

"Where's West Dean?" I politely interrupted Smith's narrative—I knew I knew it from my own rambles around the Blessed Green Isle. But I couldn't somehow place it.

"Near Chichester. Splendid glass houses and one of the finest walled gardens in all England. Truly worthy of a visit if you happen to be in that neck of the woods, as you Americans like to say. The estate fell on hard times for a while, I'm afraid, but has been brought back wonderfully under a young gardener named Jim Buckland and his wife, Sarah."

I said I was planning to attend the 2004 Chelsea Flower Show and go scout up a writer named Mirabel Osler while I was at it, who lived up in Ludlow, Shropshire. This decision had firmly come to me roughly about the Garden State Parkway the afternoon before as we ambled north toward home.

"Oh *good* for you. I expect you'll enjoy Chelsea. It's very much a grand show. The social aspect can be a bit overwhelming, but the plants you'll see are ravishing. Well worth the crowds, especially if you can sneak in on member's day. This is the Royal Horticultural Society's two hundredth birthday, you know. The queen always makes an appearance."

I didn't know this, I admitted. But this seemed like one more excellent reason to cross the pond in search of one's gardening antecedents. That and real ale pubs. Meeting the queen would be a swell bonus.

After we'd toured the rest of White Flower's emerging display gardens, which included a sensational new long perennial border filled with alliums and sea hollies by Fergus Garrett, the visiting head gardener from Great Dixter in southeast England, I mentioned to Smith about the piles of winter devastation awaiting me at home, wondering if he knew any remedy for keeping English and French lavender beds alive through the cold New England winter.

"This year was perhaps the worst year we've seen in decades for winter kill. We lost all our lavenders as well. Every *one* of them! We're at twelve hundred feet elevation, on a ridge that turns frightfully cold and stays that way often straight into June."

I was secretly pleased to learn this unfortunate news, I freely admit, taking cold comfort in the fact that even the experts at White Flower Farm had been caught unawares and lost all their lavender.

"I'd suggest you think of replacing the lavender with catmint, *Nepeta sibirica*. There are some lovely pots of it already down in the garden shop. They grow very well indeed and are rather like a poor man's lavender, just as beautiful in some opinions. You might also wish to consider some of the lovely *Baptisias* or False Indigo. There are some of those down there too, I believe."

Coming from the man who helped make White Flower Farm the L.L. Bean of flower gardening, I took the man at his word.

"By the way," I said after I'd loaded several pots of each plant into the crowded back end of the truck, "are you the real Amos Pettingill?"

Smith smiled boyishly. At that moment we were standing at the long driveway where Harris and Grant first arrived on the site nearly seventy springs ago—garden rookies who became living legends. (Boston businessman Eliot Wadsworth bought the property and firm in 1977 and has faithfully maintained it.) Both sides of the lane were now jam-packed with vaulting beds of hostas, a planting scheme that was nearly identical to the front of my own poor man's White Flower Farm up at Slightly Off in the Woods. I'd never seen this entry before now, and was mildly flattered to think all mad writers and possibly crazy gardeners think alike.

"That was the name Grant came up with purely for advertising purposes—to give the place even more of a New England personality. He had a friend from up in Maine, an admiral named Pettingill. With that man's permission, he simply changed an *e* to an *i* because, as someone said, nobody had ever seen it spelled that way before. Amos was just a classic rural Yankee name. Amos Pettingill's annual letter to customers was quickly a cherished part of the story here, something that gave people a more intimate link. It caused quite a stir when, I believe, Katherine White of *The New Yorker* broke the story that he was simply a fictitious person, a name meant to suggest the owners were true-blue New Englanders from up in Maine. People still come here asking for Amos Pettingill, and probably always will."

Proof that it was a small world after all, I explained to David Smith a short time later over a cold beer at his cottage just down the road, where I got to meet his Diana as part of the bargain, that I'd once been at a dinner party on the coast near our house where a woman down from Blue Hill claimed to have "pinched" several clumps of white Italian coneflowers from Katherine White's own considerable flower beds at the saltwater farm she shared with E. B. White.

"Well that *is* a small world," Smith observed as we sat enjoying our English beers. "Did she give you some of the coneflowers? I do hope so. Perhaps they even came from here originally. Wouldn't that be a lovely irony? Gardening, I often think, is simply a great circle of like-minded people. Wouldn't surprise me in the least."

"She did," I was happy to be able to tell him. "And I'll bet they did."

*   *   *

Possibly the happiest sight of the entire trip was waiting for us as we rounded the top of our own hilltop drive a day later, loaded to the gunwales with new spring plantings.

Halfway up the hill to Slightly Off in the Woods, we heard Lynyrd Skynyrd blaring, and suddenly there he was, Pothead Eddie, two whole months ahead of his expected appearance, grinning and giving us the peace sign with one hand, holding a hand-rolled cigarette that smelled like a smoldering Persian rug with the other.

There are crazier things, I suppose, than having a blissed-out excavator construct your new spring garden beds. For all his unpredictable reliability, Eddie really was a genius at shaping the unplanted ground of a new garden—an omen I instantly took to mean it was time to start planning our "dirty" little getaway to the Chelsea Flower Show and Mother England.

Chapter 8

Diarmuid's Balls, Gentle Chaos, and the Mad Man of Kew

A<small>FTER I HOPPED OFF THE TUBE</small> a stop too soon, I found myself running late for an important interview with Ian Hodgson, a top official of the Royal Horticultural Society at the Chelsea Flower Show, a mistake I compounded when I showed up seeking entry at the wrong spot, the "members" gate at the sprawling grounds of Royal Hospital, directly opposite where I was supposed to be on the Thames Embankment.

The crowds were already vast and surging, and the gate attendant had a long unsympathetic face only a Queen Mum could have loved.

"This says *Golf Writers of America*, sir. Not *garden* writers. You'll have to go round to the Bull-Ring gate, I'm afraid. Perhaps they can sort it out for you there."

I'd presented him my official Golfer Writer's membership card in hopes that the eagle-eyed guardian of the gate (where enhanced security measures were much in evidence) might have my name on some kind of official press list. This would spare me a time-consuming hike around the show's vast and crowded periphery that would all but assure I'd miss my chat with Ian Hodgson, the editor in chief of *The Garden*, the RHS's lovely magazine. I understood from friends of Suzy Verrier that Hodgson could not only offer a valuable perspective on the world's

169

most famous flower show, but also on the mission of the Royal Horticultural Society itself upon the occasion of its bicentennial birthday party and perhaps even offer some judicious thoughts on the direction English gardening (and thus whither my faux Sissinghurst of the North) might both be headed in the fullness of time. Gardens, a famous garden writer once observed, are nothing but evolution dressed up in birthday clothes.

"True, I am a golf writer. But I'm genuinely here to conduct an important interview about gardens. I'm also in the Royal Oaks, sir, if that would help."

I spared him the philosophical speech about how a golf course is nothing but a great big garden at heart, evolved from the same wholly unnatural British mania to shape nature. I presented him with two more membership cards, identifying me as both an overseas member of the Royal Oak Society *and* the Arbor Day Foundation, hoping to appeal to his sense of national pride and press my claim for simple human pity due to being a tardy misplaced fool. Using these quasicredentials, of course, was like trying to get into the White House press office with a Red Cross donor card. I dropped Ian Hodgson's name and title several times, hoping that might magically get me through the gate. Behind me anxious show-goers were queueing up, and someone coughed impatiently. Although the May sun was gloriously spilling on the scene, I half expected to get clouted or poked with the end of an umbrella at any moment.

According to an item in that morning's *Times*, no less than fifty thousand ticket holders and two thousand media folks from Europe and America were expected to converge on the hospital grounds this day for the member's opening of London's premier social event and the ceremonial kickoff of the garden season across Britain. Somewhere in a press tent beyond those scrolled iron gates, I noted with a flagging sense of optimism, lay a press badge with my name on it, waiting to be claimed. I promised the noble guardian of the gate that I would bring it straight back and show him following my "most urgent" chat with editor Hodgson. "It's *vital* I get there," I interjected, a small desperate note creeping into my voice.

"Dodson, eh?" The attendant considered my card, massaging his long rubbery earlobe. "You wouldn't be any relation to old *Harry* Dodson, would you now?"

I hesitated only slightly. "I am, as a matter of fact."

My great-uncle Harry Dodson was known and greatly admired from one end of Alamance County, North Carolina, to the other for the high quality of his vegetable patch and personal generosity when it came to lending out his prized plowing mule. Whether this was the same Harry Dodson he meant or not is, well, a subject for debate at another time.

The attendant suddenly offered a wintry smile and presented me back my cards, shuffling aside. "Why didn't you say you were related to old Harry? He's the reason the missus and me both went keen on the dahlias, I reckon. Nice old bloke, though. On you go, sir. Enjoy your day."

I thanked him and hustled along before anyone could raise the alarm.

Forty-eight hours before, on Yellow Book Sunday, a delightful horticultural tradition America would be well served to immediately adopt, something like thirty thousand private gardens over the breadth and span of Britain simultaneously flung open their gates and welcomed five million garden fanatics to snoop around for a modest fee that goes directly to designated charities. On that Sunday, I'd ventured down to West Dean Gardens in the chalk hills of the South Downs to see the famous restored Victorian walled garden where White Flower's own David Smith's papa had been born and reared in a humble stone bothy. He later gained moderate fame doing a BBC gardener's show and I took David at his word that West Dean was a place not to be missed as part of any voyage to the Chelsea show.

Trumping my creative entry into the show grounds was the greater serendipity of having ventured to the South Downs and discovered that the married gardening impresarios, Jim Buckland and Sarah Wain, who'd meticulously brought West Dean and its celebrated Victorian glass houses back from the brink of extinction, had been initially inspired to do so following their studies at Kew. This was largely because of the popular influence of none other than one Harry James Dodson,

RHS stalwart and famous co-presenter of a legendary BBC television gardening show called *The Victorian Kitchen Garden*, which first aired in 1987. Dodson was widely considered to be the last of a breed of estate head gardeners once widely revered and treated almost like royalty in Britain. Dodson's avuncular manner and consummate skill navigating the walled garden made him nothing less than a cult figure among British television audiences. Moreover, it was my understanding from Jim and Sarah that England's most famous head gardener was still alive and kicking somewhere out in the vanishing hedgerows of the empire. I was half tempted, after collecting my wife at Heathrow Airport later that evening, to strike off down a lane to see if we could find this celebrated gardening graybeard with such a familiar name. Given my own family's considerable horticultural obsessions and the fact that our particular North State branch had been traced all the way back to a farmer who left Oxfordshire for the New World around 1760, there was even the remote possibility we were distantly related. It was fun to think so, at any rate—marginally justifying my use of gardener Harry Dodson's good name to gain a quick entry to the Chelsea Flower Show.

As prelude to "The Greatest Flower Show on Earth," as Chelsea rather immodestly hails itself, Jim and Sarah's West Dean had turned out to be a sumptuous Sunday feast of botanical precision bordering on the surreal. To begin with, I'd found Jim, a trim, dark-haired son of North London who could have been Jude Law's older brother, seated on a kitchen chair by the gardener's cottage gate, collecting two-pound coins from a stream of visitors heading into the back garden of the old bothy. Once I'd paid my fee and identified myself as the man who'd e-mailed him, dropping David Smith's name and hoping for a look around the famous walled estate, Jim had warmly invited me to proceed into the garden and introduce myself to Sarah. She was evidently running the tea shop out of the cottage garage during the afternoon that all of Britain was happily tramping through someone else's garden.

Inside Jim's back garden, I found what British gardeners call Granny's Bonnet and wild columbine blooming in torrents of blue, as well as dreamy-headed cowslips, profuse clumps of spectacular iris, and an oval centerpiece where the narcissi and tulips had just ended but the purple alliums were regally holding on for Yellow Book Sunday.

After wandering around there a bit, feeling a little intimidated by its graceful lines and clever planting schemes, I ducked around a corner of the cottage and found a small queue of elderly folks waiting to have their tea dispensed by a nice-looking, blonde-haired woman manning a table in the open garage. I assumed this was Sarah Wain and waited until she returned change to introduce myself.

"Oh, goody," she said with a husky Australian accent, "we've been expecting you. Jim's eager to show you around the property once things settle down here this afternoon. There's a strong American connection here, you know."

"Dearie," said a woman with a cup of tea, "you've given me ten pence too much."

"Have I? I'm sorry."

"Yes, you did. If this money goes to charity I do hope you are keeping a proper account of *that*."

"So sorry, ma'am," Sarah said sweetly, plucked back the offending ten pence from the lady's spidery palm, and playfully rolled her big round Australian eyes at me as the tea drinker shuffled off to join her bus mates. There were two small tour buses parked in the West Dean car park, and gray-haired folks were wandering everywhere on the premises.

"I'm a bit preoccupied for the moment here, as you can see," Sarah said. "But why don't you use one of those illustrated maps of the grounds over there and take yourself for a little walking tour? It tells a great deal about the property. You can't get too lost 'round here. We'll come find you eventually."

The truth is, I love exploring new gardens on my own with only a tour map for company. It brings out the kid in me, reminding me of the days when I used to ride my bike for hours on end along the idle sandy footpaths of Coker Arboretum, directly behind the Morehead Planetarium in Chapel Hill. Looking at the stars in the simulated heaven of the planetarium was fun, but nothing beat roaming along those footpaths through a jungle of arching exotic trees and flowering shrubs to fire the pistons of an overactive boyhood imagination shaped by the adventure fiction of Edgar Rice Burroughs and Sir Henry Rider Haggard, whose *King Solomon's Mines* took Victorian England by storm almost the same moment the first major gardening craze struck the collective fancy of Britain's lower-middle classes. Was there a connection? George Orwell evidently thought so. If the burgeoning Industrial Age that began about then robbed many Britons of their collective ability to imagine a better life, Orwell told a gathering of scholars shortly before his death, a passion for their back gardens—a touch of the wild—may have saved the nation from extinction.

I picked up a garden guide and moseyed on through a brick archway door into the manicured grounds of a *jardin Anglaise* that many feel is Britain's finest surviving walled garden. I was nearly bowled over by the immaculate rows of vegetables and cutting flowers I found there. Trained against the brick wall were the most exquisitely groomed L'espalier fruit trees I'd seen anywhere.

The original estate dates to the early 1700s, but its horticultural apogee occurred when it was purchased by the heir of an American millionaire, named Edward James. His son William built the estate's renowned thirteen glasshouses at the height of the Victorian age, which were widely hailed as a major horticultural breakthrough at the time. William used the sprawling six-thousand-acre property, bisected by the River Lavant, largely as a weekend pleasure ground for hobnobbing with the Prince of Wales and other idle Royals on a lavish scale. West Dean was staffed by twenty-two gardeners and a head gardener who wielded almost draconian authority. Its walled garden reached its zenith "in the long Edwardian afternoon when the James's were in residence," as the garden guide summed things up, "with the house a great social centre and the demands of the kitchen insatiable." Its own arboretum dated to the estate's founding and featured some of the first North American conifers ever sent abroad.

By the time David Smith's grandfather, William, had retired as West Dean's head gardener in 1934, the First World War and changing social values had largely ended the cloistered world of the British upper classes, and places like West Dean fell into steep and lengthy decline. It is interesting to note that William's own son Edward, named for the king who abdicated, was a true eccentric in the finest British tradition, not unlike his spiritual American cousins Harry Du Pont and his tree-loving papa, Algernon. Edward continued to introduce exotic trees to the estate's arboretum until he published a peculiar novel called *The Gardener Who Saw God*—which told the tale of a young gardener who goes off to the Chelsea Flower Show and has some kind of visionary experience. Then, for reasons entirely unknown, but possibly due to the fact that he was mad as a hatter, West Dean's heir spent the balance of his days wandering around jungles in Mexico, coming home to the family estate only periodically, while the home-place slipped into decline. This was a theme to which I could certainly relate.

By the middle 1960s, the James's had the good sense to set up a trust to try and save the estate. When they handed over stewardship of it to the trustees of a newly formed artisan's college, the famous walled garden was a near complete ruin, and the famed glasshouses were sitting derelict and missing much of their glass.

That all seemed a distant unhappy memory on this warm afternoon when two hundred other garden nuts and I had come calling on Yellow Book Sunday. I found the most perfect young cabbages, brussels sprouts, and other root crops growing in such mathematically precise rows they made Jefferson's Monticello veggie beds look haphazard. When I poked my curious head into the first of the magnificently engineered glasshouses I found a hundred-year-old fig tree growing there. I then spent nearly an hour walking through the houses admiring fruit trees and vegetable vines fit for a ravenous king. From there, in the throes of serious gardenlust, I stuck my head through another arched doorway like a kid in search of garden intrigue and found my way to the most extraordinary sunken garden, featuring a three-hundred-foot pergola walk gone magnificently wild with interlaced clematis, rose climbers, and honeysuckle.

After closing time, Jim Buckland was kind enough to put me in his aging Range Rover and drive me up to the remains of West Dean's arboretum on St. Roche's Hill. Back in 1987, he explained, the region (in fact, much of Britain) was struck by hurricane force winds that leveled many of its celebrated trees, including most of the North American conifers. "But the upside of the disaster was that the storm opened up the forest and permitted us to begin a program of new understory plantings that is really quite a healthy thing." Today the interlacing dirt pathways and small maintenance roads lead West Dean visitors through an enchanting woodland that features over five hundred labeled plants and a pair of surviving Handkerchief trees, the celebrated *Davidia involucrata*, that produce large billowy, pendulous white bracts in late May that really do resemble papa's hankie blowing in the breeze. "If you have to sneeze," Jim deadpanned as I admired the blooming tree, "now's the time to do it, eh?"

After we took in a sweeping view of the estate from the brow of the hill, Jim and Sarah led me to an early supper at a nearby crowded pub and filled me in on their entertaining courtship years at Kew. She came from Australia seeking her fortune, and he mistakenly thought she was German, and somehow romance found its way among the budding gardeners. Instead of going off to New Zealand to make their fortune, they wound up first bringing another estate back to life in Hampshire and then falling under the spell of Harry Dodson's kitchen garden program. In 1991 Jim came to West Dean for an interview with the estate trustees, and Sarah eventually joined him. This culminated in their greatest collaboration, the complete and stunning restoration of West Dean, a revival that, ironically, also placed them in the forefront of British horticulture.

"Jim's a bit over the top and something of a friendly tyrant about how he runs things," Sarah joked after we'd had a fine meal and a few drinks at the pub that evening. "But it took that kind of fierce dedication to bring West Dean back to what it is today. Without his obsession there's no telling what would have become of West Dean. Gardens need that kind of passion to thrive."

"If you think I'm obsessed," Jim said, with wry smile over his steak-and-kidney pie, "you should meet our old Kew mate Simon Goodenough and his wife Deb. We used to call Simon the Mad Man of Kew. He and Deb are out on the Isle of Wight with their boys. Simon's built perhaps the most unusual botanic garden in Britain and Deb's restoring Queen Victoria's personal gardens at Osborne House. You should go out there and look them up, once you get through with the royals up at Chelsea. That would definitely give you a different aspect of British gardening. Won't see anything like it at Chelsea. I promise you that."

"I'd love to," I said, thinking once again how one thing delightfully leads to another when you meet a fellow gardening nut.

"I'll even ring him up for you," Jim said, waving us another pint.

"CHELSEA IS REALLY ABOUT EXCELLENCE in plants design, the highest quality of plantsmanship and the execution of gardens. It's not only the beginning of the social season here in London but the start of a season of special gardening shows that strikes the overall tone for all that is happening in British gardening and, depending on who you talk to about the subject, at this moment there are tremendous and possibly even revolutionary changes going on," observed Ian Hodgson, editor in chief of *The Garden*. We were seated together on a handsome stone wall, watching impossibly long double queues of patient flower show patrons shuffling along elevated observation walkways past the 2004 show's leading display gardens. The crowds were immense.

"Ten or fifteen years ago, quite frankly, Gertrude Jekyll still ruled the roost, and British gardening was largely about the herbaceous border and planting white gardens and so forth. It was all about Sissinghurst and the traditional color planting scheme—the conformity and order of Victorian gardens. The RHS itself reflected this sensibility to a large extent—a learned but rather elite society that tended to be rather reticent about reaching out to the broader gardening public. Fortunately a kind of grassroots revolution occurred that ultimately transformed the RHS into an organization that was far more inclusive and broader minded in scope and outreach, a great deal more accessible to people of all sorts who'd fallen in love with their gardens."

"What brought about this change—this so-called people's revolution?" I asked the friendly editor. I was watching an elegantly dressed gray-haired woman and a much younger woman with an infant in a pram—both wearing impressive hats and dressed as if for a day at Ascot—progressing at a snail's pace in the "slow" queue, the line that permitted patrons the closest access and most intimate view of the twelve or thirteen major display gardens of the show. In the twenty or so minutes Hodgson and I had been sitting on the wall chatting about what a mad race of gardeners Britons truly are and why, the dapper grandmother and her heirs had progressed no more than ten feet, while behind them an unshaven guy, who looked as if he might be spending the weekend watching Manchester United on the telly, exhibited an equal patience with the tedious pace of viewing. He was busy reading the official show program and making notes on gardens as they neared his point of inspection, seeming to illustrate editor Hodgson's claim that gardening's appeal is a much broader affair these days in Britain.

"In a word, gardens on television are responsible for this healthy trend. It began, I think, back in the late eighties when Harry Dodson revitalized popular interest in kitchen gardens. Now you have gardening programs that are a regular feature and gardeners who come into people's homes two or three times a week and are regarded as pop stars. Traditional head gardeners like Dodson were greatly revered figures in the old British social system, but these new TV gardeners are celebrities of the first rank, stars of the common man. The coverage of Chelsea alone will run many hours each evening on television.

"Americans, I daresay even most American gardeners I know, cannot quite fathom the huge popularity of gardening shows on television in this country, nor really perhaps appreciate the major positive impact gardening programs are having on the public at large. They're all over the airways here at the moment, influencing and inspiring ordinary people to venture out into their gardens and try new things—to strike off and follow their own creative devices. Some of the shows get a little gossipy and dramatic at times. All in good fun, of course. The pomp. The ceremony. The backbiting."

I knew exactly what Hodgson was talking about. During the two nights I'd been in London I'd thoroughly enjoyed the BBC's lively three-hour summary coverage of the show each evening, a blanket coverage that was highlighted this year by a delightfully bitchy public spat between two of the show's leading designers, a six-time Gold Medal winner and design traditionalist named Bunny Guinness and an upstart, swaggering, blue-tongued Irishman named Diarmuid Gavin, whose outrageous display garden featured thousands of brightly colored plastic balls attached to tall steel rods—he called them "lollipops"—and a giant blimp-like pod covered by several thousand small plastic lottery balls, which had all of proper Chelsea buzzing.

According to London's daily tabloids, their botanical blood feud was growing nastier by the Greenwich mean time minute, revealing the social animosity that animates and underscores most of British social life. Guinness's display garden was a classic, understated celebration of the tradition-laden Oxford-Cambridge boat race whereas Gavin's creation was an avant-garde assault on conventional garden logic. Much to the apparent delight of the press, the two celebrity gardeners had been assigned spaces directly next to each other, their respective gardens and egos separated only by a concrete wall of moderate size and insufficient height. Thus far in the running saga of their feud, Diarmuid's antics and artistic tantrums had thoroughly alienated many powerful RHS officials and even caused his original sponsors to bolt. Bunny Guinness's loyalists meanwhile kept up the stream of class warfare by noting his blithe indifference to long-accepted rules of competition. "TV Gardener falls from grace over show rules and his own little Eden," went the headline in the *The Times*.

"Diarmuid Gavin may be the bad boy of British gardening," cooed Emine Saner in *The Evening Standard*, "but old ladies love him."

In last evening's televised installment of this delightful Cheslea cattiness, Guinness, a regular presenter on *Gardeners' Question Time*, had complained to show authorities that "Diarmuid's balls" were too visible over her garden wall, a violation of the show's very clear height restrictions, she maintained, and therefore a violation of the spirit and letter of

Chelsea competition. Her first salvo weeks ago had been to label her competitor's creation "a nasty piece of work." "Bullocks," Gavin fired back, then accused her of "setting him up" for an ambush interview on Radio 4 and of having her own elitest university boats too visible from his "thoughtful pod garden," adding, "mine will move things forward and challenge people who see it. If we get the plantings right it's going to scare the hell out of every other gardener at Chelsea this year." A front-page headline in the *Sun* cried, "Snobbery in the Shrubs," after Bunny Guinness was invited to give her impressions of Diarmuid's "balls" on BBC 2 and said with a final plummy laugh, "His is more like a place I would take my children to play with their spongy balls. I like a garden to be a space one loves being in. It is rather a nice amusement area, however."

Meanwhile, according to *The Guardian*'s James Meek, the real battle royal was quietly going on inside the Great Pavilion hall where four *pelargonium* growers were determined to leave the hospital grounds with gold medals of their own. "Ask a *pelargonium* grower what a *pelargonium* is," he wrote, "and they tend to get a bit excited. The import of their reply is that whatever a *pelargonium* is, it isn't a geranium (just to confuse things the American word for *pelargonium is* "geranium"). How do you tell the difference? The simplest method seems to be to put the plant in question outside on a frosty evening and go to bed. If, when you wake up, the plant is dying, it is a *pelargonium*. They originate from South Africa and don't like the cold."

On it went, and so would I shortly—straight past the monstrously mobbed display gardens where both Gavin and Guinness were busy holding court and fanning the flames of controversy and into the Great Pavilion, where most of Britain's most celebrated private growers were assembled. I was anxious to look up my old friend David Austin and find a good daffodil expert to give me some insight on whether my winter-stunted daffodil beds (which mysteriously grew a few inches but failed to bloom) would come up again next year, as they had for well over a decade.

"So where is all this welcome gardening democracy taking us?" I put it straight to Ian Hodgson. He smiled, as if he hoped I might ask him this question.

"Have no idea, truthfully. But there are several fascinating trends taking root almost simultaneously that bode rather well, it seems to me, for gardening in my country and yours. They include a general shift away from regimented gardening toward far more naturalistic land-scapes and a great deal more attention being paid to recycling and sustainable gardening. You see this in the much wider use of ornamental grasses, popularized by the Dutch and German designers—they're *everywhere* these days. Creating gardens for wildlife habitat is also much in vogue right now. I'm happy to report there is even a move to recover our endangered hedges and beloved old forests that were vanishing quickly to advancing development until very recent times. So, in a sense, we're recovering much of what was traditionally loved here and pressing forth in exciting new directions as well.

"Gardening is as much about art as it is science, that's clearly the message most people are getting nowadays," the editor added as he escorted me to the end of the "fast" queue so I might take a peek at the show's major garden displays before I vanished into the Great Pavilion. Only 160,000 tickets are sold to the Chelsea event annually, and mine was only a single-day press badge that entitled me to roam pretty much wherever I pleased, so there wasn't a lot of time to waste. Nor room to maneuver, given the massive crowds packed into the grounds. One quick look at the display gardens was probably all I was going to get that day. A regular Chelsea goer I met in Philadelphia advised me to save most of my time for snooping about in the Great Pavilion.

Somewhere I'd read that when the RHS began limiting ticket sales and actually charging members admission back in the late 1980s, upward of ten thousand members resigned from the society in protest. Emerging from the Sloane Street Tube station just after ten o'clock that morning, I'd not only been confronted by pretty young women handing out stems of white Italian sunflowers to patrons heading to the show, but also been assaulted by several chaps scalping tickets to Britain's biggest outdoor social event. The going street price was thirty quid per ticket. What simple social mayhem over flowers, I thought—far zanier than anything I'd encountered back in Philadelphia.

"Why are the British the most ardent gardeners on earth?" I asked Ian Hodgson seconds before we parted. As it happened, we were positioned to see the vast crowds gathered around Diarmuid Gavin, who appeared to be waving his arms and happily venting like an angry anarchist at Speaker's Corner. It suddenly struck me that perhaps Diarmuid Gavin was exactly that, a gardening anarchist, symbolized by the act of showing his balls to Bunny Guinness and sticking one in the face of the traditional gardening establishment. There *did* seem to be an abundance of gray-haired ladies thoroughly enjoying his good Irish rant, however.

"Well, to begin with, we're a small nation with a marvelous climate for growing almost anything. Because of our small size and rich heritage, however, I believe we're naturally competitive about what we are able to grow and how well it can be grown. Something in the British character wants to show off. British plantsmen, as you well know, played a dominant role in finding exotic plants the world over and introducing them to gardeners everywhere. That was part of the colonial way of thinking, and it's still going on today, of course, only now we're exporting new plants and exciting ideas to you, and you are sending revolutionary plants and ideas back to us. The world has shrunk but there are still wild places. What's going on in California and much of the American Southwest, for example, is pretty exciting stuff. You're sending a whole new way of looking at gardens back to us. A very *exciting* time to be a gardener."

"So it's gone far beyond Sissinghurst," I said, thinking of my own landscape ambitions, wondering if I'd already fallen behind the times.

He smiled graciously. "Oh far beyond that, I'm afraid. Whole continents."

Hodgson urged me to enjoy the show; we shook hands, and I joined the quicker moving queue, falling in behind a handsome young and upwardly mobile couple bearing expensive digital cameras. I thought about how California might indeed be the "*new* England of cutting-edge gardening," as I'd heard some well-traveled BBC commentator assert on Radio 2 while driving up from West Dean, but dear old England still had—and always would hold—my gardening heart.

THE CHELSEA FLOWER SHOW BEGAN with somewhat perilous timing in the spring of 1913, a three-day event sponsored by the Royal Horticultural Society that featured a three-hundred-foot tent; eighty-four groups of flowers, plants, and shrubs; seventeen large rock or formal display gardens; and three hundred exhibits mounted by growers and nurserymen from across the nation. Royalty toured the hospital grounds on the opening day of the show. Among the famous plants first displayed there were several new varieties of rhododendron from China and North America, plus begonias from David Smith's friends at Blackmore and Langdon. Gate receipts from "overflowing" crowds totaled 2,150 pounds sterling.

During the Great War that soon followed, the popular event was nearly canceled and only survived at the urging and financial support of of Lord Balfour, a radically scaled-back affair that featured no exhibition tents. Alcoholic beverages were not permitted on the show grounds; the band favored Gilbert and Sullivan and Elgar over traditional beer garden German melodies; only a single display garden was available for public view; and the rather subdued theme was "Hardy Flowers for Wartime." Queen Mary, who was famous for turning out in any kind of weather, and her princess daughter came on Tuesday of show week and only a modest crowd followed. Chelsea was then suspended for two years. It closed again in 1940 due to World War II and stayed shut until 1946.

The show's resumption, according to at least one somewhat breathless British historian, marked "a much-needed revival of Britain's national spirit of optimism and visible determination to survive and prevail over adversity, as manifest in the glories of its gardens." Sir Winston Churchill, the prime minister, publicly urged the RHS to resume its annual spring extravaganza for the mental well-being of the beleaguered war-torn nation. Those who turned out to welcome Chelsea back in May 1947 paid ten shillings to be serenaded by the band of the Grenadier Guards playing Waldteufel's *Christmas Roses*.

Four years later, the RHS proudly announced the show would boast the largest marquee canvas tent in the world, covering nearly three and a half acres of the hospital's grounds. For Elizabeth's coronation two years later, the Royal Botanic Gardens at Kew pulled out the stops, built a lavish English woodland glade, and mounted the largest display of exotic plants from distant lands ever seen anywhere. The 1959 show featured a radio-controlled lawn mower you guided from a lawn chair, electric bird scarers, and the kind of in-ground watering devices that largely came about due to engineers developing advanced irrigation systems for American golf courses.

From my colonial perspective and remembering what David Smith had said at White Flower Farm, I found the Chelsea Flower Show to be perhaps a bit *too* social and over the top. I did rather like a special display garden mounted by the city of Leeds in conjunction with its sister city in Durban, South Africa, featuring a host of magnificent native heathers and ericas from that far-flung semitropical corner of the globe paired with the artwork of schoolchildren from both places. I was also greatly pleased to finally reach the scene of the show's biggest flap— Diarmuid's balls versus Bunny's boats—and discover that both competitors had been awarded silver-gilt medals for all their fuss and bother. Neither had won; both had been judged only second best.

For the next three hours inside the Great Pavilion—the scale of which was less in size, but no less awe-inspiring in its own manner than Philadelphia—I wandered blissfully from one spectacular grower's exhibit to the next. To begin with, I went straight to see the delphinium dynasty of Blackmore and Langdon, David Smith's former employer, which had shown at Chelsea since the show was held over at London's Temple grounds in 1903, and was admiring the most dazzling array of delphinium varieties I'd ever seen when I happened to fall into a conversation with an independent garden designer named Edith who hailed from Berkshire. She asked me about my own garden in Maine and in very short order conducted a full-scale inquiry to see if her professional expertise could possibly be of use.

"Tell me about your property and overall garden schemes," she demanded, sounding a little like "M" in the James Bond films. The woman clearly had the natural gift of command.

So I gave her a quick rundown that included my new Philosopher's Garden that Pothead Eddie had helped me create, a Roman rose pergola I'd also just finished building on the elevated terrace just outside my barn office, and an ambitious new Japanese side garden that was still in the early construction stages, just off our kitchen deck. During the six weeks between the world's two premier flower shows, I'd worn myself out planting these various new beds with English roses, river birches, and lots of hardy expensive shrubs.

I'd even found time to start a new southern arboretum between the rear south-facing porches of my house, filling that space with the Daylily Kings's celebrated *Hemerocallis* treasures, a trio of young tulip magnolia trees, a Carolina silver bell, and Suzy Verrier's elegant northern redbuds.

"It sounds terribly ambitious," said Edith the designer. "What sort of staff do you keep?"

I explained that I *kept* only two garden assistants. Both were essentially useless. One peed on the lawn, and the other was such a hose Nazi that I couldn't water plants without him sticking his big fat mug into the flow. Typically, more water got on Riley than got on my plants.

"They're dogs," I quickly amplified. "Golden retrievers."

"Dogs are impossible in a garden," Edith said distastefully. "You may need to limit their range or consider getting rid of them entirely." A bit worryingly, she was now writing something on a notepad she'd taken from her big canvas bag. Forget "M," I thought. She's the Lady Thatcher of British gardening.

"If I may ask, what sort of fertilizing schedule do you keep?"

"Lawn or flowers?"

She frowned. "Flowers, of course. You *must* have a regular fertilizing scheme. Surely you *fertilize*."

"I do. Occasionally. When I can remember to."

This didn't sit well with the Berkshire designer. Before I had a chance to explain to her how we were aiming to become far more organic and far less dependent on conventional chemical commercial fertilizers, even permitting larger areas of our landscape to go "native" with each passing season—a poor man's Great Dixter, if you like—she ripped off a page from her little notepad and snapped it shut. She presented me with a piece of paper upon which there was a list of traditional English perennials she felt might find a reasonable home in Maine. Most of them I already had. But I didn't dare tell her that.

"Keeping your garden properly fertilized is *essential*, young man. How would *you* like it if someone only fed you periodically? I daresay you wouldn't fancy that one bit, would you? Quite obviously, you've *much* to learn about gardening."

And with that, she hitched up her canvas carryall and set off to see a man about tea roses. As I watched her go, I realized it was impossible to disagree with Edith's verdict. I did have a great deal to learn about gardening. On the other hand, I suddenly thought I knew a little about how bad boy Diarmuid Gavin might be feeling at this moment, as he was attacked by the old guard of Chelsea.

I wanted to see a man about roses, too, but after spending the next two hours going from one incredible horticultural display to the next in the vast exhibition hall, I was disappointed when I worked my way entirely around the building and found that David Austin had been present at the show's Monday opening gala and press preview (when the queen herself came out), but hadn't yet returned to the grounds this day. By this point it was late in the afternoon, and the young woman who gave me this news offered a glossy thick Austin catalog by way of consolation.

"He'll be so sorry he missed you," she said after I explained how I'd met Austin fifteen years ago in Shropshire and thoroughly enjoyed my day at his farm and greenhouses, learning how he'd revolutionized English roses by crossbreeding them with hardy shrub species. Nice to see a man make a fortune from something he loves doing and would probably do so even if he wasn't paid to do it.

"Haven't you been back since?"

"No," I said as I flipped through the beautiful pages of the lushly illustrated catalog. Several Austin varieties had just gone into my Roman pergola garden. The trick was to see if they could handle what Maine would eventually dish out to them.

"Oh, it's entirely different there now. You must come back and see for yourself. We have a major learning center and research facility there now, and people come by the thousands each year."

"Business must be good in rural Shropshire."

"Simply brilliant. We can scarcely keep up with the demand."

For all the perfect eye-popping displays of alliums, daffodils, hydrangeas, and other all-time favorite flowers of mine, including the battling *pelargoniums*, I couldn't help feeling a little let down by the Chelsea Flower Show—but was hard-pressed to figure out exactly why. People were perfectly nice; the flowers were at their glorious peak of bloom. The lush floral and horticultural displays, as they say, were to die for. But something was missing. Maybe it was all the fancy hats and the frenzy over celebrity gardeners, and the feeling that nothing was quite as "real" as it appeared. The only thing I had to base an inevitable comparison on, of course, was the Philadelphia Flower Show, which I suddenly realized was like comparing roses to cacti.

Philly was gardening theater on a monumental scale, a grand unnatural, natural illusion—as Jack Blandy had accurately described it—made fun and accessible at the end of the day by the working mission of the PHS to inspire and elevate thousands of ordinary gardeners who flocked to the grandmother of indoor gardening shows each spring, bearing their cherished houseplants and best hopes of securing a simple prize ribbon.

Chelsea, by contrast—as the debonair cycad man had told me, with the faintest whiff of old boy condescension—was indeed very much a beautiful "show" of perfect flowers and colorful figures, all vying for the attentions of the press, and by extension a garden-savvy nation. It was also conducted out-of-doors, always a plus, which on a radiant May day like this one made the affair look and feel all the more like a big birthday celebration for the queen.

On the way out of the grounds, I considered briefly having another crack at the display gardens in the "fast" queue to see if my first impressions might be revised, but saw the line was as lengthy as ever. I decided to go the opposite way instead, heading quickly toward the exit at the gate where I'd been admitted under dubious family connections to head gardener Harry Dodson. It was the beginning of London rush hour, and I had a fairly tight schedule to keep, involving a Tube ride out to Heathrow to meet Wendy's arriving flight, followed by a return to Leicester Square and a dinner rendezvous with friends.

As I hoofed along toward the London Gate, pondering my gardening mate's happy arrival, a man standing in a bucket of water motioned me over. I was passing through the crowded marketplace section of the Chelsea show where vendors and merchants sold seeds and garden geegaws of every imaginable kind to departing and arriving showgoers. He was dressed in a handsome linen blazer and ascot, holding a flute of champagne and entertaining a group of folks. I couldn't begin to guess what he was selling. Moments before, I'd just purchased a lovely, slim, handmade English garden shovel, beautifully made and no longer than my arm, something to replace my old one with and remember beautiful showy Chelsea by. I'd always wanted one just like it for transplanting hostas.

"By the time this show concludes on Friday," said the man in the bucket like an upper-crust rake from a Noel Coward play, "these boots and I shall *both* be in the bucket, I fear. But only *they* will show no wear for the worse." The crowd tittered. That's when I realized he was selling gardening boots. Very expensive-looking, handmade Irish gardening boots.

"I have the ideal complement to your lovely gardening spade," he declared, suddenly looking at me and then pointing theatrically down at his beautiful boots. Something about the man suddenly rang a bell. He did seem a wee bit tipsy and it occurred to me that if my job had been to stand there all day in a bucket of water drinking champagne I might have been worse off than him, barely able to stand at all.

"So how much are they?" I had no interest in Irish gardening boots, of course. But half the fun of having involuntary gardenlust is finding out there's no way on God's green earth you'd ever shell out that kind of dough for a pair of boots you'd soon ruin by hiking through mud and manure. After my chat with editor Hodgson, I'd paused by the Hartley Botanic display, makers of the world's finest glasshouses and conservatories, and indulged in a harmless little fantasy of purchasing one of their spectacular greenhouses. The model I fancied was a mere eighty thousand pounds, placing it right up there with my fully-loaded mini-Bobcat tractor from the Portland Flower Show.

"Two hundred eight pounds," said the man in a tone that suggested if you had to ask such an embarrassing question, then you weren't really serious about owning handmade Irish gardening boots.

"That includes the shipping, of course."

"Thanks. They look great. But I'd just get them dirty."

He shrugged. "I promise you won't find a better price on luxury handmade Irish boots. These are the Cadillac of gardening boots."

That's when it hit me who he was: a dead ringer for the tuxedoed smoothie I'd met at the Philadelphia preview gala, the condescending cycad man himself, the botanical James Bond who tried to match me up with a priceless "living fossil" for my office.

"Say, weren't you at the Philadelphia Flower Show?" I asked pleasantly. The word *Cadillac* had done it.

The man sipped his champagne and gave a small pained smile.

"Can't say I have had that pleasure. You must have me confused with someone."

"I could swear you tried to sell me a cycad. I think I still have your business card somewhere."

"Sorry, dear boy."

I studied his florid handsome face for a moment, wondering if I'd lost my mind. "You were dead right about Chelsea," I said, in case it might be him after all. "It is far more of a show than Philadelphia. Roses to cacti. But I'm glad I saw it anyway."

"How lovely for you."

And with that he turned in his bucket to chat with an older German man who did seem very interested in buying handmade Irish gardening boots, regardless of the asking price, prompting me to hurry on my way.

THE NEXT NIGHT at a lively pub up in Ludlow, I was telling Wendy about the design brilliance of English roadside hedges—nature's guard-rails—when a middle-aged woman seated next to me on the cushioned bench at the Charleton Arms leaned over and said, above her hovering sherry glass, "Pardon the intrusion but did I hear you say you fancy old forests and yew hedges?"

"I'm sorry. Was I speaking too loudly?"

"Not at all. I know where there is a perfectly lovely one if you're in-terested. Most unusual specimen. I promise you that."

She was dressed as if for an insurance board meeting and inched closer to me on the bench seat. "Helen Thurling's the name," she said, offering a slim hand. I learned she was a local estate agent off the clock, waiting to meet her husband Ted for supper.

"You see, I'm simply mad for preserving yews and old forests and my ears pricked straight up when I heard what you two were discussing. Are you both here on holiday?"

"We're here to take Mirabel Osler to lunch tomorrow," I explained.

"The garden writer?"

"That's the one. She lives near the castle. She's agreed to show us her back garden and then let us take her to her favorite restaurant. I under-stand it has a Michelin star. The restaurant, I mean."

Even after Ted arrived, Helen and I continued chatting about Britain's efforts to preserve old growth forests and restore its vanishing hedgerows. At one point before she concentrated on her own arriving shrimp scampi starter, she told me about nearby Wenlock Forest, a spectacular unspoiled woodland where the trees resembled "creatures from a children's fairy tale."

"I can give you driving directions there too, if you like," she added most graciously. "Sometimes I just go there and wander around pretending to be a little one again."

"I THINK AMONG THE MOST VALUABLE THINGS a garden does for the human soul is makes us feel connected to the past and therefore each other," reflected Mirabel Osler. "We're all old souls, you know. People who love plants."

We were eating again, this time there were three of us. We were seated at Hibiscus, one of Ludlow's posh new Michelin-starred restaurants just below the High Street. That morning Wendy and I had wandered out the A49 into the "blue remembered hills" poet A. E. Housman immortalized. Later we located—actually, rounded a curve a bit too fast and nearly collided with—Helen Thurling's remarkable yew hedge. It was, as advertised, a monster of the species, a truly heroic specimen, swarming like a horticultural tsunami wave over a brick estate wall that followed the winding road and going on for another two hundred meters in the rough direction of Wales. After snapping photographs of the brute, we turned the little Renault around, headed back in the direction of Ludlow, and found our way through the famed Broad Gate and along a narrow busy market street to a small park and cozy town house where Osler has lived and gardened since giving up the beloved small farm she and her late husband Michael transformed in the hills just outside town into a garden spot celebrated in her classic book, *A Gentle Plea For Chaos*. Suzy Verrier had first turned me on to Osler's book, purportedly her favorite garden read of all time. Having read it twice myself, I was not only fully prepared to agree but eager to meet the author and pick her brain on one's natural urge to garden.

When *Gentle Chaos* appeared without much fanfare in 1989, it received wonderful reviews and only modest sales but kept on selling largely by word of mouth among true disciples of fine garden writing. Many today considered it a model of narrative garden writing, and the slim book had recently been reissued in a new trade paperback edition.

When I asked Mirabel on her doorstep, as we were setting off for Hibiscus, how many printings the influential little book had been through, she shook her elegantly chiseled head and sighed, "Have absolutely no idea. Truth be told, I really don't care to know, either. It just pleases me when people remember it."

"How did you come to write it?" Wendy asked. If most good gardens all had a fascinating human tale behind them, so did all great garden tales.

"It was almost an accident of heaven, a pure act of love and it came while I was looking the other way," Mirabel said. "I often think the best things in life come like that. The best things come when you're just busy . . . living."

She and Michael, a retired foreign service officer, were living and gardening at their eight-acre farm just outside town, when friends invited them to France for a weekend. "The manor house was owned by Eve Auchincloss, a lovely lady who was editor of *Connoisseur* magazine. Michael and I took various interesting plants from our farm over to her house—clematis, roses, a few things like that—and eventually I began writing Eve long letters to describe what kinds of things we were taking over and planting there in her absence. In France at that time, you see, there weren't any nurseries around, nothing like we have in this country.

"So, quite innocently, I wrote to her and she wrote me back proposing the mad idea that I do an article for her magazine about the garden I was making for her in France. Couldn't *possibly*, I wrote her back straightaway. I'd only written *letters* to friends up till then, after all." Mirabel gave a charming shudder and small smile. I judged the reluctant author to be a well-traveled woman in her late seventies.

"Eve persisted, and I resisted, so we did a brief minuet for a time, lasting nearly two years, as I recall. Then she sent me some beautiful pictures of a garden someone had made in Scotland and wondered if I might be willing to go up and see it and write about it for her magazine. Most reluctantly, with fear and trepidation, I finally gave in."

She smiled, sipping the house Merlot. "That's where it started. Before I realized it, I was working on a little book about my own garden. It is so frightening to try and make sense of your own world—particularly the world on your doorstep. You wonder if you don't sound utterly banal or silly or simply irrelevent revealing your most intimate thoughts on a subject that's very important to you. There's a sheer terror, isn't there, that nobody could possibly care about the things you do?"

"Absolutely," I agreed, admitting I felt a trapdoor open beneath me every time I set out to write a book, particularly if it concerned a subject that I cared deeply about. Making a book is not so different in this way, I added, than making a garden or raising a child. You start out with a load of good intentions and ideas and natural optimism but slowly discard one thing for another as some things fail to work out the way you hoped they might. In the end, there's no telling what you're likely to create. A suspended disbelief or something more akin to an ongoing faith is required to grow anything—garden, book, or child.

"That's the point of taking the adventure, isn't it?" she declared with feeling. "To feel yourself transformed by the experience and permit yourself to overcome the fears and simply follow wherever it's supposed to lead you! That's ultimately why I agreed to go up to Scotland and see that garden and write about it for my friend Eve. I couldn't have imagined *Gentle Plea* coming from out of that in my wildest thoughts, yet all of the feelings I had were there from a lifetime of battling with and loving various gardens." She took a swallow of her wine and added thoughtfully, "Once I got started I realized I needed to get a few things off my chest, as you Americans say, to state a few tempered opinions I didn't hear too many garden writers express." She smiled again and shook her head. "I had no idea if anyone would want to hear my silly opinions or not."

Drawing on her own experiences transforming an old farm into a garden, Osler's little book is ostensibly a collection of personal meditations expressing the author's gentle but firmly held opinions on everything from the enchantment found in trees to the intransigence of roses. Along the way she praises the generosity of fellow gardeners who are wise enough to let a garden "have its own head"; denounces the fickleness of weather and the rampant pettifoggery of so-called gardening experts; vents on the lovely tyranny of having birds in the garden; confesses to forgetting formal plant names; lauds the incalculable value of making mistakes; muses on the values of stone walls and flowing stream-

beds; advocates a sense of ever-expanding adventure and the act of perpetually shifting plants about in an effort to find the proper natural effect; and sweetly takes issue with gardening rigidity of any sort.

Her "gentle plea" for a little less regimentation and snobbery in the
garden, a little more fun and amazement at nature's divine unpre-
dictability, is told with wit, candor, and a refreshing tone of discovery
that made the little book, in my view, a treasure—something every gardener starting out should be required to read to inform them that the
journey is vastly more important than the arrival.

"How did we begin our garden?" The accidental gardening writer
admits candidly and charming near the beginning of her testimony:

> *I don't know, it wasn't deliberated. My husband Michael and I knew
> nothing, and anyway we wanted freedom to travel. Yet our very
> landscape coerced us. With one and a half acres of undulating land, a
> winding stream, stone buildings and old orchard trees, how could we
> have resisted the temptation? We didn't of course. One bulb put into
> the ground inadvertently, two or three trees planted here or there,
> we were hooked. By slow infiltration our garden began.*

And this:

> *Sometimes I wonder if gardeners like gardening. Really. I don't mean
> my sort, but the real gardeners, the dedicated ones. The seedsman,
> the propagator, the plantsman or -woman. Do they like it or is there
> somewhere a kind of perverted satisfaction that comes from doing so
> much that is hateful. Because surely, if you are truthful, a great num-
> ber of gardening jobs are pure slog.*

On the touchy subject of lawns, so near and dear to my own redneck
heart:

> *Why do experts go on so about lawns? Why all that time over the air
> or in print on the minutiae of worm casts and moss? What is the spell*

and fascination of spending such a disproportionate amount of time on this one gardening subject when so many others have more allure. Personally I equate lawns with washing up. You needn't be told twice.

The ideal garden, Osler advocates, "slips away" and blends almost indecipherably with the surrounding landscape.

Let's accept random seedling, let's accept small flowers like grace notes decorating the pavement. The corrosive vice of trimness invades everywhere. Formality is pleasing in parks, imperative at Versailles, and restful in courtyards, but why not let country churchyards be sanctuaries for wildflowers? . . . Sometime soon we must reinstate our country churchyards and country gardens before it's too late.

"Every person loves a garden for entirely different reasons, quite often for the most personal of reasons as well," Mirabel observed over lunch. "I'm always fascinated to learn what makes someone take up the gardening life. What is it the garden gives you?" she asked, looking first at Wendy and then at me. Once again, I had an inconvenient mouthful of food.

Wendy spoke up. "He loves to get filthy dirty. I know spring has come every year when I see a bush or tree go past the kitchen window. That's just Jim moving something around the yard, getting as dirty as a kid with his construction trucks."

Both women looked at me. I was enjoying a delicious morel, trying to think of what to say. Frankly I hadn't expected my subject to turn the tables so adroitly on me. But then again, having read her plea, I should have known there was a wild streak of curiosity in the woman.

I could have said I hoped someday to have my woodland garden invited to join the local garden tour; I could have said it was great when the FedEx guy looked around the property and commented how great the place was looking after all these years. I might even have said that making a garden felt a little like playing God—creating an Eden future generations might enjoy.

Instead I said, "I'm constantly surprised at how much I'm able to do, but how little I actually know." I told her about Edith, the hard-nosed designer dreadnought at Chelsea, who bluntly stated the obvious in this regard. "I'm a rank beginner and probably always will be."

"That's because you're a gardener of the heart, not the head. Tell me, what did you make of Chelsea?"

I told her it was fun, but not half as much fun as snooping around somebody's real live garden, including out-of-fashion Sissinghurst. All this talk of trends and movements basically left me feeling a little edgy, anxious to bolt for the cover of the woods, I said. I guess that was because I basically gardened by the seat of my muddy pants.

"I used to adore going to Chelsea," Mirabel Osler said with a small sigh.

"That was when when they all wore hats. Fantastic hats. I loved Chelsea then. I was writing and researching my French garden book. Then somehow, Chelsea became so commercial, so focused around the celebrity of a few rather noisy gardeners instead of the glorious plants. I began to find that so off-putting. I'm told, however, that the Pavilion remains truly exquisite. Perhaps I should venture back sometime before I die. Is that true?"

I agreed the Great Pavilion was the clear highlight for me, although my disappointment at being unable to hook up with her Shropshire neighbor David Austin was really the only one I had during my big day near the spot of the ancient Chelsea Physic Garden that provided John Bartram such a lofty calling back in the wilds of the New World two and a half centuries ago. I was beginning to see how connected everything in the garden world really is—including our debts to the past.

"Your front garden looks wonderful," Wendy chipped in toward the end of lunch, confessing how we'd actually loitered on her doorstep for several minutes before knocking simply to admire a pair of tall and elegant Italian cypresses that turned out to be Irish yews Mirabel had creatively wired up to grow in a habit that merely *resem-*

bled their Mediterranean cousins. I took a photograph of the gently chaotic entryway, thinking I might dispatch it to Jim and Jean Francis for future inspiration if they ever wound up in the entryway category again at Philadelphia.

"Very well, then. Let's go have a look at *my* back garden," Mirabel proposed. "It's a bit of a tangle at the present. You'll either like it or hate it," she added, fixing me with a glance, "because most men dearly *crave* order in a garden. That's natural male instinct for control and order, you see—the reason all those famous Victorian gardeners were men who ruthlessly attacked their lawns. If that's the case, I'm afraid you're in for trouble. You'll perhaps think I've made a living horror."

SHE NEEDN'T HAVE WORRIED her fine aristocratic head. Mirabel Osler's narrow back garden, a walled affair measuring roughly twenty by forty feet, was a veritable jungle of plants delightfully having their own head and a magnificent wisteria vine thick as a man's arm scaling up the wall and over the roof. The boughs of spectacular trees arched over a narrow path bordered by butterfly bushes and wild roses and scores of flowering shrubs that appeared to have grown into each other creating an impression of Eden reclaiming its own, leading to an arched gate that led into another section of garden that looked equally untamed and irresistible. It was England gone wild in miniature.

"When I started this garden fifteen years ago, not long after Michael died and I gave up the farm, I pulled up the lawn that was here and put down bark. Next came the trees—twenty-eight of them—and the other plants." She saw me admiring the rear gate and the unexpected *second* back garden and laughed. "That's a mirror in the gate, by the way. It doesn't lead anywhere, you see, pure illusion, placed there for the amusement of my grandchildren, an old trick from early times. The Romans were terribly clever at such things. As this particular garden runs south and east, the mirror collects the sunlight and disperses it through the shadowed areas of the garden. The effect can be quite dramatic."

"Not very British, rather un-Chelsea," I said, once again thinking that if Ian Hodgson was correct in thinking the traditional herbaceous border was dead, the British gardening establishment might only now be catching up with this marvelous grandame of chaos. In an ideal world I would have been able to introduce Mirabel to her Bay State counterpart Polly Logan and just sit back like a fly on the garden wall and listen to the two of them express their colorful opinions on the state of anything. If Polly would have made a fine first lady president, Mirabel Osler would have been an outstanding second lady prime minister. Her frankness about the state of English gardening confirmed the hunch.

"My argument at the Ludlow festival a few years ago was that traditional English gardens are polluting the world! It created quite a row of controversy but my point was this: Why must we settle for a strip of lawn with matching color coordinated borders of flowers! That's so lifeless and unnatural, the complete antithesis of man integrating with the beauty of the natural world around him! So plant the garden and please permit it to *grow*! I'd had it up to here with English gardens so I went over to California a few years ago to talk to some garden groups and the first thing they took me to see was an *English* garden! After that I simply refused to go anywhere there was an English garden someone might drag me off to see."

She made this gentle complaint as the three of us sat in her garden waiting for her kettle to boil so she could serve us a tea before sending us on our way. We planned to make a side trip through Wenlock Edge that afternoon and then drive to Southampton for an early morning ferry to the Isle of Wight. There Jim Buckland's former Kew pal Simon Goodenough had promised to show us around a municipal botanic garden some claimed was the most unusual in all Britain. That seemed like the perfect spot to conclude another fruitful garden ramble through the British countryside.

During our final few minutes together, Mirabel let on that she was debating whether or not she had the physical stamina to accept several requests to come to the United States and speak to gardening groups. If her little book is still treasured by those fortunate "old" souls lucky enough to have it placed in their hands, so are her talks about traveling through other people's gardens. "I'm thinking I may go," she let on rather impishly, "if only to see an authentic redneck."

Her American visitors both laughed hard at this. I was only too happy to confirm I had her safely covered in this department.

"If you'll agree to come speak in North Carolina I'll introduce you to my cousin James Taylor. He's a gentleman redneck and gardening fool in the nicest sense of the word." Cousin James's flower gardens, I elaborated, were always the talk of north Raleigh. As James's wife Betty once commented to me, without the slightest trace of irony, "If he could, why, James would *live* in his flower beds."

"Now wouldn't *that* be absolutely divine," cooed Mirabel Osler, rising to answer her whistling teakettle. "A gardener who never left the wild!"

"WE'RE LIVING at an extraordinary moment in the life of this planet," said Simon Goodenough. We were walking together at Ventnor Botanic Garden on the Isle of Wight less than twenty hours after leaving Mirabel Osler. All I could think was how she would have adored Ventnor, a compact public garden huddled into the lea of a south-facing coastal cliff that was simply the "wildest" public garden I'd ever laid eyes on.

"Never have we lived at a time when so much diversity of plant life is available and is crossing borders at an almost dizzying pace. The unfortunate aspect of it, however, is that as the decline of natural habitat continues to accelerate in certain areas of the undeveloped world, we're beginning to see shocking losses of plant and animal species. One reason I've been so passionate about building Ventnor is to try and make people aware of this contradiction—and understand what we're in danger of losing.

"The way we treat plants is ultimately a reflection of the way we treat each other. As they go, I'm afraid, we go as well. That's why Deb and I are both a little mad for making gardens, me here and she over at Osborne House."

If an afternoon in Mirabel Osler's gentle chaos had perhaps begun liberating me from the "tyranny" of the herbaceous border and a confining vision of the *jardin Anglaise*, our day in Simon Goodenough's extraordinary municipal garden was perhaps the most entertaining garden hike I'd ever taken on British soil.

Britain's most eclectic botanic garden is barely thirty-five years old and spread over just twenty-two acres on the former grounds of a royal diseases of the chest hospital in the Undercliff section on the southeast flank of the famous British holiday island. Ventnor began life rather quietly as a Winchester nurseryman's private vision of a traditional Victorian seaside pleasure garden and enjoyed a brief period of success before the death of its original patron and a series of unusually cold winters placed the plants there in serious jeopardy.

The garden suffered years of benign neglect. Then the island council turned to Kew Royal Botanic Gardens and recruited Simon Goodenough for its new curator. The cheerful son of a British naval commander, Goodenough grew up at posts scattered across the Far East and Africa, a self-described "maverick who loved plants, good beer, and a good party—essentially in that rough order of things," Goodenough, who once turned down Beatle George Harrison's offer to serve as his head gardener at his Henley-on-Thames estate, was then supervising the Palm House and propagation of plants at Britain's most celebrated royal botanic garden, "running a staff of ten and waiting for my superiors to either retire or shuffle off and make room at the top," when he decided to accept the island council's offer to try and save Ventnor Botanic Garden.

"My timing couldn't have been worse. I arrived in 1986 just in time for the coldest winter in more than one hundred fifty years, followed by the hurricane of 1987, a dreadful combination that killed over half the existing plants and trees here," he remembered, thoughtfully massaging the tip of his handlebar moustache over a lunch at the Mermaid Pub shortly before leading us on a tour of the garden.

Ian Hodgson, one of Simon's old mates at Kew, had been profuse in his praise of Simon's accomplishments on the Isle of Wight, an island traditionally associated with cheap holiday breaks and a famous rock festival back in the 1960s.

But the garden we spent the balance of the afternoon wandering through was a small jewel of biodiversity and ingenious design. It commenced with traditional lawns and Victorian mixed borders, but slyly soon yielded to a series of spectacular garden "rooms" that led a visitor on a magical mystery tour of the wide world botanic.

This walking tour included a set of magnificent Japanese terraces full of woody rhododendrons and azaleas, a stunning hydrangea dell that was just coming into bloom, a New Zealand garden with the most amazing "foxglove" trees and a bank of startling ten-foot-tall blue flower stalks called *Echium pininana*; a palm garden full of *Watsonias* and *Kniphofia* or "Red Hot Pokers" plants from South Africa; a Mediterranean terrace that brilliantly reproduced the landscape of a Tuscan hillside of a thousand years ago, plus a breathtaking "Americas Collection" that featured a complex understory of flowering bulbs and native North American plants and woody shrubs—familiar salvias, lupines, and purple coneflowers that grew in my own Maine garden back home—set off by a whimsical carved totem pole that featured the creator's smiling face.

The element of whimsy and self-deprecation that Mirabel Osler and Suzy Verrier believed were essential in any garden space was very much in evidence in the public garden Simon Goodenough had created on shoestring budgets over the previous decade. But his pièce de résistance was clearly a large greenhouse exhibit he'd recently unveiled that drew visitors into its mystery of nature via a mine shaft that opened into a dense jungle where nature was busy reclaiming an industrial wasteland. There, water gushed from jagged pipes, dark lagoons meandered through a twilight world of lush vines and pioneering palms, pineapple and banana trees. A broken stony path meandered through the spectacular foliage and dark mysteries of a miniature Jurassic Park where man and nature were visibly at odds.

"The message of this exhibit is that nature will always have the final say," the Mad Man of Kew explained with boyish enthusiasm, as we went along the footpath like travelers who'd suddenly wound up lost along the River Amazon.

"This place is really meant for kids—or at least the kid in all of us. It's meant to stimulate a discussion about what we're doing to our natural world by polluting it and robbing its natural resources. We make a mash of things and then just walk away. But most of the school groups come, I fancy, to see if they can spot the crocodile."

"You have a crocodile in here?"

Simon shrugged faintly and smiled, glancing around, thoroughly relishing his role as the mad scientist creator.

"Some have seen it. Big brute."

We were standing under a low canopy of an aromatic eucalyptus tree, near a small bridge fashioned from old timbers, where stunning South African agapanthus leapt up, and the dark water revealed what could have been a pair of watchful beady eyes. Simon explained he and his staff of eight started with a thirty-foot hole in the greenhouse floor, then salvaged timbers and broken piping from a new car park construction project conveniently going on over at the neighboring cricket club.

"They were planning to cart it all to the island dump and we simply told them, 'Right. We'll have all that, Love.' And brought it all in here, arranging it around a network of lagoons and waterfalls that move sixty-five thousand liters of water every minute. Like everything else in here, the water is recycled water, as well."

I couldn't help asking what it had cost to create such a magnificent and unusual garden. I couldn't help keeping an eye peeled for the crocodile, either, hoping there really was one.

"We've learned to be masters of the art of salvage here, *true* recyclers. This exhibit cost about twenty thousand pounds to develop—about a third of our entire operating budget for a year." Simon laughed. "The way the staff and I like to look at it is, the local council gives us about a thousand quid a year for every acre of the garden. That includes maintenance and anything we're keen to develop. The visitor center we came through is new, and I've got a new project on the books that will take some real ingenuity—a series of rock terraces under glass that will climb the cliff outside and feature native plants from numerous growing temperate zones around the world, huge agaves and that sort.

Quite an undertaking. We're going to be doing some major scavenging, looks like."

He had another thought as to why Ventnor had evolved into such an unusual place.

"Because we in Britain have been a gardening people for so long, there is a strong reluctance to change anything, to alter anything in an existing garden. But nature herself doesn't work that way, and, in order just to exist, we've had to be constantly tearing things up and rebuilding, using whatever is at hand." He gave us a small crocodile grin of his own. "Making a lost garden look this natural is quite a ruthless job, actually."

"How many visitors do you get each year?"

"Maybe quarter of a million—some serious gardeners, to be sure, but also lots of elderly bus groups and schoolchildren. I've often had the thought that the real attraction of a garden is that it returns you to a childlike state—perhaps that's why so many folks on the bus tours are elderly sorts. Eager to feel young again. Of course, nobody pays anything. The garden is free and open twenty-four hours a day."

As he said this, I was surprised to realize we hadn't paid a brass farthing to enter through the impressive new reception center and descend into this small hidden wonder. Kew, by comparison, claimed six pounds from a first-time visitor. I hated to sound like a naked Yankee capitalist, but what more could be achieved, I put to our genial host, if the governing council tacked on a modest one-pound admission fee? Even with that Ventnor would be among the horticultural bargains of the British Isles.

"It would certainly help," Simon said as he led us out of his man-made Lost World. "But it would no longer be a public garden open to all. It's a constant battle for survival here, to be sure, but part of the challenge and charm of this garden is that it's never closed. People come here at all hours of the day—even in the moonlight—to look at the rare flowers and shrubs or just sit and do nothing. Half the time I think that's a garden's most important function—to convince you to do nothing."

I wondered about theft or vandalism. Some of the specimens we'd seen were not only quite exotic but also rare in these latitudes. Rare plants bring out the worst in some people, as the cycad cad himself had pointed out.

"A little. But not a much as you might think." Our host laughed again, twirling his Victorian moustache with a proprietary twinkle in his mad creator's eye. "How far can they get, after all? This is an island."

For that very reason, Queen Victoria and her husband Albert chose to build their own private estate here in 1878. In the morning, following a delightful dinner out with Simon and Deb Goodenough and a refreshing sleep in the old gardener's quarters at Osborne House, Deb led us on a walking tour of the sprawling estate grounds she was systematically restoring in behalf of English Heritage who owned the glorious sandstone pile of a house and beautiful grounds. Like Sarah and Jim at West Dean, the Goodenoughs were a marriage made at Kew. Deb had been the garden's first Canadian intern. "I was up a ladder in the palm house one day in the early eighties, saw her come through the door, and thought: That's it, I'm done. Hopelessly in love," Simon explained as his wife was showing my wife around the queen's walled garden she'd recently completed putting back in operation.

Simon confided to me how pleased he was that Deb's hard work at Osborne House—reconstructing Victoria's garden "tapestry," a landscape that helped create a national garden frenzy over a century ago—was finally gaining the press and public attention it deserved. Deb Goodenough had also recently been elected secretary of the Professional Gardeners Guild, and articles were soon to be published in important British gardening periodicals extolling her handiwork at Osborne House.

"I'm admittedly something of an impatient character, whereas Deb is a tribute to the marvelous things diligence and a steady hand can yield in a garden. I think it's safe to say both of us found gardens here that were maintained, but certainly not loved the way they should have been. The key to making any garden succeed is to love it like your own family. Just never be afraid to change and grow *with* it."

Simon made this astute observation as the five us—counting the younger of their sons, Jake, a lad about my own son Jack's age—meandered along the late queen's private beach where the Goodenoughs sometimes slip down to in the evenings and have a bonfire picnic.

"You'll have to come to Maine sometime and let us show you the gardens there," I suggested by way of thanking Simon for a perfect finish to our "dirty" bank holiday in Britain.

It was, as I'd hoped it might be, the perfect ending to our travels in the mother country of gardening. Like Jefferson at Leasowes, part of me felt unexpectedly liberated from the things we'd seen and the lovely garden talks we'd had over the previous five days, and happily the feeling of being a kid was back—possibly because we were technically trespassing on a famous queen's private beach.

The womenfolk were walking ahead on the shore, talking about whatever women talk about when they're safely beyond the earshot of their husbands.

On a whim, I picked up a flat stone and skimmed it across the water toward the lights of Portsmouth Harbor, thinking how it was great to have started at West Dean and ended here in a garden built by a queen on an island four miles out at sea. I remarked to the Mad Man of Kew how sweetly ironic it was to end this particular English sojourn on the property of a monarch who sent plant hunters to every remote corner of the planet to search out the exotic and unusual, ushering in the so-called "golden age of horticulture." That world, I added, a bit melodramatically, seemed to have long ago vanished.

"Oh no," Simon said, pausing. "It's still out there, as wild as ever in places. There's probably thousands of things nobody has ever seen growing in remote places in China and Africa. The problem is, if we don't protect the environment of this planet pretty soon they may vanish before anyone ever sees them."

"Wouldn't it be great," I said, watching a ship put out to open sea, "to go on a real plant safari like that—you know, take off with great white plant hunters in search of the exotic blood lily?"

Both Simon and son Jake laughed. "I agree. But some clever bloke found the blood lily a while back. A hundred years ago, I think."

"Does anyone hunt for plants like that anymore?"

"There was a great period where nobody did that sort of thing. Budgets were cut, public interest was fairly minimal. But I think the deepening interest in gardening has revived that old profession a bit. You have to be at least as mad about plants as I am to do anything like that. Those lads get into some difficult places."

"Sounds fun," declared Jake, voicing the very thought in my head at that moment.

And with this, father and son both picked up stones and skimmed them to sea, too.

Chapter 9

❧

Stalking the Wild Pelargonium

The first decent summer rains in years made the tourists miserable, but accomplished wonders with the Elephant Angel tree. Left entirely to its own devices save a modest shot of SUPERthrive here or there from me, the severely pruned American beech put out dozens of promising new long and arching branches and, better yet, leafed out rather vigorously in a strange habit that looked more like Winged Victory than a flying pachyderm.

Summer in Maine, of course, may be the cruelest gardening time of all because you wait interminably for its arrival only to enjoy a few fine weeks of balmy weather and a handful of genuinely hot days before the season is suddenly over and heading south again for the winter. That's why I typically venture no farther than my own yard from the end of May to the first of September, unwilling to sacrifice a moment of decent "getting dirty" weather by doing silly things like sailing on boats, eating lobster, and shopping at L.L.Bean.

Besides, following my fruitful expeditions to Philadelphia and Chelsea, I had a record number of garden projects simultaneously going full-tilt on my rocky hilltop, a veritable Jeffersonian stage play of flowers to witness. First came a riot of tulips in my my new Philosopher's Garden, inspired by Brooklyn Botanic Garden's lovely Shakespeare garden and my time with Ed Pugh at Bartram's garden, under a petal snow of white blooms put forth by several *Sargentii* pears and crab apple trees. I finally found the proper spots to plant the ashes of my former garden assistants, Amos and Bailey. This drama was almost immediately followed by the debut of several spectacular Davis Austin rosebushes and a pair of climbing hydrangeas in my new Roman pergola garden and the first blooms of the Daylily King's truly spectacular *Hemerocallis* plants. By mid-July I was happily mowing my ever shrinking rear yard and admiring the way Suzy Verrier's Northern redbuds and the Carolina silver bell were taking to my new Southern arboretum. The Japanese side garden came along very nicely, too, putting out beautiful serene foliage thanks to David Smith's lovely *baptisias*. His suggestion to replace my dead lavender beds bordering the front walk with catmint and pink tea roses became the showstopper of middle summer—swarming over the white front gate and stone walkway by early July with a glorious wildness that dazzled visitors and would surely have gladdened the hearts of both William Robinson and Mirabel Osler. Due to the abundant rain, the obedient plants went quickly out of control, invading the English clematis, while my beloved hosta beds—the headline event of my front garden—grew to such staggering proportions, producing a blue haze of July flowers that resembled an impressionist painting, one visitor demanded to know what kind of mystery juice I was putting on them to produce such "mutant blooms."

I'd never been more pleased with my little flowering domain, my little redneck *jardin* slightly off in the woods. Never closer to the spirit of my inner gardening monk; never wearier of foot and lower back, to be sure. Nor happier in the dirt.

Flower gardening, I sometimes think, is far less a hobby than another form of arranged marriage. As soon as your attention drifts from one particular area to someplace else, the neglected patch goes mad with scorned growth. In late August, for example, we went away to join friends for a week on an island off the coast, and returned only to discover my new Southern arboretum overgrown with waist-high millet weeds that took me a solid week on my knees to finally clear out.

By then, Labor Day was just over the horizon and the first color was visible in the surrounding forest leaves. In mid-September, I took off to attend the first ever Garden Fare at Wintherthur Gardens, a gathering of the nation's premier gardening sources modeled after a similar event held annually in the spring in France and produced in conjunction with *Horticulture* magazine's one hundredth birthday celebration, hoping to catch a talk by Tony Avent of Plant Delights Nursery.

Once again, though, owing to an unscheduled lunch stop to read a book and an unexpected traffic jam on the Baltimore Pike, I just missed hearing him speak. I was late to Garden Fare because I stopped off to snoop around Chanticleer Garden in Wayne, a private pleasure garden that was now open to the public and every bit as sensational as Jane Pepper said it would be. The bonus at Chanticleer was that I bumped into Beth Kephart, a gifted Philadelphia writer who had just produced a lovely and poetic book about how Chanticleer helped transform her life. On the morning of her forty-first birthday, this attractive mother, wife, and seasoned deadline-writer had ventured out to Chanticleer on a bit of a lark, in search of something she couldn't quite place a name to, and found an unexpected means of seeing both the world and her life anew.

Unfamiliar with the language of flowers, unable to name the birds in the trees around her, she found herself attracted to the splendid sanctuary of Chanticleer and faithfully returned there week after week for two years. In a way, though on a vastly more intimate scale, Beth's odyssey through someone else's garden powerfully mirrored my own.

"Whenever I went to the garden I was leaving work behind," she wrote in *Ghosts in the Garden*, the little book she kindly gave me that morning at Chanticleer and which I devoured most of while having lunch at a small quiet inn in Chad's Ford, a few miles shy of Winterthur's front gate. "Words and books, the writing life, the expectations others had of me. I was forsaking deadlines and logic, a liberation I had not realized, until that spring, that I was seeking."

Beth wasn't the first kindred spirit I'd met on the garden path that year, just possibly the most lyrical, seeking a similar deeper connection to the living world. "What I had loved had become what I felt compelled to do; it was time to walk out my own front door. 'Keenly observed,' author Gretel Ehrlich has written, 'the world is transformed.' I went to the garden to see more truly. I went for transformation's sake, and to win back my talent for living plain."

AFTER A CHANCE MEETING my female counterpart in a spectacular pleasure garden and mingling with the gardening elite at Garden Fare, I knew I had to keep going to see where Ariadne's thread, the splendid garden adventure Lighty, Osler, and Suzy Verrier all spoke so powerfully about, would eventually lead me.

Several weeks later, as the first golden colors of autumn edged into the Old North State, I finally made my way down Tobacco Road to Juniper Level Botanic Garden and Plants Delight Nursery south of Raleigh. I simply had to meet Tony Avent. Denise Magnani had described him as the "funniest and most down-to-earth garden expert ever."

He was all of that and more. A witty, down-to-earth man about my own age, Tony conducted me on a long private walking tour through his magnificent Juniper Level Botanic Garden explaining how he'd been a "little plant nerd from day one." He'd tortured his mom and dad early in life by making terrariums from collecting trips to a nearby boggy woodland and forcing his parents to sell them at work, then reinvesting his profits in more plants.

"They weren't anywhere near as nuts about plants as I was but it did seem like something in the genes, maybe the only thing I would ever be able to do in life," he allowed with a laugh.

By age ten he was a "snot-nosed kid going around to local garden centers making a real nuisance of myself, informing clerks their plants were mislabeled. Just the kind of know-it-all punk you want to step on. They didn't give a hoot if it had the right Latin name, but I did. I became obsessed with accuracy but also came to realize early that most people knew more Latin names than even they realized. *Hydrangea?* That's Latin. So is *Iris, Impatiens, Lantana,* and *Hosta.* All are Latin.

But nobody ever bothered to demystify plants for people—and that really bothered me too.

"Also, I realized early on that most nurseries sold the same ten or twenty plants and there were all these amazing plants I'd read about in catalogs that supposedly wouldn't grow in zone seven. One of the most crushing experiences of my life, I'll never forget, was pestering my parents to drive me down to see Wayside Gardens in South Carolina, a legendary nursery along the lines of White Flower Farm. Their catalog was full of so many interesting things and I was certain their gardens must be heaven itself. So to shut me up my father finally drove me down to Greenwood, South Carolina, which took forever, let me tell you, only to discover there really *wasn't* a garden at Wayside Gardens—merely a warehouse for a catalog that sold seeds and plants grown from other places!

"I was one little disillusioned little plant nerd, let me tell you! I remember just sitting down on the ground thinking, *This is a crime! They're advertising a garden that doesn't exist!* That one event shaped my entire life. It was right then I decided to grow up and build a nursery of my own where there was also a real garden people could come and see and hang out in as long as they pleased."

While still under the tutelage of the renowned horticulturist J. C. Raulston at North Carolina State, Tony joined the Men's Garden Club of Wake County and heard that the director of the State Fairgrounds in Raleigh had purchased a load of nursery plants and aimed to try and dress up an otherwise drab fairground. "They had them just sitting there buried in sawdust with two-inch caliper roots coming out of the bottom of pots. So I cleaned them up and worked hard for about two days getting everything planted. The assistant manager was so thrilled he offered me a job landscaping the entire fairground. I had about a month left on my degree in horticulture, but I took the job and started at four twenty-five an hour. I thought I might stay till the end of summer. I stayed sixteen years."

Under Avent's stewardship, fighting a battle reminiscent of Simon Goodenough's perpetual struggle against the bureaucracy on the Isle of

Wight, North Carolina soon had an award-winning state fairground that audaciously featured giant agaves, banana trees, yuccas, cacti, and a rock garden nonpareil. By then, Tony was also writing a weekly garden column for the Raleigh *News and Observer* newpaper and the first of many articles for *Horticulture* magazine.

Soon the small house he shared with his wife Michelle a few blocks from his alma mater had its own surrounding gardens, where Tony not only field-tested new species of plants but also pushed the envelope on design. "That was our first venture into having a botanic garden where people could come and just wander around seeing plants they might be unfamiliar with," he explained. "It started as a pretty casual thing at first, expanding from the traditional shrubs to more adventurous things with every passing year. And suddenly it kind of overwhelmed our little place. We were like this jungle of unusual plants on this very conventional residential block and more and more people were coming to see it. I think that's when I realized we needed more room for a bigger garden, someplace I could breed and test new species—and maybe start a mail-order nursery of unusual plants to go with it."

Avent left the state's employment in 1993. By then, he and Michelle were in possession of a two-acre plot of played-out tobacco land and an old farmhouse with a spectacularly bending water oak Tony liberated from a briar patch and made the horticultural centerpiece of his extraordinary "redneck" oasis—a meandering glade of traditional and exotic trees and plants from around the world, made even more entertaining by strategically placed brooks and waterfalls and utilitarian pieces of everyday Southern life—abandoned kitchen sinks, old whiskey bottles—a witty blend of art and nature that would have warmed Samuel Johnson's heart, a modern-day Leasowes.

The Avent holdings eventually swelled to twenty acres and encompassed both a nursery where Tony could breed his beloved hostas and field-test unusual varieties of plants that challenged traditional notions about garden plants and a botanic garden that eventually featured more than seventeen thousand plants. His first *Plant Delights* catalog appeared in 1992 with a plain green cover, two years later bearing a satirical cartoon titled "America Held Hosta." That was followed by another comic gem titled "Amorphophallus are from Mars, Hostas from Venus," and a tradition was off and running. Since that time his covers had gently lampooned everything from blue- and red-state politicians to Martha Stewart to my own cherished "Lily-White Flower Farm" and developed a devoted horticultural cult following, not to mention an international customer base that was happy to pay *Plant Delight's* rather novel subscription price: "10 stamps or a box of chocolates."

"From the beginning," the man behind all this mischief explained that afternoon, as we moseyed through Juniper Level, which was already gently expiring from the cooler October nights, "I wanted a place where people could come and get inspiration and information in an un-complicated and fun way—learn, if you will, how much of a kick making a garden can really be."

"Except for all the innocent plants that have to die in the process of educating yourself," I put in, thinking of my own education as a gardener.

"My old mentor J. C. Raulston used to say if you aren't killing plants you aren't a gardener." Avent laughed. "I've never seen a plant yet I couldn't find a way to kill." His own working motto was nearly as amusing: "I consider every plant hardy until I have killed it myself at least three times."

This was music to my ears, and with the fervor of a fun-loving plant evangelist Tony showed me an astonishing array of unusual plants and trialing species that wonderful autumn afternoon, many of which he had personally collected from expeditions to the wilds of China, Mexico, Korea, Argentina, and nearly every corner of the United States.

When I happened to mention that Tony's plant passions reminded me of Dan Hinckley of the Hersonwood operation, and wondered if he perhaps knew the man, Tony grinned lazily and drawled, "Dan and I are good friends. We've even been on collecting trips together. I'm sort of the red state version of Dan and he's the blue state version of me. Our objective is one and the same, though—to help people fall in love with plants and get over their hangups."

Near the end of our friendly constitutional he showed me a huge exotic agave from Mexico and explained how he'd collected it from the wild. "I'm looking forward to seeing if we find them in Africa," he casually remarked.

"You're going to Africa?"

"That's right. South Africa," he amplified. "I'm taking a cool little group of plant nerds over there in February. That's the end of summer in Africa. We're going to go to some really neat places in the mountains and high desert where other people don't often get to in the Eastern Cape."

"Sounds incredible," I said.

"It will be. C'mon and go if you want."

He said this so casually, I wasn't sure I heard him accurately. It almost sounded like Brother Avent had invited me to accompany him to the Methodist church for the big homecoming supper.

"Surely you're joking," I said, looking at him. "*Aren't* you?"

Tony smiled. "No. We could probably squeeze you in. We plan to cover a lot of ground. It's liable to get a little crazy, though. You'd better know that going in."

"I can do crazy," I said.

"In that case, you'll be right at home. You'd get to see where plants like this came from." We were standing in one of Tony's warm and fragrant greenhouses. Already there was a noticeable nip in the air outside. The plant he pointed to was an unusual banded creature with ruckled foliage and pink clusters of flowers, the common household geranium. It turned out to be a potted geranium one of his assistants was growing, from seed.

"That's right. Pelargoniums come from South Africa," I remembered, trying out a little garden Latin I'd picked up over at Chelsea, where only crude Americans like me say "geranium."

"That and about twelve thousand other common plants and flowers," Tony said with a knowing laugh. "Who knows? You just might see this very plant growing in the wild. Half the fun is not knowing what you'll find out there."

"Stalking the wild pelargonium," I said, trying not to add *yipee* like a kid who'd been invited to pull the lever that lit up the Rockefeller Center Christmas tree.

"Exactly," Tony said.

FOR THE NEXT EIGHT WEEKS, I confess, as winter descended and I went about my usual routine of erecting large wooden protectors and covering tender plants with straw in preparation for a blizzard that would come any day, I half expected to discover Tony was only joking about permitting me to tag along to the "birthplace of flowers" with his seasoned group of plant hunters. Perhaps he was just being nice, I thought, and never intended for a gardening tenderfoot like me to sign on.

"Who cares if he was joking or not?" Suzy put the unexpected development into context when I mentioned it to her out at North Creek Farm while buying some designer garden gloves for Wendy's Christmas stocking. "I know people who would pay ten grand to go on a trip like that. If you don't go, let me know and *I'll* go."

Just days before hooking up with Tony and his three companions, Carl Schoenfeld, Wade Roitsch, and Hans Hansen, for their three-week trip to the remote highlands of the Eastern Cape, I remained half convinced the garden trip of a lifetime might never come off. In fact, on the eve of the trip, partly to confirm that I hadn't imagined the whole thing, I drove down to hear Tony speak in Boston to a packed auditorium at the country's largest gardening trade show, New England Grows, and enjoyed the sight of him breaking up the room with slides and commentary on suburban planting schemes that had gone horribly wrong, inveighing against the arrogance of the "zone five horticultural mafia" that has produced the same humdrum dozen plants seen in virtually every yard in America.

"Ready for Africa?" he asked, spotting me afterward, noting that it was only hours before we were all scheduled to rendezvous in Atlanta for the twenty-two-hour flight to Johannesburg. For weeks we'd been exchanging detailed travel information and everything was basically set except for the final seat assignments. I'd already digested half a dozen books about South Africa's violent social history and incredible biodiversity. It sounded like the edge of the known world, and I frankly couldn't wait to get there. It didn't succor my impatience one bit that four feet of hard-packed snow now lay on my sleeping flower beds.

"Are you sure you want to drag a slow-footed, nonexpert along to Africa?" I felt obliged to ask for something like the fifth or sixth time in as many weeks.

"Absolutely," he answered. "You'll be like having one of our customers along. Not backing out, are you?"

"No way. I've even packed my best pelargonium-stalking boots."

"Excellent," he said, pausing to sign a copy of his latest book for a fan, an engaging tale called *So You Want To Start a Nursery*. "I just hope we can get seats together or at least somebody interesting to sit next to. South Africa's a *long* way from Atlanta."

We shook hands and agreed to meet again tomorrow.

AN HOUR OR SO before landing in Johannesburg, as breakfast was being served, the pretty young woman seated next to me turned and observed, "These days you really can't be too careful in the cities and bushveld. In the cities they'll just rob you clean as a tooth. But in the bush they'll shoot you in the head and take what you've got. My dear Auntie Clem was driving up to see her school chum in Lesotho and got stopped by a black policeman who arrested her for having a broken turn signal. When she refused to pay the fine—a bribe, of course—she was assaulted most horribly. The policeman was later arrested and is supposed to go on trial, but my father says he never will. That sort of thing, I'm afraid, is happening almost everywhere now."

Her name was Tish. She was twenty-three and newly married, a petrochemical engineer from Houston making her first trip home to South Africa in over five years. Her father, a retired police detective, was now living in a gated seaside retirement compound just outside Durban.

To hear this pleasant policeman's daughter tell it, the end of apartheid had simply brought about a nation beset by an entirely new set of intractable problems. Even before our breakfast trays arrived, Tish went on about Cape Town's rapid descent from being the "jewel of southern Africa" to a city surrounded by settlements and "decent people living behind razor wire," describing in the starkest possible terms a country reeling from 60 percent unemployment, widespread political corruption, and the highest HIV and rape rates in the world. "It's a tragedy to see what's happening to my country," she said with a sigh as her omelette was set before her. "The outside world simply has no idea how bad conditions are, I'm afraid. Up on the borders, for example, white farmers are being killed just like in Zimbabwe. But nobody wants to talk about that problem. Part of why I came back here was to try and convince Mum and Dad to move to Texas. My husband Keith is all for it. But Dad's an old fogey. He says right or wrong, South Africa is his home."

She glanced over somberly at me, then weirdly broke into a radiant smile.

"So. Are you visiting Africa for work or holiday?"

"A little of both." I explained I was accompanying a group of world-class plant hunters who were venturing into the Drakensberg mountains and the edges of the Great Karoo desert in search of unusual plants, perhaps the garden flowers of tomorrow.

"Oh, *lovely*," Tish declared, vigorously stabbing her omelette. "You'll adore the countryside. Mum says most of the world's flowers originated here, you know. She's terribly keen on gardens. Knows everything, Dad says."

I nodded, suddenly wondering if Tish was possibly part of some South African resistance movement who moonlighted for the Bureau of Tourism. The contrast between the differing images of her homeland she gave me from one moment to the next was nothing shy of stunning, to say the least. It sounded like we were about to set wheels down in a place that was as beautiful as it was damned.

In the seat directly ahead of me, I heard Tony Avent grunt and release a small weary chuckle.

Poor fellow had had a difficult passage over the darkened Atlantic, seated as he was next to a chatty South African businessman returning from an IT conference who kept nailing down minibottles of vodka and hopping up and climbing over Tony to visit the loo, returning each time with a telltale dusting of white powder about his nostrils and a renewed desire to get better acquainted.

Now he was asleep on Tony's shoulder, snoring like a lumberjack, and Tony kept offering me darkly amused glances between the seats as he tried to eat his breakfast. Moments before landing, his seat companion suddenly sat bolt upright, demanded his breakfast from a startled flight attendant, and clambered off for another restorative shot of nose candy.

"He's planning to fly through customs," Tony ruefully explained.

WE WERE STILL LAUGHING over these oddities of arrival at dinner several hours later in an elegant but empty British dining room up the coast from Cape Town in Somerset West. A second crowded flight from Joburg to Cape Town had left us all feeling drained, and so an early evening was agreed upon. The dinner gave me an opportunity to get better acquainted with my new traveling mates and them a chance to size up a tenderfoot botanist in the wild. In the morning we were scheduled to pick up our expedition field guide an hour farther east in the town of Napier. His name was Cameron McMaster. According to Tony, McMaster was the leading expert on the complex flora and wildlife of the rugged Eastern Cape region, the poorer, wetter area that lies along the Indian Ocean coastal plain stretching two hundred fifty kilometers from the town of George to the Tsitsikamma Mountains and the Drakensberg Mountains beyond. The early leg of our travels would carry us along what was popularly called the "Garden Route" due to the lush terrain of the thinly populated district, then over the smaller Outeniqua Mountains to the Little Karoo, an arid desert valley that would lead us to the colonial Boer settlement of Graaft-Reinet.

In preparation for venturing there, I'd been reading up on the rich biodiversity of South Africa in general and the Eastern Cape and so-called Cape Floral Region in particular. In the past two decades conservationists have identified just twenty-five distinct biological "hot spots" throughout the world, areas of the planets where exceptionally large numbers of plant species are concentrated. The hottest of these designated environmentally protected spots covers only 1.4 percent of the earth's surface yet is home to almost half of all known plant species and a third of the vertebrates. Two of these so-called hot spots were on our primary itinerary: the succulent Karoo and the Cape Floral Region. The native flora of the South African biome is often described as the richest and most diverse on earth, encompassing more than twenty-four thousand species of plants in a land the approximate size of Texas. Covering a meager ninety thousand square kilometers, or less than 4 percent of the subcontinent's land surface, the tiny Cape Floral Region alone boasted an estimated nine thousand species of plants, the majority of them endemic to the region. According to John Manning, a research botanist at the National Botanical Institute in Cape Town, considered the world authority on hyacinth and iris, this narrow strip of the subcontinent was still a land in the act of yielding its best kept secrets. "Despite four hundred years of collection and study," he noted in one of the better guides I'd picked up, "its wealth is still far from exhausted, and every year new species are found and described."

This was music to a plant hunter's ears, of course. But at our opening dinner in Somerset West, I learned from Tony and the others that this expedition was going to be different in one major respect from previous plant safaris due to a rapidly changing world that is likely to make a plant hunter's life even more difficult in the years just ahead.

Rising from a controversial biodiversity conference held in Rio a decade ago, signaling fears over vanishing habitat and hoping to protect their biodiversity and assert their claim of natural sovereignty, several Third World countries, including South Africa, had recently adopted stringent new laws aimed at protecting their native plant species and sharply restricting the collection of all plant and seed materials for export.

While the United States declined to sign on to the so-called Rio Accords of 1989, concurrent with these new foreign regulations, a move supposedly aimed at stemming the threat of invasive species and the growing threat of illegal exotic plant trafficking in this country, American customs authorities adopted a policy requiring something called a Phyto Sanitary Certificate for every plant or collected seed brought into the United States from a foreign source.

In most cases, the paperwork surrounding the collection and transport of even the smallest seeds from formerly wide-open places like South Africa—where, as Manning notes, plant hunters have worked unmolested for hundreds of years—now involved a sea of bureaucratic red tape and royalty fees that were often prohibitively high. By most accounts, none of these drastic measures had yet put a visible dent in the trade in plant piracy or helped preserve a single threatened species of plant. Even so, as a result of these and other recent changes, the Avent expedition to the birthplace of flowers was focused instead on photographing and studying existing species in their native habitat and employing Global Positioning Satellite technology to pinpoint precise locations of any new finds or interesting species that could later be legally collected by an authorized collector like Cameron McMaster.

"At this point, it's basically an unworkable and unenforceable attempt to protect native species from poaching in places like Mexico and South America," explained Carl Schoenfeld, the slight, straw cowboy hat–wearing owner of Yucca Do Nursery in Texas, a veteran plant explorer whose extensive collecting vita had carried him all over the mountains of Argentina and across the remotest parts of Mexico.

During our ride from the Cape Town airport to the hotel in Somerset West, Carl had told me what a wild and dangerous place Mexico had become just in the ten years or so he'd been venturing there to hunt for exotics. Both he and his partner Wade Roitsch had been stopped at gunpoint by corrupt police and questioned on numerous occasions, had either had their plant collections confiscated or been forced to pay bribes in order to get them back. Both men knew other collectors and travelers who had been shot and killed by both drug lords and local police, and felt the day wasn't too far distant when going to Mexico to hunt for plants simply wasn't worth the risk.

"That still probably won't stop me from going," Carl allowed with a high-pitched laugh and wink. "Once collecting gets into your blood, see, you never can quite give it up. You're like a guy with a drinking problem but the liquor is the amazing plant you never thought you'd see. Maybe *no one* has."

His stories reminded me of Ernest Henry "Chinese" Wilson, the famous explorer from Boston's Arnold Arboretum who ventured a thousand miles up the Yangtze River, dodging murderous pirates and bubonic plague, and crossed a set of wild mountains just to find a single tree, the *Davidia* or Dove Tree that I'd admired in the arboretum at West Dean Gardens. Among his many horticultural introductions, Wilson introduced the kiwi fruit, the Korean stewartia, scores of rare lilies, and several Japanese paperbark maples. After a lifetime of braving jungle fever, hostile natives, lethal wildlife, capsized boats, and a landslide that shattered his leg and left him with a permanent "lily limp," the intrepid Arnold Arboretum explorer and his wife ironically died in a car mishap in 1930, closing a chapter on horticulture's wildest age of plant collecting. For some reason, Carl, with his slight build, almond-shaped head, bristling goatee, and broad-brimmed straw hat made me think of Chinese Wilson.

The need to keep up with America's insatiable hunger for new and exotic species of plants, in any case, was now gravely counterbalanced by a Third World that was rapidly closing its borders and a government of our own that didn't seem particularly interested in distinguishing between the important activities of legitimate plantsmen and scientific collectors like Tony Avent and company and plant smugglers who could pick a country clean of its traditional bush medicines and most exotic plants in no time flat.

"The Phyto certificate is a perfect example of how government attempts to solve a problem but actually only screws things up even more," Tony picked up the supper discussion in West Somerset (where the beautiful garden just outside the dining room's door was full of

American species of flowers, as sweet irony would have it, just fading in the warm summer evening air). "It's a totally misguided one-size-fits-all approach intended to stop major corporations who've done so in the past from stealing native plants for their vast medical potential. There have been some well-publicized cases of this in recent years—for example, companies that have made millions off of natural plant supplements derived from native species. The problem is, those corporations are ruthless and will find plenty of ways to subvert the system, because the governments imposing these regulations, including our own, are staffed by inspectors who are either undertrained or utterly incompetent and have little or no knowledge of what they are even looking either for or at—just a blanket regulation that says you can't bring this or that across a foreign border unless a royalty has been paid and all the paperwork is in order.

"Plant thieves simply laugh at this and find plenty of other ways to smuggle their plants into any country of their choosing, especially if the money is good, while others just put seeds in their pockets and stroll right through customs. What's to keep you from mailing a plant or seeds home? Absolutely nothing. The truth is, you could put just about any rare or exotic plant you want in a big box and mark it *gift* and I promise you it will reach its destination without anyone having ever looked inside. That's how ridiculous and ineffective these new regulations are."

"The borders of most countries are like Swiss cheese," Wade Roitsch put in. "You can slip just about anything through with a few bills laid in the right hand. Bribes are standard in the Third World."

Following roasted springbok and ostrich fillets, we were tucking into several rich British desserts. I kept glancing out the door to the darkening summer garden, having to remind myself that I was now somewhere in the Southern Hemisphere where February was really August and summer was just ending and north was now a warmer climate somewhere *below* the African equator. Who cared if we weren't going to actually collect specimens or seeds from the wild, I thought. We were going to hunt them down and see them in their wild native state. The wild green man and inner gardening monk in me felt unapologetically thrilled by this exciting prospect, turned upside down by a world in violent flux and deeply pleased to be here with a pack of modern-day Chinese Wilsons. Wherever the hell I was.

"What about China?" I asked my well-traveled companions, thinking about a new tree I'd planted in my new arboretum that previous autumn. It was a lovely young *Metasequoia glyptostroboides* like the Dawn Redwood I'd so fervently admired in Michael Payne's Wilderness Road garden, a tree thought to be among the oldest living specimens on earth yet extinct for two thousand years until a group of plant explorers found several young ones growing on a rocky ledge in China in 1947. I'd named my specimen Lilith, in honor of Adam's controversial first wife, who served as goddess of the harvest to many early agricultural peoples. I could hear crickets singing in the African night just beyond the open door.

"China's a real adventure." Hans Hansen spoke up. He'd been on extensive plant expeditions there twice, including one with Heronswood owner Dan Hinckley. "The first thing the guide does is recite you the government's new official policy forbidding any seed or plant collecting. The next thing he does is ask what you're hoping to find and then takes you straight there. The policy is ignored and never mentioned again. You get the feeling everything has a price tag in China these days, even the plants." He followed this observation up with a sad story about how, while he and a fellow plant hunters were traversing a beautiful forest in a remote mountain province, they'd suddenly noticed what was missing from the landscape. "We suddenly realized that we hadn't seen or heard a songbird our entire time in China. Our guide explained to us that this was because Mao had told people in the countryside that birds were eating all the rice, so they should kill all the songbirds. They did, and the native populations have never returned."

"All these new restrictions really do is hurt the honest plant people, the naturalists and botanists and others who have a personal and professional interest in *expanding* the biodiversity of the planet," said Wade Roitch, Carl's partner from Yucca Do. Wade was a serious, almost scholarly Texan I had yet to get a feel for. I almost got the impression he thought I was like having someone's idiot frat brother join a learned search for the elusive Blood Lily. He also sported a nifty banded straw hat that I secretly coveted, though.

Our expedition leader was finishing his Coke, still puzzling on Phytos and rapidly closing borders.

"If you look across human history," he said quietly, offering an unexpected solemnity that matched the serene buzz of the soft African night, "you find that no society or nation has ever survived for long after it closed its doors to seed plasma and plant material. Everything you eat or grow these days came from someplace else. That's an indisputable fact. It's how civilization spread in the first place. If borders are shut down and commerce in plants and seeds ceases, as some fear it may, the consequences will extend far beyond the flower world."

"The whole thing is about making money, not perpetuating species." This from Carl, shaking his head.

I wondered if that meant we might find a rare plant on this trip that hadn't been seen in hundreds or even thousands of years but nobody in America would ever get to see it. I was naturally thinking of Lilith, my "living fossil" standing just outside my kitchen door. In another seventy or eighty years, she might truly be something to see.

"It's possible," Tony said, finishing his Coke. "Assuming truly foolish people get their way."

CAMERON MCMASTER was a youthful sixty-seven-year-old amateur naturalist who'd recently retired as the director of the Dohne Merino Sheep Society to devote his time to his main passion in life: hunting down, collecting, and photographing southern Africa's vast wildflower populations.

McMaster and wife Rhoda operated a small export business out of their home in Napier called African Bulbs, specializing in the sale of exotic bulbous plants: lilies, gladioli, watsonias, amarylis, and orchids. Before picking him up and setting out for the Little Karoo, he showed the team around his modest commercial garden, and I quickly realized what a rank beginner I was about the native species we would be hunting down in the coming weeks. As the other poked about under his netted realm, oohing and aahing and photographing plants Cameron had collected from his sorties to the wild or grown from seed, he showed me a vast collection of bulbous plants that featured a wide assortment of native ledeborias, clivias, eucomis, and haemanthus plants, none of which was even remotely familiar to me, a northern gardener who had never seen anything like them save in some botanic garden greenhouse. Eucomis turned out to be the sunny-sounding pineapple lily while *Haemanthus albifos* was a lovely white Paintbrush lily.

"Do you know the *Brunsvigia natalensis*?" he asked with clear interest, glancing at me over his glasses. "The common name is the candleabra plant. I'll be taking you all to a place that should, if I'm right, be absolutely covered with them. A rare sight not to be missed."

"No," I was forced to admit, pointing to the only potted plant on his tables that was familiar to me thanks to my many years chasing a Titleist through the knee-deep roughs of Scotland. "Isn't that heather?" I adored heather; had just added a small heather and heath section to my back garden in Maine. I was delighted to discover that heather, or something that looked an awful lot like heather, grew in South Africa and possibly hailed from there as well.

"Ah, the erica family, what you may call *heaths*. There is something like six hundred varieties alone here and, yes indeed, I'm going to take you all to a place where there should be whole ridges and fields in bloom with them at this time of the year! You may even be able to see two oceans from the place I have in mind."

"Do you think we'll see King Proteas as well?" I knew the stately Protea was the national flower of South Africa from seeing an extraordinary display of them at the Philadelphia Flower Show.

"That very spot with the ericas should be simply full of them. It's a bit late in the season, perhaps, but many will surely be in bloom. A treasure to see in the wild."

I told him I would look forward to that sight and hoped he didn't mind my incessant questions. My grasp of wildflowers from this part of the world, I admitted, was limited to ericas and proteas, gladiolas and pelargoniums and not much else. I explained I came from Maine where the snow was presently about chin-deep on my snoozing flower beds.

"So you'll have much to see and learn," Cameron said enthusiastically. "Never you mind. Just stick close and ask to your heart's content."

I thanked him and immediately designated him He Who Must Be Obeyed in my mind.

By THE TIME TONY WHEELED OVER and stopped on a sharply ascending shoulder of the road winding through the beautiful Outeniqua Mountains two hours later so everyone could examine and photograph a burst of salmon peach watsonias growing in clumps of *Erica versicolor*, I'd learned enough about our field guide to know my faith in him was well placed. Cameron had been born and grew up on a sheep farm near Somerset in the Eastern Cape, in a district where his family had been for over one hundred years. After college he'd made a life in the sheep business but was unable to shake the love of wildflowers his own grandfather had given him by walking him through the bush and identifying whatever interesting thing they came across.

"When I decided to retire and sell my property near the town of Stutterheim, and Rhoda and I moved down here to Napier for reasons of security, I realized I had just as much satisfaction simply finding the flowers in the wild and photographing them as actually collecting them. Once you start doing this sort of thing on a regular basis, you see, you become hooked on the thrill of the hunt."

I asked what sort of security concerns he'd faced in Stutterheim. I'd noticed it was also on our itinerary a few days down the road, somewhere in the remoter border country above us.

On the drive out of Cape Town, the members of our group had been startled at the miles of townships that hunkered on the shoulders and median of the main coastal highway, a necklace of grim shanties that stretched well over twenty kilometers along the coastal plain. A black manager at the hotel in Somerset West had explained to me that a new law permitted squatters to set up anywhere and legally stay put if the landowner failed to have them properly removed within forty-eight hours. In a country where the unemployment rate was believed to be well over 50 percent, he said, this policy encouraged poor people to flood to the cities looking for nonexistent jobs.

Cameron gave me a much larger answer than I'd expected. The subject was obviously a tender one.

"The last few years have been difficult for many people in South Africa, particularly here in the Eastern Cape, which is more remote and far poorer than other areas of the country," our guide explained. "In formerly prosperous farming communities like the one where I grew up near Queenstown, in an effort to redistribute income and help poor black people, the government has begun systematically taking away lands that have traditionally belonged to white farmers and given it to tribal farmers who simply don't have the skill or ability to properly manage them. It's quite sad, actually. The result, I'm afraid, has been a woeful decline in the quality of the farms of the Eastern Cape, a major increase in political corruption, and a wholesale turnover in populations as families who have been here for generations simply pulled up and left. You can see the devastating effect of this political foolishness on the land and judge for yourself in the coming days.

"A direct outgrowth of that has been a tremendous increase in the crime and violence rates. There are places now up toward the former tribal lands where travelers are simply advised not to go. Robberies and shootings are quite common and the legal authorities in those places scarcely exist."

"Are we going there?" Tony asked from the captain's seat in front. He sounded like a little kid, hoping we might.

"Yes. But only with utmost caution. I'm familiar with the places I wish to take you all. There is a farmer up on the Great Kei River named Neil Potter I plan to introduce you all to who has an extraordinary story of survival. Neil's quite literally fighting for his family's survival, I'm afraid. But he's simply mad for wildflowers. He swears they keep him sane."

"Cool," said Tony. "I hope he knows where there's some interesting ferns."

✵   ✵   ✵

ON THE FAR SIDE of the mountains, a frisky wind was making dust devils in the Little Karoo. It was approaching sunset when we stopped to speak to several children gathering prickly pears from cacti on the outskirts of Graaff-Reinet. As we all bailed out of the van, reloading cameras and checking notepads, Carl explained to me that prickly pears were a North American native that had been imported during colonial times to South Africa to provide cattle with a natural food source. The plant had easily naturalized and spread, and now seemed to be almost everywhere you looked across the arid expanses. Unfortunately, so was another North American import, the small but dreaded spur cactus called *Cholla*, a Western cattleman's nightmare. Once it got into a cow's hooves, the thorns, which were all but impossible to remove, festered and ultimately disabled the animal, causing it to collapse and die from exposure and starvation.

This was the final photo "collecting" stop in a long day that had seen dozens of enthusiastic stops, first to study stunning watsonias and wild gladiolus on the upward wetter slopes of the Outeniqua Mountains, and then to examine and photograph huge exotic aloes, crassulas, euphorbias and leopard-spotted ledbourias on the drier downslopes leading into the forbidding desert grasslands of the Little Karoo. One of Tony's main objectives was to photograph and find spores from unusual species of asparagus plants, beautiful purple-stemmed shrubs with silken heart-shaped leaves that were essentially unheard-of in American gardens. The Sage of Juniper Level was on a one-man mission to find African ferns and asparagus plants and bring them into the American gardening mainstream. During this final stop, he found a huge partridge breast aloe that had all the plant nerds gasping and snapping the shutters on their digital cameras. "I've sold these in my nursery as houseplants," Tony gushed over the lovely spotted plant. "It blows my mind to find one this big and beautiful just growing in the weeds off the side of the road."

Several children had wandered up to the barbed-wire fence by the road. In their buckets were prickly pears gathered from a nearby field of acacia thorn trees. I bought a couple prickly pears for a dozen rand and Carl showed me how to open up the fruit and taste its delicious yellow flesh. A small girl and her little brother watched me carefully eat the fruit, silent and dusty-footed in the forbidding Little Karoo.

"Is he your brother? Do you live around here?" I asked the girl.

Just a shy nod from her.

"Do you speak English?"

Now a nod and small smile.

"Did you know I come in peace from Planet Hollywood?"

Suddenly a large grin from them both. I gave the big sister several rand for her trouble, and they aburptly turned and began walking toward a mud-walled house I could see off in the bush.

"Look at that slope," Cameron suddenly said to me, pointing to a dusty ridge just down the road a bit farther were there appeared to have been some recent excavation of some kind. "Do you know what you're looking at?" I shook my head, eating my prickly pear.

"Poachers dug up euphorbias there, possibly cycads as well. They cruise these remote highways, you see, and simply stop and pop them out of the ground and are gone before anyone can detect them. Only the rare few face any kind of legal consequence. A few weeks ago a group of Japanese businessmen were fined fifty thousand rand for illegally digging up euphorbias. And not long before that another collector was caught with dozens of illegally collected cycads in a shipping container, bound for California. A group of Germans recently got caught stealing dung beetles and were heavily penalized for it. But that's the exception rather than the rule. Most get away clear and are never caught."

Our guide said something to the remaining children in Xhosa, their native tongue, and they smiled at him through the wire fence.

A plant nerd hooted off in the ditch, having a minor hortgasm.

"Check out this *Aloe varigata*," Carl Schoenfeld cried from a small ravine.

Wade Roitsch was on the far side of the barbed-wire fence, squatting and photographing a perfect Karoo lily in the golden bands of fading desert light. Hans had somehow disappeared completely from sight—

no small feat in a place where you could see fifty miles in every direction with only the jagged profile of distant shadowed mountains framing the view. A dry hot evening wind continued to blow, stirring up the dust.

It was then I realized these guys each possessed an extraordinary talent for vanishing into an unforgiving landscape, a plant madness that far eclipsed my own, and decided I had better manage to find a way in the coming days to keep up with them or risk finding myself lost and lonely as a cow with a thorn in his hoof.

TWO DAYS LATER, I was standing near a tall Italian cypress in another soft African dusk in the beautiful garden at Glen Avon Farm, nursing a gin and tonic and several small body wounds. The others had yet to appear for dinner after an extraordinary day of plant adventuring that began with a sighting of springbok herds moving through the grasslands near Somerset East and ended with an arduous hike up a mountain river to see what plants flourished at the base of a spectacular waterfall straight from Edgar Rice Burroughs. Between these highlights, we'd driven up a narrow rutted mountain road lined by towering twenty-foot stalks of ancient agave plants ("They bloom once," Carl explained to me. "Then they die. It can take many years for that big one-time flowering event to happen, which is why some people call them Century plants") into a thick Afromontane forest and gathering cloud of mist (forty-two hundred feet above sea level) to the private Waainek Wildflower Reserve, where Cameron had introduced me to spitting cobras, barking Chacma baboons, and tick-bite fever, and I'd performed my dangling act from a lovely little cabbage tree to Hans Hansen's amusement over the mother of all banded pelargonium shrubs.

The other guys had enjoyed their most rewarding day in the field. Tony had climbed down the mountainside and found no less than six different varieties of ferns while Wade and Carl came upon rare Kniphofias (red-hot pokers), *Eucomis autumnalis* (pineapple lily) and an array of wild gladiolus and orchids Carl simply summarized as "pure-T *mind* boggling." Hans Hansen had shown me the world's smallest hyacinth, no bigger than the a fair-sized sewing needle, then led me off to see *Dietes iridioides*, nerines, buddlea still in bloom, and wild agapanthus growing in thick profusion in the thick grassland slopes. I'd seen my first *Bulbine narcissafolia* and wild African orchid, too.

After lunch, we'd piled into an elderly Toyota owned by Bill and Alison Brown and banged up another impossibly washed-out road behind a crazy farm dog named Benji to a spot a mile or so below the falls, then carefully picked our way upriver, hopping from one huge and slippery boulder to the next over inviting pools of swirling mountain water that made me wonder if I shouldn't have brought along my portable fly rod.

Haemanthus (paintbrush lily) was everywhere in bloom near the cascading falls, wild agapanthus hanging in bridal veils from dripping ridges, and vast amounts of *Scadoxis multiflorus* (Katherine lily, from the family Amaryllis) swarming over higher ledges on the canyon walls where Wade and Carl, showing little or no visible fatigue, immediately scampered like a pair of young mountain goats. Down below, I washed my face in a pool of cool green water, tasted it (delicious, faintly mineral), and stood with Cameron who, aware of my sudden love affair with a certain common cabbage tree of South Africa and fondness for trees in general, pointed out a glorious yellowwood tree that presided over the scene like an ancient elder of the forest. The air smelled sweetly of mist and wild mint, an Eden for all five senses. At one point I saw movement on the highest ridges of the cliff and spotted the dark shapes of swiftly moving Chacma baboons, the guardians of the falls. Soon they began throwing rocks down the cliffs at us and barking again.

"Have you survived your hike up to the falls in one piece?"

"Just barely. How high were those falls?"

Alison Brown had come out through the open door of Glen Avon's farmhouse to join me in the garden before the others arrived washed and dressed for supper. The farmhouse, simply named "The Retreat," with its yard-thick walls, handsome steeply pitched slate roof and colonial stinkwood columns, dated from the late 1800s, when Bill Brown's great-grandfather helped introduce the first merino sheep to South Africa. The empire was at its height then, and the gracious lines of The Retreat, a classic example of colonial empire architecture, reflected this far-flung glory. The current mistress's flower garden was teeming with bleeding heart and huge blue spangles of agapanthus not unlike what I'd seen growing in such native profusion up at the falls.

"Not certain, actually. Don't know that it's ever officially been measured." She drank her wine. "We did have a cow that fell from the top once, though. Terrible mess. It landed on the rocks below and simply exploded. Bits everywhere."

She smiled at me, perhaps realizing I felt like a man who'd been pummeled by a gang of angry baboons. I had more cuts and bruises on my legs than any time in my life and was possibly in the early stages of tick-bite fever. Oh, well, I thought. Tony had given fair warning.

"Cameron says these chaps are the most knowledgeable he's ever seen. They really know their plants and evidently are quite tireless in their investigations of the terrain."

"Theirs is definitely a beautiful madness. It tires me out just to tell you how tireless these gents are in pursuit of flowers."

She smiled again at me over the rim of her wine goblet. Though she was only slightly older than me, something about Alison Brown reminded me of my own mother, and her splendid garden made me think about the lost garden of my boyhood, where the seeds of what I was up to now had first been planted.

"Oh, that's enchanting. *Beautiful madness*. I shall have to use that. Is it your phrase?"

"No," I said, massaging my tick bite but otherwise greatly enjoying this tranquil moment in a fading garden of the empire. "It belongs to a monk called Brother John. He won't mind at all if you use it."

Over roasted lamb with mint and a nice claret, following happy discussions of euphorbias "as big as hedgehogs" and excited talk of the day's other discoveries, Bill Brown explained how his ancestor Robert

Hart stepped off the boat at the Cape of Good Hope in 1795, penniless as a beggar, and served eighteen years as a private in the Argyleshire Highlanders attempting to tame the colony's wild eastern frontier. After a brief return to Britain, Hart returned in 1807 as a commissioned officer in a mixed regiment that included British, Boer (the Afrikaner descendants of original Dutch settlers of the sixteenth century), and native Khoikhoi fighters (a fair-skinned people who are believed to have originated in the Cape bush) under the command of Colonel John Graham, a hard-nosed military man who set out to exterminate Xhosa tribes filtering down from the Great Fish River to the north, outer remnants of the great Zulu nations. Graham's war was a decisive moment in the history of South Africa because, as historian Frank Welsh noted, all the frontier inhabitants of the Zuurveld region of the Eastern Cape—white, Khoikhoi, and Xhosa alike—had existed more or less peaceably since the days of the founding Dutch colony. Graham's systematic campaign to exterminate the *Kaffirs*—a slang term meant to describe the nomadic cattle-tending Xhosa—or at least drive them above the Great Fish River, set off a period of bloody frontier warfare. "Graham had raised the stakes, and ensured continued strife," says Welsh, "not to be settled for another half century, and to which there could be only one eventual outcome. Not that negotiations and co-existence abruptly ceased—the very next year Xhosa were allowed back into the Zuurveld to raise a crop—but the exercise of imperial power had demonstrated that a solution could be enforced in the teeth of any reisistance."

The next war came at the end of the century against the Boers, and by then Somerset East was a prosperous farm town that had been settled by Scottish farmers. Robert Hart's farmstead had the only grain mill for a hundred miles in any direction. Glen Avon farm boasted flocks of merino sheep and vast citrus fields as well.

Six generations later, Hart's descendant Bill Brown was struggling to hold on to his family land in the face of a nation that was once again undergoing systematic change. Life below the Bosberg, the mountain where we'd found so many incredible wildflowers in the clouds, had become its own struggle to survive. "Right now I have three rifles out protecting my sheep," Brown explained. "One is for jackals, lynx, and caracels, another for dogs. The third is for stock thieves."

He explained that a new government policy might soon require him to give a portion of his land to a neighboring black farmer whose own ancestors had come from hundreds of miles to the north in the traditional tribal lands. "As a rule, these are people who have little or no understanding of modern agricultural methods, so the land quickly degenerates, the sheep die or are poached, and the farmer goes broke and must turn to the government for financial assistance. This sort of thing is happening all across this district, I'm afraid, not just next door to us."

"It's happening all up and down the country," put in Cameron somberly. He was in a unique position to know, because he worked with sheep farmers all over the eastern districts of South Africa. As he spoke, Cameron looked at the plant nerds to make his point, each one individually, including the expedition rookie.

"If you don't think this sort of rapid destruction of habitat and beautiful farm land will have a powerful negative impact on the future wildlife and native flower populations of this country, you are tragically mistaken. Every year the problem becomes worse. The local politicians become richer while the people out here, black and white alike, grow poorer."

Facing a merino wool market that had been depressed for two years and the financial hit incurred with the potential loss of their land, the Browns had decided to open the doors of their beautiful colonial retreat as as an upmarket guesthouse.

"In some ways it's been a terrible strain on our family," Alison Brown said to me back out on the porch as we stood together admiring a night that seemed to be very alive with distant calls and exotic rustlings. An Egyptian duck waddled past us, and there was a new brown pup who was chewing on the laces of my boots. "My biggest fear, I suppose, is none of our sons will be able to carry on the farm after us. One is very keen to do so, but there may soon be nothing left here for him to farm. This place has been a paradise for us in every way. But these days you see once-splendid farms like this just sitting abandoned by the roadside. It breaks one's heart."

She smiled and wondered if I might wish a nightcap. I declined, but thanked her for such gracious hospitality, thinking of two Advil before bed. I didn't know what else to say, so I added, "You have a spectacular garden, Mrs. Brown."

"Thank you," she said, visibly brightening. "I'm terribly glad you think so."

IN ADELAIDE THE NEXT NOON, we stopped for biltong, a popular dried meat of unknown origin that tasted like beef jerky. The morning drive from the upper Zuurveld toward the high Nico Pass through the Amatola Mountains had provided a morning bounty of stunning high grassland flowers and multiple hortgasms—nerines and haemanthus in bloom, patches of pineapple lily, aloe striata, and several beautiful grasses from the genus *Cymbopogon*. Near Cathcart, where Cameron grew up and his brother Hugh still ran the family's sheep interests, we climbed around a patch of huge boulders that looked as if they'd been left by a receding Ice Age and found gigantic clumps of euphorbia Carl estimated to be at least one hundred years old. Tony found several patches of wild asparagus ferns, both terrestrial and epiphytic; Wade found stunning species of dwarf kniphofias; and I tagged along after Hans, who led me to a dazzling plant in full cry of bloom, a huge electric pink *Brunsvigia grandilflora*, popularly called the candleabra flower for obvious reasons. Nearby there were beautiful stalks of gladiolus and even a wild hibiscus nestled in the thick purple fringed grass that turned out to be *Simba pogon*, or turpentine grass. Thinking how nice it would look bordering my Philosopher's Garden, I asked Tony if he thought it would be cold hardy enough for life in Maine.

"Possibly," he answered, taking yet another GPS and elevation reading as we approached a specimen I knew and loved, a handsome young *Cussonia paniculata*, or common mountain cabbage tree, like the one that had saved my skin up at the Waainek reserve. "Most of what we're seeing here wouldn't even work as a houseplant back in America because it has a die-off or dormant period. American gardeners, as a rule, don't like that. They want big flowers and lots of bloom all year long, because they've been conditioned by nurseries and fertilizer companies to think that way. But even plants need periods of rest, and the result of that time of regeneration is stunning flowers like these. Our job is to educate people and help them get with the natural cycle of life. If that happens, plants like these could just take off in America."

He suddenly gave me one of his famous lazy Juniper Level grins and told me an idea that had just come to him. Most travelers came to Africa hoping to see one of the so-called Big Five game animals—elephants, rhinos, water buffalo, lions, and giraffes. "I'm thinking at the end of the trip we should each vote on our own Big Five from the plant world here—the things that really knocked our socks off. So you might start making your list and thinking about that."

In Adelaide, as we waited outside a butcher shop where Cameron ducked inside to buy biltong, several black youths lingered around the van. One tall young man wearing a bright orange vest over a faded blue suit stationed himself directly beside the open door of the van and said something to Hans and me in Xhosa. The towns and landscape of this district had grown steadily shabbier and neglected as we progressed toward the foothills of the southern Drakensbergs. There were African National Party slogans brightly painted on walls promoting "Liberty" and "Freedom" but there were also boarded-up shops, refuse in streets, and hillsides of bleak settlement shanties at both ends of town. A sign in the window of the butcher shop read: NO CHEWING OR BLOWING BUBBLE GUM ALLOWED.

"He wants to guard the car for you for a few rand," Cameron said as he came back, climbed in, and dismissed the young man with a few gentle words of Xhosa, clicking his tongue the way the native peoples did. Officially, South Africa has eleven languages. Cameron spoke three of them, including the fading Boer language of the old Afrikaner nation.

Turning along the Kat River Valley toward the Nico Pass, we began passing citrus farms that must once have been stunning but now were being quickly reclaimed by the wild. Farmhouses like the ones Alison Brown had described sat huddled and empty and decaying in the late summer heat, old machinery rusting in the dooryards. "This is one of the areas where the government, in an effort to cut the poverty rate, bought out farms and gave them to the local black politicians to redistribute. Xhosa farmers are generally cattle farmers of a nomadic nature. The cow is almost sacred to them, and they permit their herds of cows and goats to wander wherever they wish, eating everything in sight. As you can see, overgrazing is a major problem, as the livestock has eaten the grasses to the roots and now there is nothing but bare earth in many places. Citrus groves need much attention—water, fertilizer, proper pruning, and spraying. These new farmers had neither the expertise nor money to do any of that, so the land has slipped back to nature. Most of these farms have simply been abandoned."

He shook his head, staring over at a hillside where cultivated lemon trees had been overrun by other species of larger trees and brush. I asked him what the word *Xhosa* meant.

"Destroyer," he translated, distantly. He glanced at me and smiled a little. "Pretty ironic, that."

We passed the abandoned Chicory Hotel, dark and leaning in on itself on a sandy pitch just off the highway. The building's windows were blasted out, a volunteer palm was growing on its doorstep. "I used to go this way to my school in Queenstown," Cameron observed quietly, still watching the neglected landscape. "Another problem around here is telephone wires. They rarely have decent telephone services because people steal the telephone wires for the copper in them."

In the town of Seymour another large ANC sign showing people on the march read TOGETHER FIGHTING POVERTY! Seymour made the neighborhoods around John Bartram's garden in West Philadelphia look like Walt Fisher's Bryn Mawr. We passed a crowded afternoon market and I saw a man sitting beneath a large wood crate that was missing one end. He was watching a small TV on a stool, oblivious to the dogs and crowds kicking up dust around him. The crate appeared to be his place of employment. He was advertising funeral services and Nike sportswear.

Carl wondered how much this region could decline before civil war broke out.

"In some ways, it's already happening," Cameron said. "There are strikes and protests happening in many towns out this way. Services and jobs have been promised but never delivered. The whole system is degrading so rapidly, I'm afraid, if something isn't done to reverse the disintegration you're going to see the kinds of things presently going on up in Zimbabwe. The successful farmers here, black and white alike, will all eventually pull out, and there will be no one to replace them."

We passed more awful settlements spanning an angry red hillside. Children played in a large mud puddle and TV aerials sprouted from dozens of rusting corrugated roofs. Young men and teenage boys sat in junker cars, smoking, staring. I found myself looking at a field of peculiar mounds with odd bits of statues and flowers and realized I was looking at the settlement cemetery. It was vast. Several fresh graves had been dug, the hard red earth peeled back, and a group of people were standing together off in the distance, possibly burying someone.

At Whittlesea, groups of women were walking along the hot highway tarmac with bundles on their heads and children were herding cows directly on the road shoulder. There were no wildflowers to see because the cattle and goats had eaten every visible bit of green down to the hard red ground for as far as we could see on either side of the road. At one point, a large emaciated cow stepped into the highway. Tony sharply braked and swerved, causing me to wind up on Hans's lap. "What's the penalty for killing a man's cow?" I asked Cameron, climbing off the amiable Minnesotan.

"Fairly severe, I think. Owning a cow here is a sign of status."

"But at least you get all the free biltong you want," said Hans, who was quick with a joke when we needed it most.

Queenstown, a large market town where Cameron had attended boarding school as a boy, had once been a colonial beauty. You could see that in the elegant lines of its Victorian courthouse and handsome buildings. Now it was crowded, congested, and dirty. I didn't see a single white face among the afternoon shopping crowds, but I saw people laughing and talking on street corners, mothers with umbrellas chastising misbehaving children in shop doorways, old men watching the world go by.

It was good to reach the Mountain Shadows Inn on the upslopes of the Drakensberg Mountains, near the outpost town of Elliot. The word *Drakensberg* meant "Dragon mountain" and we were sitting on the dragon's tail. By then the settlements had ceased and the rolling green land had resumed, evidence that the farms in this district were still in reasonably good shape. The inn, set in the lea of a hill, was vintage 1950s American motel—spare, clean, a little down-at-the-heels—with a dining room that was friendly and superb. We ate black bean soup, fried fish, fillet of lamb, homemade crusty bread. In the bar after dinner, Hans and I chatted with a man from Joburg who worked for Volkswagen and was scouting out places to shoot a commercial spot. The vast otherworldly expanses of green hills backdropped by the stony Drakenbergs, he explained, were perfect for "showing off the power of a new road machine." BMW and Porsche, he added, also used the area for commercial shoots.

"How do you get your vehicles here?" Hans asked him. It was over eight hundred kilometers to Cape Town, at least a twelve-hour drive.

"We fly them in, of course. Military transport planes."

As we left the bar and passed through the hotel's orange shag-carpeted entrance foyer, Hans pointed up at the huge giraffe head hanging on the wall.

"Look," he said cheerfully, "one of the Big Five. Only four more to go."

CAPE TURTLE DOVES WERE CALLING just after dawn in Rhodes, a beautifully preserved Victorian village set on the banks of several clear trout streams near the highest mountain pass in South Africa.

The prim valley town is named in honor of Cecil John Rhodes, a charismatic businessman who made a fortune in the Kimberley diamond fields and used the backing of powerful gold mining and diamond interests to become prime minister of the Cape and a virtual dictator in 1890. The town was now a haven for trout anglers and pleasantly lost in time with its grid of neat gravel avenues, Dutch Reformed church, and distinctive gingerbread green-roofed Cape houses with their well-kept gardens.

From what I'd read about Cecil Rhodes, the little place that bore his name was the picture of everything he'd hoped South Africa might someday be. Dedicated to the idea of bringing an area of Africa about the size of western Europe directly into the sphere of the British Empire's influence, Rhodes conspired to topple the Boer government of the Transvaal (where gold had been discovered in 1886, leading to a flood of British prospectors) that led directly to the two neighboring Boer republics declaring war on Britain in 1899. By then, Rhodes had been forced to resign from office due to charges of cronyism and was devoting his considerable wealth and influence to creating the country of Rhodesia in his own image. Another legacy of his wealth and influence was the creation of Rhodes Scholarships. He died the same year the Boer War ended and Britain established the independent Union of South Africa.

I stepped out of the Walkerbouts Inn with my bird book just as the sun was coming up and found Cameron McMaster waiting there. Every morning before joining the others for breakfast, I'd begun taking short hikes to try and see birds and limber up my legs, easing my own "lily" limp directly attributable to the rigors of trying to keep up with this wild bunch of plant nerds over the previous six days. I'd been pleased when Cameron asked if I would fancy a companion on my dawn stroll about Rhodes, because his knowledge of Eastern Cape bird life was the match of his plant expertise. I'd begun keeping notes on the beautiful exotic birds he'd pointed out to me in the field. They included the great sacred ibis like those seen on ancient Egyptian tombs, a helmeted guinea fowl, redbilled woodhoopoe, crested barbet, and a stunning African goshawk. I also wanted to know more about our field guide and how he had changed from an ordinary sheep farmer into a world-class amateur naturalist who had discovered two butterflies and a flower in the wild and had them named for him. The *Cyrtanthus McMasterii*, a small red lily, was found on a high ground above the Kei River, our destination in two days' time.

"So, what did you think of yesterday's little mountain adventure?" he asked pleasantly as we set off together into the deserted avenues of Rhodes with a friendly hotel cat tagging along.

"Pretty exciting stuff. Luckily we survived it."

"Those *Kniphofia caulescens* and *Dierama robustum* were quite extraordinary, weren't they? Carl and Wade seemed very pleased to find oxalis and delospermas in such profusion."

"I'm talking about the drive up."

He gave a gentle snort. "I tried not to notice, in case we didn't make it. Quite worrying at moments."

Arriving at Walkerbouts Inn in Rhodes around ten in the morning the previous day, we'd immediately set off in the van toward a high and lonely prospect called Tiffendale, which was home to South Africa's only ski resort and only fifteen kilometers from the Lesotho border. Tiffendale was reportedly host to some of the most stunning high-altitude wildflowers on the planet, but getting there was no easy feat. The narrow dirt road ascending to the ski resort just past Rhodes was marked by a sign that warned us to proceed at our own risk and used an arrow to indicate the current road conditions ahead. Before leaving Walkerbouts, Big Deb on the desk had warned Tony, "Whatever you do, Love, don't stop. If you stall or stop, you're likely to be a goner. The slope is a sixty percent grade in places. Mind how you go. A group went off the edge just last spring."

She hadn't exaggerated the challenge. For the better part of a half hour, the six of us sat tense and quiet as Tony hurled our six-passenger Mercedes van up the loose scree of sharp switchbacks in a howling lower gear, spewing rocks and tossing a hubcap over a cliff at one point in the wild carnival ride. I felt a nudge and turned to see my pal Hans smiling at me and pointing out his side of the van. Fifty feet below was a rusting vehicle lying upside down in the weeds. "I'll bet that's the last group of plant nerds who tried to get up here," he remarked with a thin smile.

Our reward for reaching the summit had made the anxious moments worthwhile: whole fields of red-hot pokers suddenly in flower as far as the eye could see, stunning vistas of ornamental grasses filled with perfect pineapple lilies and wild gladiolus. After convincing a lone employee at the closed resort to make us lunch, we each wandered off to explore the astonishing flora growing on the banks of a meandering stream running down the alpine grasslands at nearly eight thousand feet. Up that high, the only sounds were made by the wind, darting birds, and the clicking cameras of the plant nerds. Hans showed me a stunning black orchid he'd found, and I wandered off by myself with Else Pooley's field guidebook to wildflowers and found wild pelargoniums and sedums, small starflowers and African bluebells.

Sometime in the late afternoon, I was sitting peacefully in a beautiful patch of purple-fringed grass wishing I had it growing back home in Maine and watching the most amazing iridescent green bird with the longest tail I'd ever seen flit through the waving grass tops, half-daydreaming at the top of the world, when Cameron came up quietly and observed, "That's the malachite sunbird. Beautiful creature, isn't he? That long tail is his breeding plumage. He's trying his best to impress a lady friend. And, oh, *look*—that smaller dark bird there is the Drakensberg sisken. I've never ever seen one of those in the wild. *Wonderful!*"

A few moments later, he showed me a small satyrium orchid, named for the Satyr of mythological fame. This made him visibly happy, too. During the careful ride back down the steep mountain road to sleepy Rhodes, my companions had been ecstatic about their discoveries that day, proclaiming Tiffendale the best stop yet on our plant safari. "It was almost too much excitement for such thin air," joked Carl, removing his big straw hat.

For our dawn walk around Rhodes, the birds were singing their late-summer hearts out. Within three blocks of the sleeping town Cameron pointed out a Natal robin, a greater-collared sunbird, a capped wheatear, and a Karoo chat.

"And if you look sharply there," Cameron said excitedly, pointing to a meadow just behind a cottage, "you'll see the secretary bird, a bird of prey who eats snakes. The quills behind his head make him resemble a secretary with pens behind the ear, you see?"

We suddenly came upon a lady hoeing in her vegetable garden. Eleanor Waterson had the most magnificent cabbages and tomatoes growing in her veggie patch, where the earth was black as embers from basalt and other minerals. "Whatever I don't use I sell to the local black people," explained the owner of the aptly named Garden Guesthouse. "We're totally organic and never have any pests except perhaps the odd snail, which Zuki and I simply pick off by hand." Her bordering agapanthus was even nicer than Alison Brown's.

She was a Scot from Caithness who'd suffered a serious accident when her horse fell on her while riding up to Tiffendale, crushing one leg. "They took me over to the hospital a hundred miles away at Bluemontaine," she explained. "That's five hours from here and basically meant I had to close the guesthouse for a time." She told us she had been forced to give up on Rhodes and was relocating to open a guesthouse down in Cape Town, hoping to take her housekeeper Zuki with her. She said she loved Rhodes but simply couldn't make the numbers work during the long isolated winters. The resort up at Tiffendale only saw about four hundred hearty skiers on a good weekend but new chalets were being built to provide more accommodations on the mountain.

"Are you American anglers?"

"Not this trip," I replied. "I'm just out to stalk the wild pelargonium."

"He's a lucky fellow traveling with a group of exceedingly knowledgeable plantsmen," Cameron amplified in my behalf. "They're finding all sorts of amazing things in the wild. They don't miss a single thing, these chaps."

"Oh, splendid. We just had a group of American plantsmen through here a week or so ago. Botanists and birders, I believe. They went up to Tiffendale too. Then on to Lesotho, I believe. Do you know them?"

"No ma'am." I did recall Tony explaining that another group led by a renowned botanist from the Denver Botanic Garden had preceded us by mere days into South Africa. I'd also read somewhere that expert guided forays like this one were one of the fastest-growing segments of the travel industry, especially as native habitat declined and climate changed.

"Well, cheerio. Good fortune finding beautiful flowers," Eleanor Waterson said, and offered me a flawless tomato just picked from her garden. I accepted it and said thank you and wished her good luck in Cape Town.

"I'm told I'll need it," she joked with a husky laugh. "I hear the place is an armed camp these days."

I ASKED CAMERON how he'd come to be so crazy for plants and birds and butterflies.

"One thing leads to another, doesn't it? After agricultural college I returned to my family's farm in Cathcart, but soon found myself working for the sheep society full-time for a living and residing with my young family in Stutterheim. I plan to take you all there in a day or so, by the way, and show you all a marvelous waterfall in an extraordinarily pristine forest. You will be particularly interested in the trees, I feel. In any case, it was getting my own little patch of ground that finally did it. You start looking for interesting things to plant, and the next thing you know, you're out in the field looking at things and learning about the origin of plants and looking closely at every living thing that passes in front of your nose.

"Rhoda and I are a second marriage, and for both of us, plants are a major love interest. The African bulb business is frankly a little more than either of us would prefer at the moment—the demand is so high—and being out in the field like this or writing about what we've seen in the bush is really what I live for."

He explained that he would need to leave us after Stutterheim and journey back to Napier to host a group of visiting Australian sheep farmers and take them around to see several outstanding sheep farms. Their gain was our loss, I thought.

"I tell my farmers that they are only temporary custodians of a land that people one thousand years from now will need and want to see," Cameron mused as we completed our waking loop of Rhodes and approached the windows of the dining room where the other plant nerds had assembled and were already eating eggs. Everyone but Tony was drinking the aromatic local bush tea. Tony's drink was Coca-Cola, morning, noon, and night. By my count, confirmed by Hans, he consumed about five or six bottles a day.

"As a result, I tell them, they have a responsibility to care for it, for as you've seen on the ride up here, land can degenerate so quickly and easily. I also tell them they should find out everything they possibly can about the land they own—what sort of plants and animals reside there, what kind of biodiversity exists in their little bit of the world they have stewardship of. For if they understand that, they'll understand how we're all linked by nature and every species is almost entirely dependent upon the other."

Pausing by the inn door, He Who Must Be Obeyed gave me a hard look. "*That* pretty much explains why I eventually grew so mad for plants and butterflies and birds. The thread that holds our world together is very fragile, I fear, and people must know that before it's too late and the damage we're doing is irreversible. Frankly that's what's so appalling about all these new restrictions and threatened closures of borders. The way habitat is vanishing, if some of these plants don't get into horticulture soon, I fear they will simply vanish for all time. The people in charge of making such ludicrous policies think they are perpetuating biodiversity. But the truth is, they are contributing to the extinction of many plant and animal species."

As the door creaked on its hinges, a large feeding bird exploded from the overgrown meadow a few yards away.

"Another secretary bird," Cameron said. It appeared to have a small breakfast snake in its talons.

"I'd hoped it might be a watted crane. I have the keenest hope of seeing one of those in the wild someday."

Chapter 10

At Play in a Garden of Heaven

THE END OF SUMMER RAINS finally caught up to us at Woodcliffe Farm, turning the unpaved roads to a soft red goo in the lush farm valley just outside MacLear. I thought I could detect the expedition approaching an emotional crescendo. In the fog on top of the Sani Pass, at Naude's Neck, one of the highest elevations in sub-Saharan Africa, more than eight thousand feet above sea level, the nerds had once again fanned out and vanished in the mist, botanizing for hours on remote cliffs and ledges.

Tony showed me how to collect spores from a lovely fern species he found, purple-stemmed shrubs with delicate opalescent heart-shaped leaves, using the blade of a penknife to scrape tiny brown specks tucked into a fold on the back of the leaf onto a small square of specimen paper. There was discernible excitement in his voice as he explained how, as far as he knew, no plantsman had yet introduced this beautiful plant to the American gardening marketplace—possibly anywhere. If he was eventually able to reproduce plants from spores our guide was legally permitted to collect under the vague new regulations, assuming they produced viable plants and successfully passed their field trial at Juniper Level, Tony might well be the first to do so.

The economics of such a simple botanizing act were potentially eye-opening. Several years back, Tony paid a call on a plant pathologist at his remote university laboratory in Hawaii in search of *Colocasia*, or elephant ears, a fairly common tropical plant. Elephant ears are so common, in fact, it was widely believed there was no viable market for them. "This man, however, had been breeding them for over thirty years with little or no attention to his work. His plants were incredible, stunning cultivars that had never been outside the building." The two men struck a deal and Tony returned to North Carolina with over two hundred different varieties to breed and field-test. With Tony's help, several of the unusual *Colocasia* wound up in the national Proven Winner's trial program possibly to be sold at leading nurseries and plant outlets across the country. For his trouble, Tony was permitted to be the first to sell certain patented elephant ears to his Plant Delights customers. The original breeder will be entitled to a royalty of seven cents off every plant sold, and when I asked Tony how many pots of elephant ears might be sold under such an extensive program, he smiled and replied, "Could be millions."

At the big New England Grows nursery industry trade show in Boston, I'd run smack-dab into another story where discovery meets commerce, this one involving a little shrub I was particularly fond of, something called the Endless Summer hydrangea. According to a manager for Bailey's Nurseries, University of Georgia professor Dr. Michael Dirr, America's leading expert on woody plants, was visiting the big Minnesota-based plant supplier when he noticed something unusual about a particular plant that a Bailey employee had collected from the backyard of an elderly gardener in the Northwest. Dirr took several cutings from the *Hydrangea macrophylla* home to his Georgia lab and soon found that the answers of Northern gardeners like me had been answered. The little hydrangea turned out to be a perpetually flowering cold, hardy, big-leaf hydrangea shrub that would bloom on both old and new wood virtually all summer—the grail, as it were, of many commercial plant breeders. Since the introduction of Endless Summer in 2003, Bailey's had sold an estimated 1.4 million of the plants, including five to me for forty bucks apiece. Endless Summer was presently the biggest-selling single plant in the commercial horticulture world.

Thinking of this as we squatted together there in the mist at Naude's Neck, it was easy enough to imagine the stunningly beautiful wild asparagus shrub quickly taking root in disciminating gardens everywhere. Including my own.

Halfway down the other side of the mountain, exactly the point where the clouds abruptly stopped and a broad sun-lit valley stretched out breathtaking for a hundred miles, Cameron had suddenly shouted us to a stop. He'd hopped out and scrambled up a bank and over a barbed-wire fence, dropping to his stomach like a man who'd been shot. Hans, Carl, and Wade were hot on his heels, cameras clicking, following by the two back-stragglers of the group, Tony and me. "Look at these orchids!" Cameron cried, aiming his own small digital camera. "These extraordinary plants are a pure indicator species of the pristine conditions found on this side of the mountain. You might have difficulty finding a more ecologically pristine place in the world than this very spot."

The grassy slope on the far side of the fence was also thick with stunning orchids abloom, and with other treasures—gladiolas, banded pelargoniums, *Agapanthus campanulatas*, and stunning crassulas. Moments later, Wade found hypoxis, pineapple and bottlebrush lilies while Carl was having hortgasms over ledbourias and aloes half a slope away, among a scree of small boulders. Snooping about with Hans, I came upon a series of huge hard mounds hiding in bursts of ericas. They resembled overgrown fire ant colonies. "African termites," Cameron amplified.

"Prehistoric African termites," said Hans. "Let's don't knock and see if they're home."

A bit farther down the winding road, the shoulders of which were lined by at least four different varieties of kniphofias and gladiolus, Carl pointed out a grove of magnificent shaggy pines beaded silver with condensation from the wet air, explaining they were introductions from the forested slopes of Mexico, probably only twenty or thirty years in age, a rapidly growing pinus clearly being grown for their timber value. If anyone would have known this, it was Carl Schoenfeld. He's made more than one hundred collecting trips to Mexico.

The biggest thrill came ten miles or so down the mountainside, however, and this time it was Hans who let out the war shriek to stop the van. "What?" said Tony, "Did we hit a televangelist?"

"No. Holy cow!" Hans cried, "Check out the field, guys!"

The field above the ditch to our right was full of iridescent pink *Brunsvigia grandiflora* at the peak of bloom in the lifting mist, hundreds of huge candelabra plants with two-foot spans of arching pink flowers, looking like a botanist's picture of heaven, a horticulturist's field of dreams. I honestly closed my eyes and opened them again to confirm the extraordinary sight. Then I snapped a dozen photographs of my own.

We arrived in the dark—weary, hungry, dirty, and mentally drained, roaming around for what seemed like an eternity along a series of narrow rutted roads that split head-high fields of grass in a tropical downpour, half expecting a water buffalo or rogue elephant to come charging out of the grass at any moment. In fact, so hungry I was even munching on Cameron's foul biltong, it was at this very point I asked our guide if any of the Big Five were still roaming about—the kid in me who'd been weaned on Rider Haggard and Edgar Rice Burroughs certainly hoped that was the case. "Afraid not. Once upon a time, just a hundred years ago or so, this river valley would have been full of large game animals—elephants, lions, zebras, giraffes, very likely water buffalo too. You'll see that reflected in the remarkable cave paintings of the San people. But the animals were systematically hunted and killed and ultimately made extinct in this part of southern Africa. A great shame, in my estimation. You can see what a paradise it would have been for them, can't you? Who can say how long they had been here before man first set foot in this lovely river valley. The animals were the rightful heirs—revered and worshipped by the San people. You'll see that on the walls of the cave tomorrow."

Phyll Sephton made us a delicious dinner of roasted lamb, shepherd's pie, creamed peas, and cauliflower. Phyll's first husband had passed away from cancer a few years earlier. She had remarried and now lived two hundred kilometers away, but returned to the family home every so often. Woodcliffe had been in her late husband's family for generations and the tale wasn't quite so severe as down at Glen Avon, but the mistress of Woodcliffe told tales of how local officials appointed friends to important jobs and the district superintendent of schools—who couldn't read—had tripled his own income while council members now paid themselves seventy thousand rand a month and drove Land Rovers while cutting road services to outlying farms around MacClear. "When my husband was growing up here as a boy," she explained, "it was very different then. He used to take off from a high pasture in a small airplane with his father to fly over the mountains to school. People had jobs and were kind. There was little or no violence like today. My children worry that it is unsafe for me to come here alone. Just last year I drove home through a village I knew well in the Transkei and the next afternoon a car was hijacked and the owner murdered. We have the highest carjacking rate in the world. But I still come here because it is our family home. We always drive two cars now, so you can get away in the other if you must. The wild animals have all disappeared but the humans are wild now. It's another kind of Africa."

As I listened to her talk, I was reminded of my favorite book about Africa, *West with the Night*, by pioneering aviatrix Beryl Markham, who grew up on a similar farm in Kenya at the turn of the previous century and wrote in her memoirs, "To see ten thousand animals untamed and not branded with the symbols of human commerce is like scaling an unconquered mountain for the first time, or like finding a forest with roads or footpaths, or the blemish of an axe. You know then what you had always been told—that the world once lived and grew without adding machines and newsprint and brick-walled streets and the tyranny of clocks."

WE WOKE in the guesthouse to the sound of burros braying and set off after breakfast up a rain-washed track in the farm "Bucky," a ramshackle

Nissan truck driven by Phyll Sephton's head man who spoke only one discernable English phrase—"Yes boss"—and seemed to be named, as near as I could tell, Mbuko. Everything I said to Mbuko, who wore knee-tall rubber boots, someone's cast-off Regent Street plaid suit, and a porkpie hat, prompted a gleaming white smile, brisk nod, and quick "Yes boss."

"Is it true *National Geographic* sent a team to photograph these cave paintings?"

"Yes boss."

"Tell me, Mbuko, do you think we might see rhinos and elephants and maybe lions dancing on cliffs on our way up the river to the cave paintings?" In my mind, I was still with Beryl Markham in another Africa.

"Yes boss."

The track came to a halt where a culvert had blown out from rushing water off the slopes. Mbuko waved his arm to indicate that we would have to walk from this point on, perhaps a distance of two or three miles, we calculated from Phyll's descriptions at dinner. The Xhosa guide picked up a large stick and set off at a smooth pace and we dutifully fell in behind him, tramping through the deep mud and passing through a cow pasture where several mixed-breed bulls eyed us suspiciously. Beyond another livestock gate, the river suddenly came into view, bending magnificently through an alley of high limestone cliffs aproned by lush jungles and dense wet grasslands.

It wasn't long before Tony, Carl, and Wade had laid back to botanize the grasslands while Hans and I struggled to keep pace with the head man. Hans was wearing a T-shirt that read SEND IN THE CLONES. The other nerds had been remarkably patient with my incessant questions but Hans's quick wit and juvenile sense of humor more or less matched my own. Earlier in the trip I'd given him my old canvas L.L.Bean fishing hat with the large floppy brim because Hans was far more fair-skinned than me and he'd wondered if he would suddenly have a hankering for lobster. When Carl saw him wearing the hat, he grinned and called Hans "Umbrella head."

As we hiked along, jumping streams and climbing over boulders on the rapidly narrowing track, I learned that Hans was the middle-child son of a dairyman who had grown up in a small farm town of four hundred fifty souls in southwest Minnesota, graduated in a class of twenty-three, and gone off to a branch of the University of Minnesota to study environmental horticulture. Following an internship with a rose propagator in his native state, he'd wound up working his first job at a cut flower wholesaler in Australia, then went on to learn about tissue culturing at a lab in New Zealand—essentially cloning plants and growing them in a test tube. "I remember being so fascinated to discover that what you could produce in one year in a lab might take eight or nine years in the field," he said, explaining how he'd eventually returned home to Minnesota to work for a private nursery called Shady Oaks that specialized in his first love, hostas—yet another thing we had in common.

I knew from Tony that Hans was one of America's top hosta breeders, with several of his own varieties patented and in broad commercial distribution, but I was pleased to learn how passionate the subject of breeding new hostas and naming them was to this lanky son of the American prairie. "Hostas are such a friendly plant," he observed as we went along. "They're easy to grow and divide easily, don't demand a lot, and make any garden look better. Just about anyone can have great success with them. I love giving them to friends. That's the best-kept secret pleasure of gardening, I think—giving plants to your friends." Several of Hans's creations, including "Old Glory" and "Stained Glass" were best-selling hosta varieties; I'd learned from Tony that "Stained Glass" had recently been designated as the "Hosta of the Year for 2006" by the American Hosta Growers Group. Hans would never had revealed this to me. His love was in creating and distributing unusual hostas—not in basking in their popularity.

One of his greatest professional pleasures, however, he admitted, was preparing Shady Oak's annual sales catalog. "There's almost always a nice human story behind every plant. For example, we had a wonderful new hosta called 'Green Eyes,' a very popular plant, yellow with emerald edges, and I asked the man who bred it why he'd named it that. He simply pointed to his wife. Her eyes were the greenest things ever."

The wet grasslands we were suddenly wading through, following the sight of Mbuko's porkpie hat, suddenly entered a grade that was suddenly pitched and treacherous. The river was now a frothing torrent fifty feet directly below us, and several times we had to stop and try to determine which way our guide was headed through the perilous landscape.

We paused to take a breather and admired a prehistoric grasshopper with scarlet and yellow armor plates, large as a child's toy, and lost sight of Mbuko completely. That's when Hans spotted a magnificent King Protea and stopped to study and photograph it.

I was still in the romantic grip of Beryl Markham, I confess, and eager to lay eyes on those ancient San cave paintings, so I bid my companion adieu and pushed on to try and catch up with our guide. Over the shoulder of a ridge where the river sharply turned, I regained sight of him, higher up on the grassy slopes now, crossing over a large boulder's dome and mysteriously whacking the waist-high grass as he reentered it.

The point from which I saw Mbuko, however, appeared to be a dead end for any hope of a trail. Before me lay a large flat rock tilted at a severe angle toward the edge of the cliff a dozen yards below. Beyond that was now a hundred feet of air rising off the misty surface of the boiling river.

Perplexed, I stood there for several moments wondering what to do, to proceed or wait for the others. There was no visible path anywhere above the rock, but a slight indentation in the grass directly across where *something* large had gone ahead of me. I got about halfway across the wet surface of the rock, wedging the tips of my fingers into fissures, when the toe of my lead boot slipped and began sliding down the rock, heading for the edge of the cliff, at which point I dove for the far side of the rock and managed to grab a sharp edge and stop myself from going over and into the river. The only real damage was a skinned knee and a sudden case of self-loathing at my stupidity in not waiting for my mates. Something slithered off in the grass below the rock I was gripping, and I suddenly realized why Mbuko was beating the dense grasslands with a large stick.

I sat on top of the rock for probably five or ten minutes feeling my racing heart finally slow down to a reasonable gallop and regaining my composure, recalling Cameron's reassurances that just about every poisonous snake in Africa except for the lethal puff adder would hurry to get out of an intruder's way. With this in mind, I set off, climbing slowly hand over hand up the steep grass slope, singing an old James Taylor song about faraway Carolina, hoping some black mamba or puff adder wasn't a music critic as well.

By the time I reached the first cave, several hundred feet above a spectacular oxbow in the river, Mbuko was relaxing on a limestone ledge, enjoying a cigarette, his snake stick leaning against the wall. He gave me a gleaming toothy smile as I hoisted myself up, huffing and sweating from the final climb, picked up his stick, and pointed to a crude figure of a human being done in russet tones; the crude figure was clearly pursing a horned animal I took to be an eland or springbok. What little breath I had, the painting took away.

"Wow," was all I could manage at this point, still sucking the damp air into my aching lungs.

"I realize why you have that stick," I said after a moment, to Mbuko.

"Yes boss."

"It was for snakes, huh?"

"Yes boss."

"Did you hear me singing?"

"Yes boss."

"I'll bet you thought it was really James Taylor climbing up here to see these paintings, didn't you?"

"Yes boss."

One by one, the others arrived. It turned out I'd somehow missed the main trail and wound up taking myself on an unnecessary tour of lower Mambaland. Always hold tight to hand of nurse, goes the wise Victorian admonition, for fear of finding something worse.

CARL SCHOENFELD GREW UP on a ranch in the rolling hills north of San Antonio. "Looking back, my sister Shelly and I had wonderful childhoods that were completely out in nature," he told me in the middle of a hot morning two days later. We were exploring a large dry boulder-strewn hilltop not far from the town of Stutterheim, where Cameron promised to lead us into a rare original Afromontane forest near his former property later that day. When I spotted what looked to be a huge cycad, I asked Carl for a confirmation, and he'd explained to me that the specimen could easily have been fifteen hundred years old. He also told me about the peculiar indigenous growing characteristics of cycads—when droughts come, they simply cease growing on top and grow *downward* instead—prompting me to tell him about meeting the James Bond of rare plants at the Philadelphia Flower Show preview gala and then possibly seeing him again selling gourmet Irish gardening boots at Chelsea.

"There are a lot of people feeding off the popularity of certain exotics right now," Carl observed, "and a lot of them care far more about the quick money they can make than the perpetuation of any species." He smiled, shook his head, and added with a self-deprecating chuckle, "You can always tell the real plant nuts by the way they behave out-of-doors, especially in the wild. The reason we have such long days in the field is that we're basically paranoid about missing something incredible, maybe life-changing. In the back of your mind is this constant fear that if you get tired and quit now, the instant you do so you'll miss the most extraordinary plant you could ever hope to see. So we drive ourselves from sunup to sundown, as long as there is light. That's something that got in my blood, I'm afraid, as early as the second grade. Plant hunters are all just overgrown children at heart."

That was the Christmas his sister Shelly received a pony and Carl got a bonsai kit and the *Exotica Encyclopedia of Gardening*, filled with pictures of rare and exotic plants from Madagascar, Tasmania, and Africa. "All of the images were tied to faraway places and there was a cool map of the world showing people hiking over some mysterious exotic terrain like this one. I grew that bonsai from seed and collected rocks and started hiking off on my own through my father's ranchland to find unusual cacti and other plants. I brought them home and planted them around our house, wedging them into rocks to mimic nature. The land there was almost magical. But it was really that book that put me on this path, the mystery and adventure of world plant exotica. I still have the book."

By high school, Carl was growing his own exotic plants in a greenhouse his father built from the windows of a bank building taken down in San Antonio. "My mom and grandmother and I began growing orchids. None of my friends really understood the attraction, I suppose, but my sister and I grew up without TV and the things most other kids had. Now I look back and realize what a special gift our parents gave us—entertainment as vast as the outdoors."

By the time he was studying environmental design at Texas A&M, Carl knew he would wind up making some kind of life in horticulture. "If I hadn't had a roommate who got drunk one night at a college party," he said with a chuckle as we explored the dry hilltop just outside Stutterheim together (at one point finding several large recently shed cobra skins), "I might never have found my direction in life. My roomie was supposed to drive out to Hempstead and help a professor of his do some work on a small nursery he was thinking of selling. But he was so hungover I went in his place and met my future business partner. He offered me a job designing gardens and doing maintenance at Peckerwood Gardens, which specialized in rare and exotic plants for zone eight-A, and soon I was doing just about every job there. I dropped out of Texas A&M just six hours short of my environmental design degree and never went back."

In 1987, Carl made his first plant expedition to the hill country of northeast Mexico. "That was the remotest and most unexplored part of Mexico, an area largely left alone by collectors for the Arnold Aboretum and other big outfits. Some of the mountains there were nearly eight thousand feet. Probably twenty percent of the plants I found there would have been found growing in the Appalachians as far up as western Massachusetts. What a surprise and delight that was to learn. It was like finding a lost plant kingdom hidden in the mountains of Mexico, my own little Eden. That's why I kept going back there to explore and collect. It was like something from the *Exotica Encyclopedia of Plants*. I was living my boyhood fantasy."

A decade later, Carl purchased the small commercial nursery he and his former partner had eventually started on the side to complement Peckerwood Gardens, Yucca Do Nursery, and hired Wade Roitsch to work as a propagator and shipping manager for their catalog. Like a handful of the elite catalogs, including Plant Delights and Shady Oaks (wholesale only), Yucca Do specialized in shipping live, mature, healthy plants to its customers. Wade Roitsch was also the son of a Texas cattle-man who'd fallen for plants while working his way through college. His first trip to the high traces of northeast Mexico came shortly after he arrived, and he too was bitten by the plant exploration bug. The two had made dozens of collecting sorties there together and also explored the jungles and grasslands of Argentina and Brazil. On the heels of this South African trip, Wade told me, he was planning to accompany Tony on his first venture into Thailand and Vietnam. "There's a feeling those places may also eventually close down their borders," Wade said in his solemn and straightforward manner. "So I really want to see what's there if there is any chance of that happening."

He told me this as we were scaling through the dense vines of a rare surviving tropical rain forest to Leopard Falls that same afternoon. Above us towered magnificent yellowwood trees Cameron had said were home to families of indigenous mataloe mountain monkeys. The understory was thick with stunning flowers in bloom—scadoxis, haeman-thus, and an amazing climbing African onion called *Bowiea volubilis*. Tony found at least six varieties of ferns and soon disappeared down a trail near the top of the roaring falls. The others melted away too, into the web of the jungle, drawn by the dense green foliage and tropical lushness. At one point on the steep ascent over mossy logs and jutting stones, I glanced up and suddenly had to freeze. I was inches from the largest spider's web I'd ever seen, as large and shimmery as a silk flag. In the middle of the web sat a large iridescent green spider with golden legs, quite a handsome thing. I just happened to have my field guide in my pocket and pulled it out. The spider turned out to be from the Oxy-opidae family of arachnids, something called a Lynx spider. *Active hunter on vegetation*, pointed out the guide. *Slightly venemous. Leaps consid-*

erable distances. I took a photograph and gave the beautiful African spider a friendly berth.

A few minutes later I was standing on top of the roaring falls gazing upward at the extraordinary massive yellowwoods, thinking I was living out *my* boyhood fantasy, when Cameron came up beside me, abruptly dropped to his knees, and lowered his mouth to the pool above the falls to drink. He had been showing me wild salvias to die for and pointed out a tiny rare epiphytic orchid growing from the moss that had accumulated on the bark of a witch hazel tree leaning over the water, an entire self-sustaining ecosystem. "Four and one half tons of debris falls from those trees to the forest floor here every year, creating one of the most biodiverse environments on this earth. The monkeys are merely the showmen of this rain forest. You won't see them at this hour of the day, I'm afraid. But trust me when I say they are always watching you."

"Is that water safe to drink?" I said above the din of the noisy falls.

"Perfectly so. Water must simply cross seven stones before it's safe enough to drink. This water comes from far on top, you see, filtering down through a large and pristine grassland that serves as a giant water filter. The problem is, the local tribes have recently been permitted to graze their cattle up there, so the grass is rapidly vanishing. We're battling to save it, for if the grass is destroyed, this entire unique ecosystem will be compromised and soon the thousands of life-forms that rely on the water and each other will begin to die off, beginning with those majestic trees you are so passionately admiring. It's as perfect an example of how all life-forms from fungus to birds are delicately linked in the web of life. There's probably more undiscovered fungi here than anyplace in the world." He drank again and then repeated what seemed to be a theme with him:

"Flowers and trees are a pure indicator of a country's political and social life—and habitat is directly related to the state of the nation."

I nodded and he added, with a lighter tone, "In the evenings, beautiful Cape parrots fill these trees above the falls here. I once brought a friend of mine from the university to this very spot, a fellow naturalist who invited the beautiful daughter of one of his colleagues along to help him collect. She was a very beautiful girl in her late teens. It was a hot day and we paused here to drink. The next thing I knew, the young woman had stripped off all her clothes and dived straight into this pool. It was like something out of a movie. What an unforgettable day of plant collecting that was!"

"Incredible," I said, staring at the vast rain forest canopy around us. Through the trees I thought I could make out wild iris spreading down the slopes, thousands upon thousands of "walking" iris plants carpeting the damp jungle floor. Cameron confirmed it.

"Try a drink," He Who Must Be Obeyed insisted. "Taste the original water of southern Africa before it disappears as well."

So I dropped to me knees and drank from my second African river with cupped hands.

"What do you think?" He smiled almost like the proprietor of a shop. "Like heaven up here, isn't it?"

"Fantastic." The water was delicious. But I was still thinking about what he'd told me about both the naked Jane and the race to save the jungle. "Do you think this place will survive?"

Cameron shrugged, cupping more water. "Who can say. Time will tell. We're in the fight of our lives to save it. You saw the town below, my old town. It's filled with poverty and falling apart. The place I'm taking you tomorrow up on the Kei River, however, overlooking the tribal border lands, is an even more perilous tale of survival. Neil Potter's place is where I found the cyrtanthus named for me.You won't believe what he is up against. Quite frightening. He's battling both man and nature, I'm afraid. Beautiful flowers are one of the things that keep the man going."

On that note, I cupped my hands and drank from the delicious endangered river again.

NEIL POTTER'S PLACE was an hour or so out of Stutterheim, in the steep rugged mountain highlands overlooking the winding Great Kei

River. The road going in was a nightmare of potholes and washouts, the worst terrain we'd seen yet.

Neil Potter was the son of one of Cameron's former schoolmates, a fifth-generation sheep and cattle farmer whose forebears had been farming in the district even before the black tribes filtered down from the Orange Free State at an earlier part of the previous century. He was a muscular, quick-smiling former officer in the South African army who pleasantly explained, as we banged and jostled torturously upward in his elderly Isuzu 4X4 to a prime collecting spot where Cameron had found the rare cyrtanthus that would officially bear his name in field guides starting in 2005, that all he had ever wished to do in life was return to his father's land and breed sheep and cattle and raise a family of his own. I was riding alone with Neil in the front cab when he told me this, pointing to the roofline of a pretty but isolated farmhouse on a distant hillside, linked to the main road by a winding yellow clay track at the lower elevations.

"That's where we used to live before my family was attacked," he said almost offhandedly. The others were jostling around in the flatbed behind us, and I could hear them laughing about the insane terrain the truck was ascending. In places there appeared to be no road whatsoever, only evidence of a steeply rising sheep trail twisting around huge boulders and rock outcrops.

I asked Neil who had attacked his family.

"It was five men who came across the Kei River one night two years ago. My wife Carmen and I were watching TV rather late. Our sons Dylan and Morgan were in their beds. I was alerted by our dog that something was up outside and I stepped out to investigate with my twelve-gauge shotgun. We have a lot of predators up here, you see. I was surprised and jumped by the five of them. They were armed with knives and pistols. Luckily I managed to break free and get a shot off, killing one of them on the spot. I got another one in the jaw before they fled, taking the body of the dead man with them. They just vanished back into the bush."

He told this harrowing tale so simply, so calmly, it almost sounded like part of his daily work routine. Like everything we'd seen in Southern Africa, nothing was small or predictable, including the plants and the people.

"Did they find the men who did it?"

"Yes. They eventually found the men who did it—they came from a tribal village you can see from the top of the mountain—but not much was done against them. Truthfully, I was fortunate to have escaped going to jail myself."

"*What?*"

Neil gave a faint smile over the wheel of his violently jostling Bucky. "If they'd found the dead man's body, without question I would have been arrested and tried for murder and probably have gone to prison, possibly for life. That's the kind of frontier justice we have up here now, I'm afraid. Fortunately for my family's sake, they never found the dead man's body. They must have buried him in the jungle. The men who attacked my family were only charged with nuisance trespassing. They claimed they only wanted to steal my farm dog. I have no idea if they were even fined. That's when Carmen put her foot down, and we took a safer farm down below on the main road, next door to a lovely black farmer who can tell you equally horrifying stories about the decline of life in these parts. He has nothing kind to say about the local authorities. Farming is in such terrible condition in these parts, he now operates a funeral home on the side." He gave a quick grin and shot me a glance. "Burying people is a fairly reliable business, seems like."

THE TOP of the mountain was like a swelling green bosom crowned by a dense jungle of short tangled trees and vines. It was a considerable hike up a very steep grade to reach the tree line, and my legs immediately began protesting. Cameron's cyrtanthus was somewhere over the crown of the hill, but my weary legs just said no go. Fortunately, so did Tony's. While the others set off with Cameron in the lead, projecting a round-trip hike of at least four hours, Tony, Neil and I ventured down the opposite slopes toward a high, grass-topped cliff overlooking maybe twenty miles of the tribal lands and winding Great Kei River. For a place so utterly and violently under seige, it was simply one of the most arresting landscapes I'd seen.

Tony found asparagus ferns and indigenous ficus and was thus quickly in high-altitude rapture, while I poked about and found several baby cycads that probably could have paid for a nice new riding mower if I'd sold them at the Philadelphia Flower Show. After an hour or so on my own, I came across Neil kneeling near the edge of the cliff, photographing a huge, exotic plant whose leaves exploded, fanlike, from a large brown bulb that appeared to be only half buried. I asked him what it was.

"Cyrtanthus of some kind. I don't recall the Latin."

"Like the one Cameron found?"

"Exactly. I should know, but it's this photostatic memory of mine. It copies for a moment and then vanishes."

"So you fancy wildflowers too?"

Neil gave me a softer look. "Oh, very much so, though it's late in the game for me. In the past few years flowers have become my passion. Cameron got me hooked on them. Before that they were just plants and interesting bushes. Now every time I'm out in the bush I carry two things—my field guide and my thirty-eight. Once you start looking at plants that way, a whole new world begins. The more you learn, the more you realize there is to learn. It just draws you in. I've recently started bringing my sons up here on wildflower hunts. They absolutely love it and we spend hours looking for things. Cameron says there are undoubtedly species that have never been found on this mountain. The environment here is still that undisturbed."

As we sat together on the cliff, feeling a cool wind from two thousand feet below rise off the Great Kei River and brush our sweating faces, I asked Neil how long he realistically expected this upland flower paradise to stay this way. Below us a couple hundred feet, large birds of prey were circling on the upward thermals. They looked like vultures.

He flashed one of his large and friendly smiles, although I could detect a sadness behind his natural cheerfulness. "The next twenty years will tell the tale. AIDS has wiped out the middle-aged people in this part of Africa, so you have only old people and very young men, who basically have no training or knowledge of farming practices. If we can create a generation of educated young blacks, however, I think all of this can be saved and preserved for my boys and other generations. If not, it will be lost very quickly, I fear."

"Is there any industry or jobs along the river?"

"I'm afraid only the sheep and cows I loan them." Another quick, sad smile. "In the old days if you had a sheep stolen, you simply went across the river and had a word with the chief or head man, and everything got straightened out. No more, I'm afraid. Now they take my cows, too. They use them in their funeral services—butchering the animal on the spot and having a barbecue that often lasts several days."

"How many cows have you lost this way?"

"Too many." He smiled and tossed a rock over the cliff. "Thank God for my boys and my flowers, eh?"

On the climb together back up through the dense grasslands and rocks, he told me more Xhosa customs and showed me the Cape browsing bush, pulling off several leaves and inviting me to chew them—"a natural appetite suppressant and energy stimulant, makes a lovely Bushman's tea as well"—and we found patches of wild gladiolus, Rock fig, and Cape willow, the bark of which Neil harvested and ground to sell to a local physician. Among other things, aspirin came from the bark of Cape willow, he explained as we climbed, and a local doctor believed it could be used to cure various kinds of cancer. Neil was harvesting the bark and grinding it for the doctor, and tests were underway. At one point he took my arm in his iron grip, as a snake slithered away just ahead of us.

He grinned and released my arm. "Think it might have been a spitting cobra. Nasty bugger. You have to shoot them before they shoot you."

AFRICA COULD HAVE ENDED for me right there—on a pristine flower-strewn summit high above a beautiful winding river that was older than man's time on this earth. Metaphors for the beautiful and damned didn't get much more spectacular than this.

Hours later at our pretty hotel on the outskirts of Stutterheim, everyone collapsed from exhaustion, bone weary, with aching muscles and filthy piles of clothing. We had been gouged and stung from two weeks of acacia thorns and insects. Over dinner that night, Tony told me every plant expedition reached a point where the adrenaline simply "gave out," and this was it. Cameron had left us to be with his Australian sheep growers, and we were on our own for the final days of botanizing. "It's difficult to imagine anything more amazing than what we've seen," Wade observed. Together he and Carl had already snapped thousands of photographs.

"Hey everybody," said Hans, lifting his ginger beer. "It's Valentine's Day. Did you remember that someone special?"

I hadn't, and for the first time that night, ironically enough, I attemped to use my international cell phone to call a florist back in Maine to order flowers for my wife. The signal was faint and then vanished altogether in a blizzard of hissing white noise.

Two days later, reasonably rested and washed, we pushed on to Addo Park to see the wildlife, the dusty herds of elephants and zebras. Addo Park is one of the few unqualified successes of rural South Africa. We stayed overnight in a strange Afrikaner hotel, where I went to ask about the astonishing tree growing over the empty car park. It was big as a California redwood, with smooth bark veins as large as a man's thigh and gorgeous green foliage. I thought it might be the famed Tree of Life of ancient Africa and wound up in the bar talking to several tough-looking men with lots of tattoos and scars on their faces. I guessed they were local Boer gentlemen out to share a friendly pint and catch the big Valentine's weekend rugby match on the telly. They were South Africa's version of the unreconstructed redneck so near and dear to my own and Tony Avent's hearts.

"You bunch Americans?" the biggest tattooed and most visibly scarred Afrikaner asked me with a grunt. South Africa was playing New Zealand in the World Cup quarter finals, I deduced entirely on my own.

"That's right." I ordered a pint of Guinness and manfully downed half the glass in one swallow.

"Tourists?" said a short fireplug of a fellow wearing a cockeyed straw hat on his flat head.

"Nope. Hunters. Probably the finest in all the world."

A new respect appeared in their eyes. The big one wanted to know what we were hunting and where. Maybe he was an out-of-work big-game guide.

"All the big five," I said, waited a beat, then ticked off a few of the species I was contemplating for the final balloting of our Big Five Horticultural vote.

"We're talking *Cussonia spicata* and *Erica mammosa*. The Pineapple lily also made my list, too, of course. What an amazing little thing." I took another hearty slug of Guinness.

They stared blankly at each other and then at me.

"You mean fuckin' flowers?" the little one thought to ask; his Dutch lager was suspended in midair. So was his belief.

"That's right," I confirmed and finished my beer, in case I needed to make a sprint for my bungalow. The big guy grinned, though, and suddenly clapped me warmly on the shoulder.

"You mates, like, came all the way out here just to look at our flowers, eh?"

"That's right." I added that I might shove my own grandmother down a flight of church steps just to have that big beautiful tree from the car park growing in my yard back in Maine.

"That's a Cape chestnut," Big Tattoo said, and offered to buy me another round. As I had a pocket full of rands, though, I bought the next round.

"Where the hell is Maine?" wondered the Small Tattoo, still pondering the mystery of why grown men would come all the way to South Africa to hunt for flowers.

"A little north of Boston and well below zero," I said in my best Bing Crosby.

Big Tattoo touched his pint to mine. "Good luck to you boys," he said warmly.

Before turning out the lights that night, I heard on my room radio that there were violent protests breaking out in the Orange Free State due to lack of government services. Some white travelers had been hijacked and murdered on a busy road just outside of Durban.

When I stepped outside my room around midnight to try my cell phone again, the massive thunderstorm that had knocked out lights at dinner was still rumbling and spitting rain. I stood barefoot in the rain, dialed my home number, and finally heard my wife on the opposite end. It was snowing hard back home in Maine, she said, and my daughter Maggie wanted to say hello.

As Maggie and I chatted, fading in and out from each other half a world away, I suddenly saw a lone figure walking toward me through the rainy darkness. When the lightning flashed I saw he was armed with a rifle. When he got within a few yards away, I saw he was a young black man.

"Good evening," he said politely.

"Good evening," I said to him. "You the night watchman?"

"We have had several robbers, sir. It is probably not safe to be out of your room."

"I understand."

"Please lock your door, sir."

"Absolutely no problem there."

"Who's that?" my daughter demanded half a world away.

"Very polite fellow with a small elephant gun," I told her and laughed, hoping I'd somehow make both of use feel a little less queasy.

THE NEXT DAY in Grahamstown, a bustling university town, I took a break from the nerds and wandered the crowded streets by myself. It was both market day in the district capital and the first day of the new school term. Students were queued outside of the only bookstore in town, and the two Internet coffeehouses were packed with young people—black and white—e-mailing on their laptops. While the nerds botanized a beautiful dry slope outside town, I wandered down a narrow, crowded alley into a street bazaar and talked with a group of native women who'd brought huge melons and pumpkins to town to sell. Since I failed to get flowers to my wife for Valentine's Day, I bought her a lovely Zulu fertility mask carved from native stinkwood.

"If you make her wear this," the skinny black woman who sold it to me for twenty dollars assured me with a wild toothless grin, "she will grow very fat and have many babies for you."

"Just what I'm sure she's hoping for," I told her and said thanks.

After that I lily-limped into the crowded bank across the street to cash a travelers check and get more rands for my fellow plant geeks while they scoured the local hills. I somehow managed to reach the front of the very long line only to discover I was queued up to purchase funeral insurance.

We traveled for several more days, swinging back across the high Swatzburg Pass—the edge of fynbos country—frightfully fogged in as we ascended up a shapely winding asphalt road where there were no guardrails and nothing but sweet eternity a few yards either left or right. Every so often one of the nerds would suffer a halfhearted hortgasm, and Tony would stop on the narrow shoulder; they would climb out and investigate interesting aloes or crassulas in the dry acidic soil. I would hang out among the beautiful king protea and sudden croppings of erica—the two plants I put third and fourth on my own Big Five list, just behind the humble common cabbage tree of South Africa. In mymind I confess, I was already heading home. The Philadelphia Flower Show began exactly thirteen days from the morning we were lost in the fog on top of the Swatzberg Pass for what seemed like a small lifetime. Finally we reached the top, and there was a helpful sign that announced *Die Top*. By this point we'd lost two more hubcaps off the Mercedes, and the suspension system where I was seated in back was making a funny scraping noises from hitting too many potholes time forgot. After lunch at a beautiful inn down in Prince Albert, we wound along a dry valley road lined with magnificent limestone ledges where colonies of baboons stood watching. We found whole hillsides covered in unusual aloes, and Wade found a gigantic turtle. At one point the largest brown snake I'd ever seen lay coiled on the asphalt road's shoulder near a dry culvert.

Tony and I poked it with a stick and found it was dead. Moments later there was a noise and a silver BMW rocketed past us going about ninety. Snakes never had a chance along that beautiful valley road. I half expected to see a film crew in a helicopter giving hot pursuit.

In Oudtshoorn, once more on the edge of the Little Karoo, which calls itself the ostrich capital of the world, we found a restaurant that served grilled zebra and other big game delicacies. On our drive back to Napier to reunite and have a farewell dinner with Cameron and Rhoda McMaster, we passed through a natural hot springs area that resembled the surface of Mars—a barren haven for huge desert succulents. The only sign of habitation for miles in any direction was a joint with a large neon sign planted in the rock scree off the side of the road: JUST AHEAD. RONNIE'S SEX SHOP.

There was no room for me at the local inn where the others stayed that night in Napier, so I got to spend the night at Cameron and Rhoda's place. We stayed up late drinking a little sherry and talking about the worrying legislation that was threatened to uniformly end all legal trafficking of plants and seed from South Africa to the world. "The amazing thing is, it's about two or three hundred years too late," declared Rhoda with feeling. "Other countries, particularly the Europeans, have made fortunes off our native flowers and plants for so long, but the folly is these plants left here long ago. The politicians simply don't seem to grasp that the only people they will hurt are true plant lovers here and abroad. We're legally selling them flowers and seed as it is. Once you shut it all down, only the thieves will be in business. And they will take what they want, without anyone knowing they have been there."

Despite this gloomy forecast, I thanked the McMasters for their incredible hospitality and informed Cameron that it was the unanimous opinion of the others that Cameron was the most able field guide they'd ever met. He seemed very pleased by this information, especially after I added that I'd placed *his* name on my own list of Africa's Big Five Horticultural stars.

"Here's to your garden back home in Maine," he proposed, lifting his glass to me. "Long may it grow. Is it spring there yet?"

"Not quite. Should be happening sometime around July."

The next day we stood in a breathtaking meadow, high above two oceans and vast fields filled with King proteas and blooming ericas. Our host was a local farmer named Thys De Villers who still spoke with such a thick Dutch Afrikaner accent I could scarely make out a word he said. He clearly relished his role as sacred keeper of an 11,000-acre fynbos haven and he gave me a huge grin and thumbs-up when he saw me break off several different species of blooming heaths and hold them up for Hans to photograph.

"For the heart, eh?" he said to me thickly, sounding like an early Dutch settler.

"For some friends in Philadelphia."

Dag hammarskjöld was supposed to have said there is South Africa and then there is Cape Town—a beautiful European city lost at the edge of a continent.

What we found there over the next couple days was both disturbing and inspiring. The roads leading into the city were lined with grim and sprawling townships. Our hotel on the edge of the center city was a four-star affair with a ten-foot concrete fence topped by three feet of coiled razor wire. "Is that to keep them out or us in?" Hans tried to break the tension by asking the reception clerk this as we were checking in.

The young black clerk stared at us, unamused, and politely explained that it was strictly unadvisable to walk the streets after dark or go to places unaccompanied.

A friend of mine once lived in an artsy corner of Cape Town, though, and fondly described it as a Third World San Francisco. So while the others ventured out the next day to look at Jackass penguins on the coast near Simonstown, I ignored the hotel clerk's advice and set off on foot to explore the city on my own.

This was the day after we'd spent an enchanting afternoon wandering around world-famous Kirstenbosch Botanic Garden, which sits at the foot of Table Mountain, where down drafts of tropical warmth and moisture off the mountain help create the wettest spot on the Cape and a unique gardening environment. The extensive gardens are planted entirely in South African species, laid out in classic landscape presentations that displayed the leading plants of the nation. My problem, if seeing stunning plants anywhere is ever a problem, was that I'd seen many of these aloes, brunsvigias, ericas, pelargoniums, proteas, and cycads growing wild in their native habitats during a journey that had carried us more than ten thousand miles across southern Africa and finally brought us to a world-famous garden. Seeing the plants suddenly arranged in such neat and cultivated borders and perfect tree-lined avenues was something of a muted pleasure for me. Perhaps the gardener in me had finally gone a little wild, as well.

I had a wonderful if slightly unnerving day on my own in Cape Town. Passing through a derelict district, I followed street map to St. George's Cathedral, Desmond Tutu's Anglican mother church. I briefly took refuge there from the heat and listened to a young black man practicing hymns on the pipe organ. Then I went back out into the heat of the day and hiked up through the Company Garden toward the African Museum, passing old Cecil John Rhodes on his pedestal, facing north toward the hinterlands where we'd just been, piegon droppings on his extended pointing finger.

The Company Garden, the first spot the Dutch planted in the 1500s when they set foot on the Cape to colonize it, is the oldest garden spot in the nation. For my money it's also one of the loveliest. There were yellow finches darting through the blooming agapanthus and hundreds of dozens of black schoolchildren laughing and playing tag on the grass there. For a while I followed a pure white albino squirrel, and he led me to a perfectly maintained rose garden where every bush was in bloom. There were huge hibiscus shrubs throwing out a wonderful scent, too. I didn't spot another white face anywhere, but I felt entirely at ease in the ancient Company Garden.

Alone in the vast and empty African Museum, I read about how the first settlers to the Cape had eaten gladiolus bulbs roasted over a fire in order to survive their first winter on the continent. The local Khoi tribesmen showed them this neat trick and others. At one point one of the early settlers sent a plaintive letter home to Holland that took more than a year to reach its destination. "There is such abundance here and we are joyfully at work and play in a garden not unlike heaven itself," he wrote to relatives. "Though I don't know if I should ever be graced to see my beloved home again."

I WAS STILL THINKING about that unknown homesick gardener in a brave new world the next afternoon when the five of us drove up Table Mountain hoping to see what grew there and take a last long look at the jewel of the southern Cape. Coming here had clearly changed something in me, too. Or perhaps merely set it loose.

The road, in any case, was closed due to landslides, so we took one last long hike up the winding asphalt road to a point near the summit. There ornamental grasses were waving in a stout ocean wind, and all of Cape Town stretched out before a very blue sea. We took a few final photographs, all shook hands, and Tony announced the official results of everyone's Big Five balloting.

Aloe, brunsvigia, kniphofia, haemanthus, and agapanthus had won. Not counting Cameron, I had two that made the list.

"If it helps," Tony attempted to console me on the top of windy Table Mountain, "we all considered the common cabbage tree a sentimental choice since it saved us from having to carry you off to a hospital."

Chapter 11

※

I Was Here

"SOMETIMES IT'S THE GOING BACK that takes us forward," Philadelphia writer Beth Kephart wrote in her poetic little book about the two years Chanticleer Garden opened her eyes to a deeper lived-in world and helped her find grace in just letting go of the past. "What I found most here in this garden," she told me in a conversation weeks after we met by chance that morning before Garden Fare, "was a way of releasing my own ghosts and looking at the future with clearer eyes. A garden just keeps going and reminds us to do just that."

Less than forty hours after arriving home from Africa, I stepped through the doors of the 176th Philadelphia Flower Show eager to see old friends and find out what they'd been up to in the year I'd been off on my own private odyssey of garden discovery.

It was once again Friday afternoon on the eve of the show's gala preview party, and I didn't waste any time in hunting down my friend the Botticelli of Bulbs, Walt Fisher. He and Linda and the Straws, Jim and Keith, were placing the last of tulips in the pots in their new competitive class, Container Gardens. The theme of this year's show was "America the Beautiful" and featured, among other things, the original White House gates in a display garden that would greet the thousands expected to flock to the exhibition hall, starting Sunday morning at eight.

Walt's big news was his knees. "Had them both done exactly one hundred eight days ago," he anounced with the timekeeper's precision I would have expected from him. "So now if we've forgotten to add something important at the last minute I can *sprint* to find it and bring it back." He explained that the Inforcers were up against even more daunting competiton this year, including renowned plantsman Ray Rogers and a major gardening foundation. When I asked Walt where the Amey siblings were, remembering how I hoped to have a word with the show's "first family" of gardeners, he pointed down an aisle crowded with workers and said, "They're over in Condo class this year, up against your friends the Francises."

I'd arrived late and some workers were already beginning to knock off and head home to wait out to the first round of official judging. Union crews were already sweeping up the floors as the setup phase had evidently come off with even more precision than usual under the guidance of the show's new designer, Sam Lenhenny. After chatting with them for a while and filling them in on my own adventures, I went off to find Jeanne Francis.

I suddenly knew what Walt had meant a year ago when he observed that coming back every year to the Philadelphia Flower Show was like attending a reunion of good friends. That's exactly how being here suddenly felt.

I found Jeanne Francis on her knees "flower fluffing" primroses and sunflowers in Condo class. Her entryway was a novel "Native American" theme. The moment she saw me, Jeanne gave a little shriek of delight and hopped up and hugged me like a long lost friend.

"Where have you been?" she insisted with her jolly wood sprite laugh. "We thought for sure we would see you entering something in the show this year. This year a plant, next year your own exhibit. That's how it goes. I warned you about this addiction of yours."

I explained I'd just gotten off a plane from southern Africa only a few hours before and was still having difficulty adjusting to the twelve-hour time difference, not to mention the crazier pace of life.

"What were you doing *there*, hon?"

"Searching for wildflowers with five plant hunters."

"Oh . . . my . . . *god*! Was that incredible or what?"

I agreed it was, although already the sojourn was beginning to take on the quality of a fine dream. Had it really happened or was it merely a lovely winter dream I had while my flower beds slept beneath their burial mounds of snow, awaiting spring's reluctant return? Fortunately, I already had several photographs of the trip to show Jeanne, including those taken near the end on Thys De Viller's incredible evica-covered hilltop.

Jeanne's big news for the year was that she and her business partner Alicia McShulkis had completed their labors on the abolitionist schoolroom project, become certified historic garden restorers, and even taken a joint field trip down to Monticello. "We just keep *evolving*," she declared. "We now dress up like colonial babes and give a PowerPoint program on the botany of Lewis and Clark. If I may say so, it's a hoot. Garden groups eat it up. We've never had so much fun."

I told her I wasn't the least bit surprised to learn this and nodded over at the exhibit of the vaunted Amey siblings, a spectacular traditional Philadelphia condo entryway. None of my phone calls to the Amey family over the previous twelve months—at least three or four attempts—had been returned as hoped, which led me to think they might be either shy about interviews or simply in a class by themselves.

"Is that the Amey siblings?" I asked Jeanne. Two young women were in discussion with a PHS official.

"That's them. Their father Stan is somewhere around here, too. You should try and speak to him. He's a major player in Philly gardening circles."

"Where's Jim?"

She laughed. "Off eating again."

Jeanne and I chatted pleasantly for a dozen more minutes about my African wildflower hunt and her latest ambitions to broaden her garden club lecturing career. When I looked over where the siblings had just been standing, however, they were gone.

"Looks like you missed them again," Jeanne said, chuckling.

"Guess I'll never know for sure if they got their plants last year at Home Depot," I said.

She patted my hand consolingly. "In plant competition, hon, some things are probably better kept a sweet mystery."

I FOUND JACK AND JOE BLANDY in the nick of time, just before they knocked off and took their crew out for their annual flower show setup dinner in Chinatown. Their entry in the major exhibit class was a spectacular "American Woodland Garden" that featured deer-resistant trees and shrubs. According to Jack, Pennsylvania's two and a half million white tail deer did five million dollars' worth of damage to the yards and gardens of the Keystone state every year. The only way to fight back was to plant things they wouldn't eat, an approach I felt sure Ed Pugh, wherever he was, would wholeheartedly endorse.

Since I'd last seen them, Jack and wife Jane had been to India on a special Rotary Club program to vaccinate poor children against polio. During that same time, son Joe had finally become a registered landscape architect, and both men had recently been advised that they would soon be inducted together into Temple University's Ambler School of Horticulture's Hall of Fame.

"Not bad for an old English major who accidentally fell in love with plants, I guess," Jack said wryly, as we stood admiring his handsome deer-resistant woodland. He added that business was so brisk he'd been forced to recently take on a new project manager. "Joe has all sorts of big plans to expand the business in ways I never even thought of," he said with an unmistakable note of pride. "Pretty soon I'll be working for *him*."

We shook hands, and I wished him good luck and then spent the rest of my time hanging out in the Horticourt looking at exquisite euphorbias, crassulas, ledbourias, and nerines, remembering the way they looked in the wild.

"I just saw this plant in the wild," I said out loud at one point to nobody in particular—to myself, actually. It was a lovely banded pelargonium not unlike the one I'd nearly flattened when I dropped from the common cabbage tree to see the world's smallest hyacinth.

"Really? Where?" A show volunteer, an older lady in a yellow scarf, was on duty at the registration table nearby. The Horticourt had thinned out, too.

"A foggy mountaintop in South Africa."

"Lucky *you*."

I couldn't disagree.

Once again i was among the first to plow through the doors of the Pennsylvania Convention Center when the 2005 Philadelphia Flower Show opened for business. It may have been my imagination or the result of nearly a month in the bush, but the jostling crowds seemed even more enthusiastic and determined to see who'd won what in the mother of all plant competitions.

Jack and Joe Blandy's splendid deer-resistant American woodland garden had placed second overall, but captured an important new prize from the Bartlett Tree Company along with several smaller awards for best use of trees. "Next year we'll be out of the competition," Jack surprised me with the news. He grinned and added, "That's because we've been asked to do the Central feature for the 2006 show."

The theme would be "Enchanted Spring" and his mind was already working overtime on the floral extravaganza. It was going to have three major components, he said, giving me a glimpse into his thinking. "Fire, wind, and water. We're planning to have a tropical volcano with a lava flow made from plants, a water feature like nothing anyone's done before, and maybe kites in a spring meadow."

"Sounds challenging," I said.

"Come back and see it," he insisted. "Same time next year. That's the joy of being at Philly."

I promised I would and went off to find the final four Inforcers.

They'd finished a close second to Ray Rogers in the first phase of judging. "It's hard to be too disappointed," allowed Walt. "Ray is a show legend, one of the finest plantsmen in America. But it would be nice to go out on a win. Doesn't look like our group will be returning next year."

I was shocked to hear this. He kindly elaborated. "Linda and I want to do something smaller again, and the Straws are so busy these days. That's okay. We've had a grand time and a great run."

I wondered if this meant there would be no more springtime bursting forth in his basement in Bryn Mawr. He laughed and shook his head.

"Oh yes. There will be bulbs. *Plenty* of them." He explained that he'd already ordered fifteen hundred spring bulbs and would have his pots dutifully planted by Veterans Day. "I'm going back to my roots a little bit and enter individual plants in the Horticourt," he explained.

The added bonus of not competing on the larger scale, he said, was that he could do a lot more lecturing on bulb forcing around the Delaware Valley and still photograph the show the way he'd done for years. The requests for lectures, Linda put in, was growing every year. She invited me to come again for lunch before the 2006 show and I promised I would do that, too. The lady makes a mean tuna on marbled rye.

Finally, I went to find Jim and Jeanne Francis in Condo class.

The surging crowds were already standing three and four deep there, firing flash cameras at the beautiful condo entries.

The delightful couple who'd begun their courtship at the Philadelphia Flower Show more than thirty years ago had finished in fourth place, just behind the Amey siblings in the first round of judging. "It's a moral victory for us," Jim said, adding that only half a point separated them from third place, and a couple more points would have tied them with the blue ribbon winner, an Oriental-themed condo entry done by a local garden club.

"The most important thing is the whole class scored in the nineties," Jim explained about the sliding point system. "We'll improve for Wednesday and probably at least win a class award now. We may even move up to second or third."

"Next year we're going to give Jim a break," Jeanne informed me. She and her partner were probably going to sign up for a smaller undertaking, a slot in Balcony class. "I'm already thinking about a balcony full of daffodils out on Nantucket," she said, rolling her eyes, then laughed. "Who knows. It's crazy. But we'll figure out something."

Rather touchingly, Jeanne took my arm and wondered if I would be back.

"You're supposed to be *hooked,* hon. That's the secret way they keep this thing growing, you know."

Once again I promised her I would be there, but only if she agreed to show up on her floral balcony wearing one of her fetching colonial dame outfits.

THREE WEEKS LATER, still waiting for my own ground to thaw, but encouraged by the large number of faintly swelling buds I saw on the Elephant Angel tree's new branches, I once again set off for North Carolina, aiming to catch the enchanted spring on its final northern advance.

Sometimes it's the going back that takes us forward. Once more I had both a mission and garden destinations in mind—places I'd lost but needed to rediscover and finally somehow let go of.

On the way there, I stopped off at Longwood Gardens to see my friends Denise Magnani and Dick Lighty at the Delaware Center for Horticulture's 25th Anniversary Rare Plant Auction, an event I understood might possibly turn out to be the largest rare plant auction in American history. The evening festivities included Dr. Michael Dirr and Dan Hinckley of Heronswood Nursery as celebrity auctioneers, a pair of gardening goodfellows I'd never actually met, but felt I knew from my travels through other people's gardens. The honoree that evening was none other than Dr. Richard Lighty.

I ran into the man himself while silently bidding on a young "Golden Dawn" *Metaseqouia glyptostoboides*, hoping to procure a healthy young life mate for Lilith, my own living fossil back home. I also penciled in a rather daring bid on a regal "Royal Frost" birch. Assuming my bid won, I would need one of Jack Blandy's trucks to get the strapping young tree home.

"So tell me where you've been and what have you've learned," the evening's guest of honor demanded to know in a charming, booming voice. I gave him a brief rundown on my year's activities following our lovely spring afternoon at Springwood, an adventure that commenced in a Bryn Mawr basement full of blooming spring flowers and ended on a dramatic African hillside half a world away, covered with blooming proteas and heaths. I even showed him the little sprig from Thys De Viller's spectacular meadow. As he examined the little piece of erica, I explained that I'd taken his advice and followed the splendid narrative of gardening all the way back to the birthplace of flowers.

"What a wonderful journey," Lighty said, clearly pleased. "And to think it's really just getting started for you! What a marvelous way to begin."

Moments later, I ran into his star pupil Denise Magnani, another late-in-life gardening soul who, like Jefferson and Harry Du Pont, had created a garden for the ages.

Denise's big news was that she was thinking of leaving Winterthur and venturing off on her own to start a garden design consulting business, specializing in children's gardens. "People have been urging me to do it for years, and I guess now is the moment to do it," she said. "Gardens change and so do the people who make them. It's a big leap, but I'm excited about the possibilities."

Winterthur's loss, I assured her, would be some future gardener's gain. Especially for the children of wherever she wound up creating her next enchanted garden.

Following the live auction, I went up to say a quick hello and introduce myself to the celebrity auctioneers, Dirr and Hinckley. Dirr was pleased to know I knew Michael Payne down on the Wilderness Road in Virginia, and Hinckley was happy to hear that I'd just been off to Africa with Tony Avent and Hans Hansen, two of his former traveling mates.

None of my silent bids, alas, was successful, but a funny thing happened on my way out of the auction collection tent. I ran into the attractive Alabama blonde who'd been with the James Bond of rare plant dealers exactly one spring ago at the Philly preview party. She was toting a handsome "Huron" viburnum I secretly wished I'd seen first. An older woman at the silent auction had told me the only way to assure you got the plant you wanted was to "grab a cocktail, plant yourself by the one you want, and outbid anyone who comes close. You've got to be *ruth-*

less, sweetie. Silent auctions are warfare with pencils." Obviously, I should have heeded her advice.

"I hoped I might see you here," I said to the belle of Alabama. "So where's your English friend Humphrey?"

"Oh," she replied vaguely, "he took off a while back. I think he's back in London these days."

I didn't have the heart to ask any more than that or to inform the lady he might be selling expensive Irish garden boots from a bucket of water. I just said it was good to see her again and wished her luck with her lovely "Huron" virburnum.

A FEW WEEKS BEFORE THIS, just a few days after arriving home from Philadelphia, I learned from Anthony Brown that his mama, Sweet Alice, had slipped away to some old soul's needy garden in eternity. He and his two sisters, he said, hoped to soon buy Sweet Alice's place in Ashe County and begin fixing it up. "Lots to be done. It'll never be like it was when mama had it," he said, "but we all grew up in that garden, see, and it will always be our home."

I told him I knew exactly what he was talking about and thanked him for reconnecting me with his mother one spring ago. It amazed me how quickly my year in the garden had passed.

"Did she actually remember you?" he wondered.

"Not in the least. But she remembered my mom. That's the most important thing. She gave me a little redbud tree, too. Actually—made me steal it from her yard."

Anthony had a good laugh at this. "That's mama, all right. She used to pester me to go dig up some big old bush she loved and bring it to her. Can't remember its name . . . some kind of camelia, maybe. She wanted to plant it in the front yard so she could see it out of her window at the rest home. I kind of wish I did that, you know?"

I said I knew, and added that I had a lost garden to try and recover, too.

A couple days after this, I secured the number of the woman who'd bought my mother's house and phoned her up and brazenly asked her if

I might stop by in the coming days and spread the ashes of my mom's old dog Molly in the lily of the valley beds in the back garden. I half expected her to hang up the phone at such a strange request.

Like everything else that year, though, she surprised me.

"I have an idea," said Nancy Wilkinson. "Why don't you come for Sunday brunch, and I can show you what I've done with your mother's garden. We can have brunch in her garden."

I got to Greensboro early that beautiful Sunday morning in May, a whole hour early as it turned out. On a lark, to fill the time before I made my way to Dogwood Drive, I drove over to my old elementary school to see if I could find any traces of my Eagle Scout project from 1970, the ambitious nature walk I'd built through the woodland dell at Archibald D. Murphy Elementary, the first garden I ever designed and built.

Given the rampant growth of the Gate City of the Piedmont, I was prepared to find the woods long gone; the landscape forever changed.

But the woods were there and, rather miraculously, so was the woodland nature trail I'd created thirty-five years ago. I started down the path into the woods and followed it down to the small creek and back up the other side through thickets of blooming wildflowers. The tree and shrub signs I'd carefully made in my father's workshop, à la young Tony Avent, to identify each specimen by its formal Latin and common usage name, had vanished but the trees and shrubs were there and growing magnificently. I found a dogwood, a white ash, and a redbud I was certain I'd put there.

I was blinking my eyes when I emerged from the little woodland garden half an hour later. The trail looped right back to where it began, just like I'd planned thirty-five years ago. It wasn't the sunlight that made me blink but the mother and small boy who were approaching the start of the trail as I came out probably thought so.

"Hello," I said to them.

"Hi," she said cheerfully. The boy was probably four or five, wearing blue sneakers that looked brand new. I'd had nearly identical sneakers at his age. Seeing his reminded me of mine.

"What a beautiful day," I said.

"Isn't it?" They stopped. The boy still held his mom's hand. She glanced at the Carolina blue sky.

"I was just checking out this old trail . . . to see if it was still here. I used to come here as a kid," I explained, leaving it at that.

"It's a great place," she said. "Like a little secret garden in there. Everything's so wild and beautiful. Tommy loves it."

"I'm glad," I said, still blinking. "Maybe someday he'll be a gardener, huh?"

"Maybe," she replied. "He already knows the names of some plants."

THE INSIDE of my mom's house had been altered very little, but the one place Nancy Wilkinson wanted me to see first was the upstairs party room in the attic where my brother Dickie and I used to have the occasional teenage party. The walls back then had been painted with crazy '60s slogans like *Free Love!* and *Go Naked!* But Nancy had painted over most of the silly teenage grafitti save for one mysterious slogan near the north end of the room where she'd set up a large table and several racks upon which she now grew beautiful orchids.

"I was so taken by the haunting quality of the message I decided to leave it. It sounded so personal I just couldn't cover it up."

I WAS HERE, read the slogan. Nancy smiled, looking at the juvenile lettering. "I love that," she said simply. "Like a message in a bottle."

Out back, I was pleased and relieved to see little or nothing had changed. The old brick planters I built for my mom's ferns back in 1969 were still there and still crumbling from my inexpert teenage masonry; the lily of the valley beds were larger and more beautiful than ever, the bamboo at the back of the property had spread along the back fence and screened out the adjoining property; and several of mother's old peony beds were already producing the first luscious blooms of early summer.

I asked Nancy about the redbud in the side yard, and she explained it was gone when she moved in—had never realized one had been there, in fact.

"You have no way of knowing this," she said suddenly, "but this house and your mother's garden were a godsend for me." She explained that she bought the house following a difficult divorce and shortly after the last of her children had grown up and moved away.

"It was like having to start life over for me," she said quietly, offering me a delicious wedge of the quiche she'd baked that morning and filling my wineglass with a chilled Chardonnay. "When I got here, to be truthful, I was something of a wreck. But your mother's garden was so beautiful that I could tell someone very special had lived here and loved this place."

She took a sip of wine, blinked her eyes, and added, "Little by little it drew me out of my sadness and helped me get back the life I needed to have."

As she told me this, I blinked my eyes too. But, once again, it wasn't from the warm spring sunshine.

As we ate, I told Nancy I knew my mom would be very happy to know her garden had been passed along to her.

I could see how this remark touched her. "I'm happy you think so," she said. "And I'd like you to come back in the fall so I can give you some of your mother's peonies. We'll dig them up, and you can take them home to your garden in Maine. Everyone in the neighborhood says your mom was so generous with her plants."

"Most gardeners are," I said, thinking of Hans Hansen on a muddy path in Africa. "Sharing plants is the sign of a true gardener."

"You're welcome here any time," she added.

"Thanks." I almost couldn't speak now.

She smiled and pointed to the attic. "Were you the author of the slogan on the wall up there in my orchid room?"

I shrugged, unable to speak, figuring I probably had been.

"You still are," she said, and then wiped her own eyes.

MY EXTRAORDINARY HOST had another lovely surprise. After we spread Miss Molly's ashes through the lily of the valley beds beneath the towering tulip maples where she used to guard the yard and snooze on hot summer days, the gate swung open and Merle Corry and Ginny Franks came around the corner. They were my mom's longtime neighborhood chums. We hugged and kissed and had a grand old time catching up and then the gate opened a second time and Andy Miller from next door joined the party.

The gate opened a third time, and it was none other than James Thornton, my mom's longtime yardman. As James had reminded me more than once over the years, he never called himself a "gardener" because my mother did all the "real gardening."

After the little garden party ended, I offered to drive James home. He asked me instead to give him a lift over to the shopping center where his grandson was supposed to pick him up.

"It's good you brought old Miss Molly's ashes home where she belongs," he observed, looking at the handsome spring-filled yards as we left Dogwood Drive. "You know, that dog guarded your mama's garden for many years. She lived for guardin' that garden." James suddenly smiled, showing a single gold tooth.

"I know for a fact she took the pants clean off the UPS man at least twice!"

We both laughed at this picture of the old girl.

"You shouldn't stay away so long," James said as we shook hands and said good-bye.

I promised him I would try and avoid doing that from now on, and pointed out I'd be back in the late fall to fetch some of my mother's peonies for my garden up in Maine.

"Maine . . ." James said, shaking his head wonderingly. "What's that like?"

"Wonderful," I said. "Just like here only much colder. Molly despised it."

I MADE ONLY two more stops on my way home to Maine.

The first was to say hello to Polly Logan. She made me sit on her garden loggia and tell her almost every detail of my journey through other people's gardens. When I finished, she gave me a robust Phyllis Diller laugh and made me promise I'd come back and tell my story to her garden club. I promised I would do this and asked how she was feeling and whether she'd beaten back the red-meat neocon in her party's big election. I also wondered if her larcenous gardener had by any chance ever met justice.

"Oh, I won," she said, as if the outcome had never really been in doubt, "and they managed to catch up with him out in Ohio. He'd grown a goatee and was working in a carnival. The jewelry, of course, was long gone. But I'm pretty lucky. Evidently he'd shot his way out of a courtroom in Kansas and was still wanted there."

Then, as usual, she laughed.

MY FINAL STOP was to see my garden guru Suzy Verrier at North Creek Farm, to buy a new "Iroquois" virburnum and whatever else she might have on hand that was new and interesting and just might find a permanent home in my northern woodland garden. If another spring had come, so had a load of outrageous stone wall schemes and gardening plans that might or might not ever get built.

As usual, she was delighted to see me, filling me in on her plan to expand her own garden and giving me the big news that *Real Simple* magazine planned to feature North Creek Farm in an upcoming edition of the magazine.

I congratulated her on this forthcoming debut and thanked her for helping save the Elephant Angel tree and having the wisdom to set a gardening novice on a meandering path of discovery through other people's gardens. I'd met some of the nicest people on earth and learned just enough to understand I still had a lifetime of learning to do.

"That just means you're a real gardener," she said as she walked me out to the truck with my new virburnum. "We're all learning. That's the beauty of this thing. You don't own a garden. It owns *you*. The more you give, the more you get. Besides, we're all show-offs at heart."

I reached home an hour before dark and made another nice discovery.

Pothead Eddie was working late on his tractor, pushing around piles of rich dark soil and grooving to Neil Young on his boom box.

When he saw me suddenly appear, he gave me the peace sign and grinned slyly as if to say, *See, bro? And you thought I'd never show up till Labor Day.*

I waved back and didn't waste what light was left by going inside to change out of my travel clothes. For the time being, I was still here, and this was the garden that owned me. I merely opened the door to the house, let my latest two garden assistants out for an evening romp, and took myself straight off to the garden shed to fetch my new English garden spade to begin transplanting hostas and getting gloriously dirty.

Acknowledgments

THE ONLY REGRET I HAVE regarding this unapologetic ode to the gardening spirit is that I couldn't begin to mention all the generous gardeners I met in my travels into one narrative tale, including an unforgettable afternoon spent with garden writer extraordinaire Barbara Damrosch and her husband, Elliot Coleman, a pioneer of the sustainable food movement, on their amazing saltwater farm near Blue Hill, Maine. My good friend John Powers and wife Jane Waddle were kind enough to permit me to tag along with them to the thrilling finals of the Giant Pumpkin Growers Championship where John's one-thousand-pound pumpkin captured a top prize, a feat that probably deserves a book of its own. Also, regrettably, you won't get to read about an inspiring road trip I took to the Chicago Botanic Garden's extraordinary annual plant sale, a three-day plant extravaganza conducted each spring at one of America's true treasures of a public garden. Many thanks to Julie McCafferty of the CBG and Director of Plant Collections, Galen Gates. Your generosity won't be forgotten anytime soon.

As for those who did make these pages, and agreed to read the manuscript so I wouldn't embarrass myself too badly, my first and deepest gratitude goes to Suzy Verrier for her long years of botanic encourage-

ment, earth wisdom, and sheer enthusiasm, and to plantsman Tony
Avent, a remarkable man whose infectious passion for plants and will-
ingness to drag a novice gardener from Maine along to the wilds of
Africa makes him either all the more special or simply crazy. Ditto four
other gifted horticultural goodfellows named Carl Schoenfeld, Wade
Roitsch, Hans Hansen, and Cameron McMaster. You guys are the true
"Big Five" of Africa. Thank you, Rhoda McMaster, for your hospitality
and insights.

The Pennsylvania Horticultural Society is an infinite resource for
every American gardener. I must thank PHS president Jane Pepper for
her enthusiastic support and great suggestions, as well as Steve Mauer,
the society's tireless public relations director, for placing me in the company of some special folks at the heart of the Philadelphia Flower Show.
They include Walt and Linda Fisher, Jack and Joe Blandy, Morris and
Cynthia Cheston Jr., Keith and Jim Straw, Jim and Jeanne Francis, Walter Off, and dozens of other show competitors, officials, and volunteers
who met an unending stream of questions from a Show rookie with un-
failing politeness and generosity of spirit. Thank you, Jim Rohr of PNC
Bank, for your kindness and support of plant lovers everywhere.

Dr. Richard Lighty, first director of the Longwood Graduate Program in Horticulture at the University of Delaware, shaped a lot of my
thinking and treated me to an afternoon with a true plant philosopher,
as did his talented former pupil Denise Magnani at Winterthur Gardens. Curator Joel Fry of Bartram's Garden will forever have my gratitude, as well. I would like to thank Dr. Michael Payne for showing me
his incredible Wilderness Road garden and John and Faye Shooter of
Marietta Daylilies for dropping everything to enlighten an unannounced visitor to the pleasures of growing daylilies. Many thanks, as
well, to David Smith for the cold beer and walking tour of White Flower
Farm, Chanticleer Executive Director Bill Thomas for inviting me into
one of America's greatest family pleasure gardens, and the lively colonial dames of the Community Garden Club of Cohasset, in particular
their unsinkable founder, Polly Logan, and her generous pal, Pat Chase.

Thank you, Nancy Wilkinson, for lunch in a familiar back garden I won't soon forget. You are the rightful keeper of that place now. Thank you, poet-writer Beth Kephart, for sharing your powerful insights on the magic of gardens, and friends Nick and Maggie Niles, Benita Ryan, Col. Bob Day, Randy Jones, Rayburn and Jane Tucker, and Rennie Reynolds, for introducing me to numerous other gardeners and their gardens. I'm also indebted to Parker Andes, Director of Horticulture at Biltmore Gardens, Asheville, North Carolina. A most special thank-you, too, to Isabel Correll and Peter Hatch of the Monticello Foundation.

England will always own a large piece of my golfing and gardening heart and I have several important folks to thank in that direction, including my longtime golf pal and fellow gnome garden traveler, Charles Churchill; Jim Buckland and Sarah Wain of stunning West Dean Gardens; gracious Ian Hodgson of the Royal Horticultural Society's *The Garden* magazine; the ageless and inspiring Mirabel Osler; Andy and Beth McKillop; and Simon and Deb Goodenough of the Isle of Wight. The beer is on ice, the lobster waiting—all of you please come to Maine and I'll show you what you helped inspire. Thank you, Kate Bennie, our family's beloved Queen Mum, for your many years of gardening and life wisdom. And editor Brian Tart—thank you for once again believing I had a tale worth telling.

Lastly, a heartfelt thank-you to the world's most supportive gardening mate and wife, Wendy Dodson, for understanding my need to get filthy dirty every spring and fall and shout violently at the skies whenever the damned rain won't come.

I'm an old man but a new gardener, and therein most indebted to you and the dogs.

Jim Dodson
Topsham, Maine
November 2005